# 'TWO SOULS ALAS'

## Jung's Two Personalities and the Making Of Analytical Psychology

**Mark Saban**

The Zurich Lecture Series

**Volume 2**

CHIRON PUBLICATIONS · ASHEVILLE, NORTH CAROLINA

www.ChironPublications.com

Interior and cover design by Danijela Mijailovic
Printed primarily in the United States of America.

ISBN 978-1-63051-748-9 paperback
ISBN 978-1-63051-749-6 hardcover
ISBN 978-1-63051-750-2 electronic
ISBN 978-1-63051-751-9 limited edition paperback


Library of Congress Cataloging-in-Publication Data

Names: Saban, Mark, author.
Title: 'Two souls alas' : Jung's two personalities and the making of analytical psychology / Saban Mark.
Description: Asheville, North Carolina : Chiron Publications, [2019] | Series: The Zurich lecture series ; volume 2 | Includes bibliographical references. | Summary: "In his memoir, Memories Dreams Reflections, Carl Jung tells us that, as a child, he had the experience of possessing two personalities. 'Two Souls Alas' is the first book to suggest that Jung's experience of the difficult dynamic between these two personalities not only informs basic principles behind the development of Jung's psychological model but underscores the theory and practice of Analytical Psychology as a whole. Mark Saban suggested that what Jung took from his experience of inner division was the principle that psychological health depends upon the avoidance of one-sidedness - a precept that underpins Jung's seminal notion of individuation. In practice, this process requires again and again that any one-sided position, approach or belief is brought into tension with a conflicting 'opposite' position, in order that a third position can be achieved which transcends both of the earlier positions. In the second part of the book, Saban takes up this principle and uses it to perform an internal critique on Analytical Psychology as enshrined in Jung's Collected Works. He suggests that in certain arenas Jung's personal one-sidedness - specifically his persistent tendency to prioritise the inner dimension of psychological work, and to downplay or ignore the outer dimension - undermined Jung's capacity to fully follow through the 'logic' of the two personalities. Saban argues that, as a result, Analytical Psychology has failed to find a stance from which it can creatively engage with political, social and historical matters. This book opens up a new direction for post-Jungian psychology, and indicates some ways in which, by following the logic of the two personalities, the one-sidedness that has long shadowed Jungian psychology can begin to be corrected"-- Provided by publisher.
Identifiers: LCCN 2020016263 (print) | LCCN 2020016264 (ebook) | ISBN 9781630517489 (paperback) | ISBN 9781630517496 (hardcover) | ISBN 9781630517502 (ebook)
Subjects: LCSH: Jung, C.G. (Carl Gustav), 1875-1961. | Jungian psychology. | Personality. | Polarity (Psychology)
Classification: LCC BF173.J85 S23 2019 (print) | LCC BF173.J85 (ebook) | DDC 150.19/54--dc23
LC record available at https://lccn.loc.gov/2020016263
LC ebook record available at https://lccn.loc.gov/202001626

# TABLE OF CONTENTS

I dedicate this book to my darling wife,
Penny, the love of my life.
Without her help and support it
couldn't have been written.
Without her presence in my life
I would not be the person who could write it.

# ACKNOWLEDGEMENTS

I am very grateful to Roderick Main and Matt Ffytche who supervised the PhD thesis that formed the basis for this book. Despite (or because of) their lightness of touch, I have never found their wise and scholarly interventions less than wholly helpful.

Kevin Lu's contribution has been essential. I owe him a great deal and I am proud to count him as a friend.

The book would not have taken the direction it has without Andrew Samuels.  He involved me (against my will!) in the organisation of the first Analysis and Activism Conference in 2014, and the editing of the book that came out of it, and eventually even I couldn't avoid appreciating the crucial importance to Jungian psychology of the relational and the political. I have a great deal to thank him for.

Finally, I would like to offer my profound thanks to Murray Stein and Steve Buser for giving me the opportunity to deliver the Zurich lectures on which this book is based, and to Jennifer Fitzgerald for midwifing it into print.

# INTRODUCTION

At the outset of this project, my aim was to write about "the problem of opposites," something Jung refers to in nearly everything he ever wrote. As far as I was aware, nobody had written a full-length work that focused directly upon this theme. But before going any further, I thought that I needed to work out what opposites really are, and this question led me in the direction of Heraclitus and Aristotle, Schelling and Hegel—all thinkers who had something deep and important to say about "the opposites."

After a year of this difficult, complex, and fascinating reading, I realised that I had wandered a long way from Jung and, more importantly, a long way from psychology. By pursuing "the opposites" in this way, I had made the kind of mistake it is easy to make when working therapeutically with clients. I had listened to and responded to the manifest content of what was offered instead of wondering what might be going on in the background. Reading Jung's repeated references to this rather abstract idea—"the problem of the opposites"—I had snatched at it, lost my balance and fallen into a philosophical hole that had gotten me nowhere.

What I needed to do was to ask a more basic and more personal question: What did this "question of the opposites" mean to Jung? Why was he so concerned with it that he returned to it again and again in all kinds of different ways?

In a 1935 lecture at the Tavistock Institute in London, Jung made this point: "I consider my contribution to psychology to be my subjective confession. It is my personal psychology, my prejudice that I see psychological facts as I do. I admit that I see things in such and such a way." (Jung, 1935, par. 275) In this book I use this important insight as a lens through which to interrogate this problem of the opposites. Of course, when Jung pointed to the status of his psychology as subjective confession, he certainly didn't mean to suggest that it was "nothing but" an expression of his personal equation. What he meant was that the only way to create the conditions necessary for true communication was to acknowledge the personal, subjective nature of our perspective and thus become aware of the differences between our own perspective and the perspectives of others.

In order to write a book about Jung and his psychology, I needed to open up a potentially transformative field of negotiation between me, the reader/writer, and Jung, the reader/writer of his own life. Jung's own meetings with (and reading of) both inner and outer others—Philemon and Freud, Salome and Spielrein—are paralleled, therefore, in my own meeting with (and reading of) Jung and his two personalities. The primary aim of such a meeting is not to learn something or absorb something or appropriate something that can at some later point be instrumentally utilised—though that may happen. More importantly, it is the very event of engaging with (conflicting with, even being wounded by) the other that constellates (and performs) the event of transformation. The examples of this that we will be focusing upon here are Jung's meetings with his inner (and as we will see outer) others. But my point is that the same has been my experience of meeting (reading/writing) Jung.

One of the things I aim to show is that this notion of the transformative encounter with the other underlies Jung's psychology, and it particularly underlies the individuation process, which I take to constitute the core of that psychology. As I intend to show in the first few chapters, Jung's experience of the two personalities led him to an understanding of how he was (and we are) made by that process. All Jung's psychological work, it seems to me, even that which predates the moment when Jung and Freud went their separate ways, revolves around and explicates the workings of the dynamic, energetic logic of individuation. The particular way in which Jung developed these ideas and these practices was inevitably conditioned by his own personal equation, or as he it puts it in several places, by his personal myth. Although the experiential dimension of this personal equation is what lends his psychology both energy and focus, it is also the factor that limits and confines it.

# Introduction

Jung famously said, "Thank God I am Jung and not a Jungian!" (quoted in Hannah 1976, p.78). He meant that since he was the creator of Jungian psychology, he was also, in a sense, free of that burden of Jungian dogma that the rest of us have to carry. No line can be drawn between Jung's individuation process and the individuation of his psychology, and that fact reprieved Jung from being a Jungian. He didn't have to wrestle with the paradoxical situation by which one individuates (becomes one's truest self) through a psychology that takes its shape and its content from someone else's individuation process. Jung may (or may not) be a genius, but your (and my) individuation process will always be yours (and mine) *and not his*!

However, there is a further problem with this idea. If Analytical Psychology, the psychology that Jung created, is to outlive him, if it is to remain alive and to continue to interact meaningfully with the culture, history, and politics of the 21st century, then it must *itself* continue to individuate, and that means changing, transforming, reacting to, and engaging with the world around it. What will get in the way of that process (and I will argue that this is exactly what has occurred) is the sedimentation and hypostatisation of Jung's ideas, as formulated in his published texts. As soon as we say or assume that Jung has said everything there is to say about psychology, then we have created a closed system. Under these circumstances, to be a Jungian means merely to know how to apply this ready-made system to new clinical and cultural situations.

However fruitful such a process may be, the closed nature of the Jungian system, i.e., its reliance upon a set of fixed hermeneutic terms such as "archetype" or "trickster," means that the transformation or renewal *of these very notions* (the archetype, the trickster, etc.) is made all but impossible. In effect, this means that Analytical Psychology itself remains frozen. This calcification of what was once a living psychology seems to me to be in flagrant conflict with the central idea in Jung's psychology—that of individuation. If individuation (and life) are to continue, what is required is for the known and the fixed to be constantly challenged and brought into conflict and tension with the unknown and the fluid. If this is true of me and of my clients, why should it not be just as true of Analytical Psychology and the ideas that make it up?

I shall argue in this book that although Jung's psychology itself places an emphasis upon the crucial importance of correcting the tendency of the psyche to become one-sided, Jung's own personality suffered (inevitably) from a powerful and persistent one-sidedness, which took the form of a bias in the direction of introversion, interiority, aloneness, secrets, and unrelatedness. This bias is important because it has shaped the theory and practice of Analytical Psychology. We can see it in the persistent difficulties Jungian psychology gets into when it tries to meet the outer world—in the form of outer relationships, groups, society, and the political. These are some of the particular limitations that, it seems to me, need to be analysed and tackled if the individuation of Analytical Psychology can proceed. If we want to engage with this problem, we need first to acknowledge it. My hope is that this study is a contribution toward that acknowledgment.

As the reader will discover, the second part of the book (particularly chapters 5 and 6) utilises the findings of the first half as a means of critiquing Jung's psychology as found in the *Collected Works*. Rather than bringing to bear a critical model that originates outside of Jung's psychology, such as, for example, psychoanalysis, I use what I understand to be Jung's own model of individuation to provide an internal critique of the particular version of Jung's psychology that has come down to us and remains fundamental to Jungian training organisations throughout the world. I am, in effect using Jung to critique Jung.

In Chapter One, I perform an initial survey of Jung's experience of the two personalities and bring it into tension with his notion of the personal myth. Having set the scene in this way, in Chapter Two, I examine the ways in which Jung set about developing a model of the psyche within which the dynamics of the two personalities can be properly understood. Chapter Three looks at Jung's attempt to process an encounter with personality No. 2 via his crucial relationship with Freud, why that relationship failed, and what that failure had to do with his early experiences. In Chapter Four, Jung's relationships with a series of important women are looked at in detail, with special attention given to the way in which Jung tended to internalise aspects of his outer relationships and to appropriate them for the purposes of his inner development. In Chapter Five, I focus upon Jung's emphasis upon the inner dimension and neglect of the outer, a theme I develop in Chapter Six, where I examine some of the ways in which Jung's one-sided approach shows up in clinical work and political analysis.

# CHAPTER ONE
# Jung's 'Personal Myth' and the Two Personalities

Parts of this chapter have previously appeared in *Narratives of Individuation*, (Routledge, London 2019).

Zwei Seelen wohnen, ach! in meiner Brust,
die eine will sich von der andern trennen:
Die eine hält in derber Liebeslust
sich an die Welt mit klammernden Organen;
die andre hebt gewaltsam sich vom Dust
zu den Gefilden hoher Ahnen.

In me there are two souls, alas, and their
Division tears my life in two.
One loves the world, it clutches her, it binds
Itself to her, clinging with furious lust;
The other longs to soar beyond the dust
Into the realm of high ancestral minds.

Goethe, Faust part one, lines 1112-7

(English translation: Goethe, 1987, p. 35-6)

When Jung came, at the end of his life, to write what he described as his "so-called autobiography," *Memories Dream Reflections* (Jung,1989) (henceforth *MDR*), his intention was not merely to offer the reader a chronological itemisation of significant experiences and memories. He also wanted to throw some retrospective light upon the psychology he had created by offering the reader some fresh insights into those events of his life in which, as he put it, "the imperishable world irrupted into this one." (Jung, 1989, p. 4) He knew perfectly well that he was thereby enabling his readers to deepen their understanding of the fundamental concepts that make up the psychology he created (to become known as Analytical Psychology) by providing them with a subjective account of the personal experiences that lay behind that psychology.

The reader of *MDR* discovered, for example, that the anima archetype was not merely an abstract idea or concept dreamt up by Jung but emerged instead from the specific event of Jung hearing the anima speak to him. She had the voice of a real woman known by Jung, and one day, out of the blue, she struck up a conversation with him (Jung, 1989, p.185). With this example, and many others, *MDR* revealed to the uninitiated public a dimension of Jung's psychology that had until this point been available only to Jung's inner circle.[1] It turned out that the 20 volumes of Jung's *Collected Works*, and the psychological system they contain, had originally emerged from a core of personal and subjective experiences.[2] The particular aspect of that personal core that I want to look at in this chapter is Jung's experience of having two personalities, an account of which dominates the first three chapters of *MDR*.

In 2013, I wrote a paper that drew attention to what I saw as the critical importance of Jung's treatment of his two personalities in *MDR* (Saban, 2013). It seemed to me that Jung's account of this experience offers us a red thread that, followed through, brings us seamlessly to Jung's most important idea: the concept of individuation. By looking closely at the different ways in which Jung engaged with this question, it seemed to me that we might get some insights into some of the problems that have emerged in and around Analytical Psychology in the hundred years since Jung's foundational "confrontation with the unconscious." In short, the topic of the "two personalities" gives us a real chance to "dream forward" the individuation of Jung's psychology.

This book represents my attempts to substantiate an intuition that this particular dimension of Jung's life and work provides us with a crucial lens through which to revision the ideas of Analytical Psychology. For this reason, I want to start by reencountering the two personalities—but in a specific context, that of Jung's "personal myth."

## Jung's Personal Myth

When, in extreme old age, Jung overcame his initial resistance to the idea of an autobiography and finally began to write down what he remembered from his early years, he was surprised to find that he had become enthused by the unexpected turn the project had taken. As he wrote to his secretary Aniela Jaffé:

> This 'autobiography' is now taking a direction quite different from what I had imagined at the beginning … it has become a necessity for me to write down my early memories. If I neglect to do so for a single day, unpleasant physical symptoms immediately follow. As soon as I set to work they vanish and my head feels perfectly clear. (Jung, 1989, p. vi)

For Jung, this new direction offered a fresh standpoint from which to revision his whole psychological life. As Jung became caught up in the writing of his memoir, Jaffé wrote excitedly to the publisher, Kurt Wolff,

> [S]omething so wonderful and meaningful happened . . . Jung himself is writing his autobiography all over again . . . so much had become clear to [Jung] and especially the meaning of his life which he had apparently not seen to its full extent. (Bair, 2004, p. 595)

Jung's exhilaration seems to have derived from a burgeoning awareness that the writing and remembering of his early years was not only shedding light upon his life and his work but was also illuminating the relationship between the two and thus providing a new way to understand both. When he came to compose the prologue to his memoir, he chose to articulate this insight in a characteristically Jungian way by telling his readers he was about to narrate his "personal myth." (Jung 1989, p. 3)[3]

This term, "personal myth," is very striking because it conjoins two quite different worlds of meaning. "[S]trictly speaking…" as Lucy Huskinson has observed, it commits "a category error." (Huskinson, 2008, p. 4) While the word "personal" refers us to a subjective dimension that concerns individual human experience, the word "myth" points us toward a universal dimension which, in Jung's articulation, takes an archetypal form.[4] Interestingly, the term "personal myth" also performs what it signifies, in that it brings together precisely the two ingredients that the narrative in question—the story that Jung tells us—insists upon putting into tension.

As we enter the early chapters of MDR, we meet these two dimensions again, though in the guise of Jung's two personalities. For Jung, the tale of the two personalities qualifies as a personal myth because it is a story that on the one hand expresses Jung's subjective experiences, while on the other, it simultaneously reveals a universal dimension. As we will see, the tension between these facets runs through the whole psychology that Jung developed. Under the broad headings of "personality No. 1" and "personality No. 2," Jung explores a whole range of different motifs, ideas, and images. However, the central problem he interrogates through the telling of this narrative myth can be summed up in the one question which Jung's psychology never ceases to address: How can a human being function day-to-day as an individual person in the world, without losing touch with the dynamic, numinous, timeless aspects of existence that are essential for a meaningful life?

I am going to argue in this book that it was as a way to engage with, explore, and articulate this problem that Jung created and developed Analytical Psychology. My argument is going to involve me in looking closely at the specific ways in which Jung's personal struggles with this issue unfolded.

First, however, I want to ask a more immediate question: What does Jung mean in MDR when he emphasises the *mythic* importance of his *personal* experiences?

## Jung and the Personal

When he was 75 in 1950, Jung contributed a new foreword to the book which had in 1912 precipitated his split with Freud and thereby birthed Jungian psychology. *Symbols of Transformation* (in German

*Wandlungen und Symbole der Libido* [Jung, 1912b]) had immersed Jung in a wide-ranging psychological amplification of world mythology. He tells us in the 1950 foreword that when he had completed the book, he found himself beset by inner turmoil. The mythic structures Jung had inherited from his pastor father—that of Christianity—had long since lost their ability to hold him, and the mythic structure he had taken from his latest father figure—that of psychoanalysis—had now also lost its sustaining significance for him. Staring into this abyss of meaning, Jung asked himself, "What is the myth you are living?" (Jung, 1967, p. xxiv)

"I did not know that I was living a myth," Jung reflected, "and even if I had known it, I would not have known what sort of myth was ordering my life without my knowledge." (Jung, 1967, p. xxv) In that moment, he says, he set himself a "task of tasks. ... I took it upon myself to get to know 'my' myth." After all, Jung asked himself, how could he make "due allowance for the personal factor, for my personal equation, which is yet so necessary for a knowledge of the other person, if I was unconscious of it?" This "task of tasks" was to become a lifetime's work for Jung, since even in his 83rd year, as he set about writing his autobiography, the nature of that myth remained, it seems, far from settled.

Jung's comments here are reminiscent of warnings we find littered throughout the *Collected Works* about what he calls the "personal equation." (e.g., Jung, 1921, para 9; 1934b, para 216; 1934c, para 351; 1947, para 421). This factor has the capacity to warp not only personal and therapeutic relations, but also, should it remain unrecognised, the entire project of psychology as a scientific endeavour. The best that any psychological researcher can achieve, Jung implies, is to make sufficient allowance for a subjective bias that is both inevitable and ineradicable: "The demand that [the psychologist] should see only objectively is quite out of the question, for it is impossible. We must be satisfied if he does not see too subjectively." (Jung, 1921, para. 10)

If, as Jung claims, the personal myth can obscure our "knowledge of the other person," (Jung, 1967, p. xxiv) we might have expected him to be urgently searching for ways to minimise the danger. After all, as Jung tells us in *Psychological Types,* his typological system was developed precisely in order to transcend this kind of problem, originally identified in the impossible conflict between the respective personal equations of Freud and Alfred Adler (in Freud's case that of one-sided extraversion and in Adler's that of one-sided introversion) (Jung, 1921, para. 91).

But in *MDR*, there is no sign that Jung regards his personal myth as a distorting factor at all. In fact, he sees it as a red thread running through every aspect of both his life and his psychology, ineradicable from any understanding of either. In fact, Jung's implication is that we are intended to understand his personal myth as in some sense, *relevant us all*.

This dissonance brings into sharp focus the curious nature of the tension within which Jung's psychology is situated: On the one hand, it is a kind of "subjective confession" grounded in Jung's own experiences, and on the other hand, it claims to be an objective and universally applicable body of ideas. What Jung requires us to accept, implicitly or explicitly, is not only that his personal experiences are in some sense exemplars of human experience as a whole, but also that the myth that conveys the essence of these experiences can offer everyone insight into their own lives.

But how can this be? How can a factor that Jung himself has repeatedly trumpeted as the source of considerable and profound distortion simultaneously constitute the very factor that provides us with the central meaning to our lives?

In order to answer this question, we need to undertake a deeper analysis of the relationship between Jung's personal equation and those aspects of his psyche that he was to come to understand as universally human. Our problem is that if we directly utilise Jung's own writings to guide us in this discernment, we may well fall into error, since everything Jung writes is, of course, coloured by his personal equation. The way to locate the blind spots in Jung's psychology is to employ a kind of *via negativa*: allowing its manifest content to reveal what might be being left out. By looking closely at the narrative of the two personalities in *MDR*, I hope to shed some light on this problem.

## The Split

As a child, Jung seems to have experienced a disturbing sense of inner division: "Somewhere deep in the background I always knew that I was two persons" (Jung, 1989, p. 44). In *MDR*, Jung usually expresses himself in nontechnical language and avoids utilising the jargon of Analytical Psychology. However, what is striking about this passage is the way he not only resists the use of psychological terminology to describe this duality of personality, but, more importantly, he refuses to retrospectively pathologize himself. The conflict between the personalities, he tells us, "has nothing to do with a 'split' or dissociation in the ordinary medical sense. On the contrary, it is played out in every individual." (Jung, 1989, p. 45)

Jung's experience of possessing two personalities was not, he implies, constellated by a quirk of his own psychological development. On the contrary, for Jung this inner division represents *a fundamental dynamic of human psychology*. Far from being a mere contingent detail of his childhood, the encounter between Jung's personality No. 1 and personality No. 2 is to be understood as active within the psyche of every human being.

It is far from clear how we should interpret this extraordinary assertion, because in the immediate context of *MDR* Jung fails to spell it out or to develop it into a full-fledged theory. Jung's writing in *MDR* is not theoretical, although it is psychological. He makes his psychological points via the narrative itself. It follows that the tale of the two personalities, as contained in the first three chapters of *MDR*, must be intended to illustrate its own point. As we have seen, the work of recalling and transcribing his early memories newly illuminated for Jung "the meaning of his life which he had apparently not seen to its full extent." (Bair, 2004, p.595) I shall argue here that Jung's newfound perspective derived from a realisation that the dynamic tension between his two personalities was of central importance for the unfolding of his own individuation, in that it played a critical and ongoing role in his personal myth and therefore in his whole psychology.

This dynamic, I shall argue, first emerged in the form of a problematic feeling of division between two personalities, a split that recurred throughout Jung's early life in various different shapes and eventually showed up in the form of what Jung describes in his mature psychology as the "problem of the opposites"—a problem that Jung came to see as universal, since, for him, it constituted the core dynamic within the process of individuation.

It is characteristic of Jung that, when confronted by what can seem merely pathological, he assumes an approach that tends toward the teleological. Jung interprets his early experience of the two personalities as significant not because it was caused by (or caused ) traumatic early damage that required later repair, but rather because it functioned as a crucial initiation, not only adumbrating the character of his onward path, but also indicating the means by which he (and by extension we) might reach his (and our) goal.

## The Two Personalities

I am not going to describe in detail the specific values, motifs, and images Jung associates with the two personalities (the details of which I assume to be peculiar to Jung and his time) but instead I want to concentrate upon 1) the dynamic nature of the tension between them and 2) the way in which that tension played out in the context of Jung's life. Nonetheless, in order to grasp the particular character of the contrast between the two that Jung draws, I shall survey and summarise the key aspects of each personality as described in *MDR*. Jung tells us there that before he identified the two personalities in himself, he noticed them first in his mother:

> There was an enormous difference between my mother's two personalities. ... By day she was a loving mother, but at night she seemed uncanny. Then she was like one of those seers who is at the same time a strange animal, like a priestess in a bear's cave. Archaic and ruthless; ruthless as truth and nature. At such moments she was the embodiment of what I have called the "natural mind." (Jung, 1989, p.50)

When Jung was 3 years old, Emilie Jung's mental difficulties led to her entering a care home where she remained for months (Bair, 2004, p. 21). Although Jung does not attribute any infantile disturbances of his own to his mother's absences, he does acknowledge, when discussing his mother's two personalities, that as a child he "often had anxiety dreams about her." (Jung, 1989, p.50) In Emilie's case, the two personalities seem to have been radically different and mutually exclusive (Jung, 1989, p.49). Jung makes it clear that as a child he felt it would be wrong to draw attention to this difference; to do so would lead only to her denying it, because personality No. 2 was, as he describes it, an "unconscious personality." (Jung, 1989, p.48) When she occupied her personality No. 1, Emilie Jung was a "kindly, fat old woman, extremely hospitable, and possessor of a great sense of humor." These conventional virtues in a mother were in extreme contrast with her No. 2 qualities: uncanny, archaic, ruthless, unexpected, and frightening (Jung, 1989, p.50). As we shall see, there are important parallels between Jung's two personalities and those of his mother. I shall return to some of the implications of this fact in Chapter 4.

## Personality No. 1

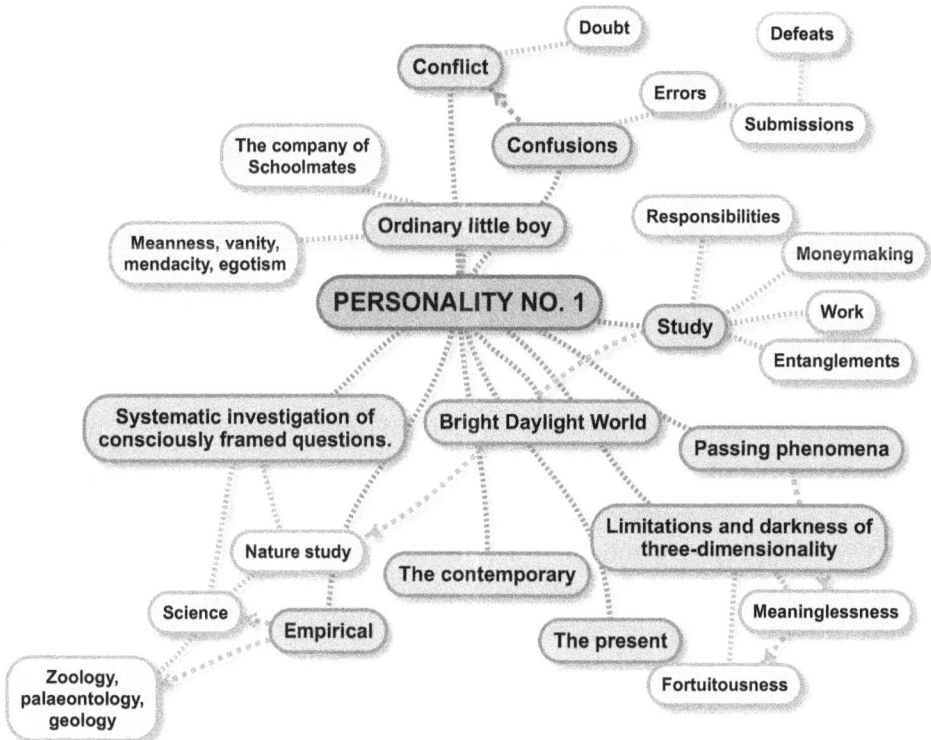

*Figure 1.* Personality No. 1

Jung's personality No. 1 corresponds to his identity as a conventional and ordinary child and adult. In *MDR*, Jung associates
personality No. 1 with the familiar, the everyday, and the reliable: the
"bright daylight world" of normality (Jung, 1989, p.19). Compared with
personality No. 2, there is a sense of limitation and superficiality,
stemming from personality No. 1's involvement in the time-bound
phenomena of everyday life. Jung associates it with the mundane
shadow qualities of meanness, vanity, mendacity, and egotism (Jung,
1989, p.45). As personality No. 1, Jung existed as merely a grubby,
naughty, and lazy little "schoolboy who ... deserved his punishment, and
who had to behave to his age." (Jung, 1989, p. 35)

In academic or intellectual terms, personality No. 1 was concerned
with the systematic investigation of "consciously framed" questions
(Jung, 1989, p.68), and represented Jung's attraction to facts, "concrete
things" and empirical science (Jung, 1989, p.82).

It should be emphasised that Personality No. 1 was the dimension
that involved Jung in the world of outer relationships, both personal and
collective, in the context of family, school, and work.

## Personality No. 2

In *MDR*, as Renos Papadopoulos has pointed out, what was later to
achieve fuller articulation as personality No. 2 is foreshadowed in the
various treasured secret and meaningful events of Jung's childhood. These
include the giant phallus dream, the stone on which Jung sits, wondering
if he is sitter or stone, and the secret manikin and its soul-stone
(Papadopoulos, 1991). Although Jung describes these experiences and
objects as "secret," he makes it clear that this was not the kind of secret
that could ever be revealed. It involved the child Jung in a realm of
impenetrable mystery and unanswerable questions.

Jung related his personality No. 2 to what he calls "God's world" (Jung,
1989, p.67): an experience of nature in wild and cosmic form: earth, sun,
moon, weather, the night, and dreams (Jung, 1989, pp. 44-5). According to
Jung, No. 2 "knew God as a hidden, personal, and at the same time
suprapersonal secret." (Jung, 1989, p. 45) Later, it brought with it a sense of

Frightening

Importance  Mysterious  Strange

Greco-Roman  Dignity  Ruthless  Death

Egyptian

Archaic  Authority  Uncanny

Medieval  The Past  Ghosts

History  **PERSONALITY NO. 2**  The Old Man

Eckhart  Destiny  Fate  Imperishable

The Inner

Philosophy  Knowing God  Secrets  Solitude

Nietzsche  'God's world'

Schopenhauer  Stone on which Jung sits  Subterranean Phallus dream

Trees  Stones

Timeless  Carved Manikin

Animals  Sun

Weather  The Abyss  Secret Fire

Infinite space and time  Moon

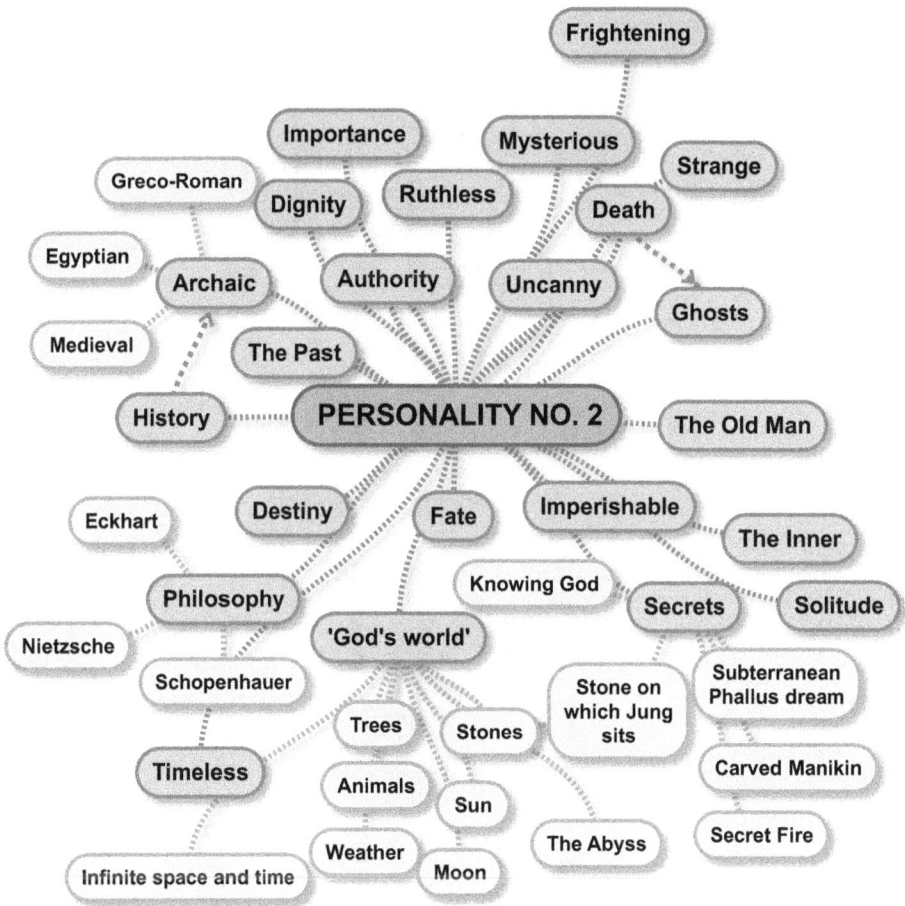

*Figure 2.* Personality No. 2

timelessness, infinity, and the imperishable, or as Jung puts it, "superhuman dazzling light, the darkness of the abyss, the cold passivity of infinite space and time, the uncanny grotesqueness of the irrational world of chance." (Jung, 1989, p. 72) Personality No. 2 was sometimes experienced in the form of "intuitive premonitions." (Jung, 1989, p. 68) It was often drawn to the search for meaning and was later associated with philosophy (especially Eckhart, Schopenhauer, Kant, and Nietzsche). Other personality No. 2 interests included a romantic nostalgic sense of history (Jung, 1989, pp. 68ff.), Greco-Roman, Egyptian, and prehistoric archaeology, and comparative religion.

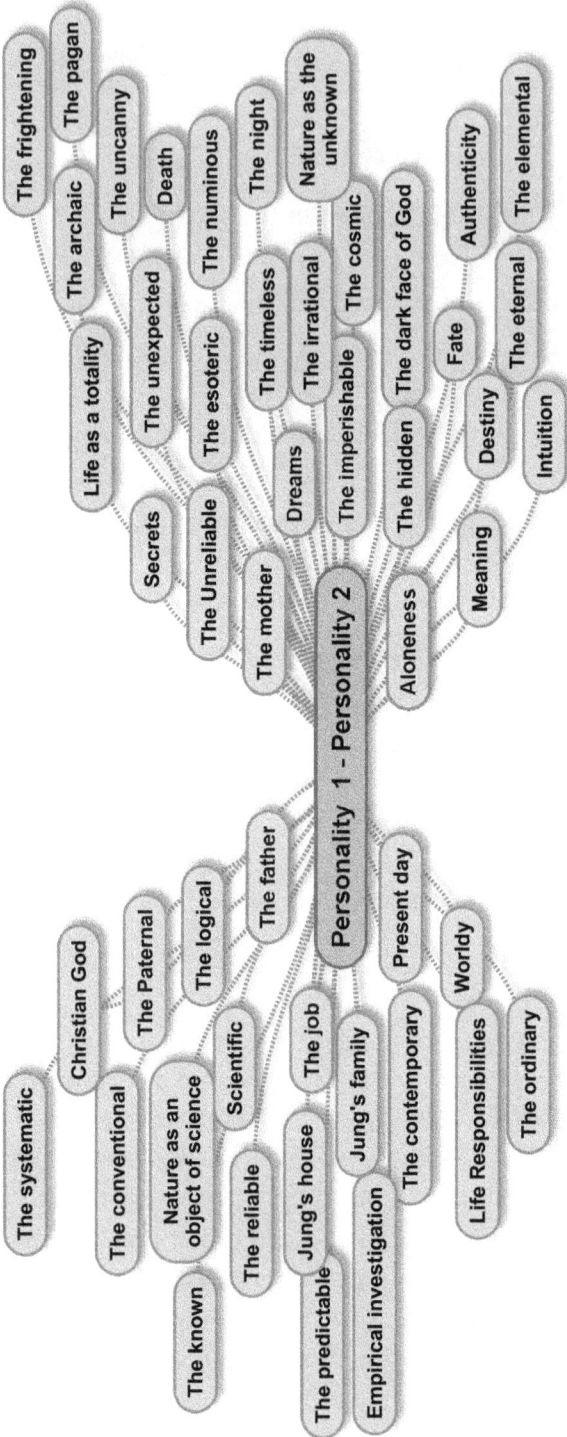

*Figure 3.* The Two Personalities

The frightening
The pagan
The archaic
The uncanny
Death
The numinous
The night
Nature as the unknown
The elemental
Authenticity
The esoteric
The cosmic
The dark face of God
The eternal
Life as a totality
The unexpected
The timeless
The irrational
Fate
Destiny
Intuition
Secrets
The imperishable
The hidden
Dreams
The Unreliable
The mother
Meaning
Aloneness

**Personality 1 – Personality 2**

The father
The logical
Present day
The Paternal
The job
Worldy
Christian God
The conventional
Scientific
Jung's family
The contemporary
The systematic
Nature as an object of science
Jung's house
Life Responsibilities
The reliable
Empirical investigation
The ordinary
The known
The predictable

In contrast with personality No. 1, No. 2 was emphatically inward-facing and invariably experienced by Jung when he was alone. In practice, Jung's No. 2 seems to be almost completely nonrelational, except in an intrapsychic context.

## The Interactional Process

This is not the place to exhaustively map the respective domains of the two personalities because, for our purposes, what matters more is the dynamic relationship between them. We can explore this dynamic more fruitfully if we trace the shifting ways in which Jung found himself relating to the two personalities over time. These were the experiences that made Jung aware of the differences and contrasts between them, and they eventually enabled him to negotiate a path that avoided falling one way or the other. As we will see, what was never to recede was a proneness to the magnetic attraction of personality No. 2 (e.g. Jung, 1989, p.20). As a result of this powerful influence, the avoidance of one-sidedness was to become an enduring challenge for Jung until the end of his life.

In his early years, Jung's sense of self seemed to reside primarily in personality No. 2, and as a result, personality No. 1 was felt to be alien (Jung, 1989, p.19). He experienced personality No. 2 as a zone of safety and security into which he could retreat, reassured by the comforting knowledge that he alone possessed its "secret." As Jung puts it, "This possession of a secret had a very powerful formative influence on my character; I consider it the essential factor of my boyhood." (Jung, 1989, p. 22) In Chapter 3, we will take a closer look at this "secret" at the heart of personality No. 2.

It is important to note that from a young age, Jung found the outer world—the world of other people—far more challenging than he did his inner world. When at school, for example, with other children, his experience of inner division was exacerbated; the personality No. 1 realm of outer relationship and sociality "alienated me from myself":

When I was with [other children] I became different from the way
1 was at home ... It seemed to me that the change in myself was

due to the influence of my schoolfellows, who somehow misled me or compelled me to be different from what I thought I was. The influence of this wider world, this world which contained others besides my parents, seemed to me dubious if not altogether suspect and, in some obscure way, hostile. (Jung, 1989, p.19)

Not surprisingly, Jung's desire to shelter in personality No. 2 resulted in a tendency to avoid school and the company of others, and this avoidance reached its climax in a series of fainting fits that overtook him for six months. Allowed to stay away from school, Jung became completely absorbed in the "mysterious realm" of No. 2 (Jung, 1989, p. 22) and whiled away the hours deep in nature, dreaming, drawing, and reading. Although he relished this opportunity to dwell in the realm of No. 2, even at the time he "had the obscure feeling that [he] was fleeing from [him]self." (Jung, 1989, p. 31)

This period ended with what Jung describes as a "collision with reality." Overhearing a conversation in which his father recounted the crippling effect that Jung's "illness" was having on the family, Jung suddenly understood the necessity for him to reenter the world as an active person (Jung, 1989, p.31). At this point Jung's sense of self made a significant shift in the direction of personality No. 1. Shortly afterward, he describes an experience of "having just emerged from a dense cloud": "I knew all at once: now I am myself! … Previously I had existed too, but everything had happened to me. Now I happened to myself. Now I knew: I am myself now, now I exist." (Jung, 1989, p.32)

The way in which Jung hammers the word "I" in this passage eloquently underscores the stage of ego development he had reached. Indeed, this conscious and deliberate entrance into egohood seems to have reinforced his ability to explore and achieve differentiations that had hitherto been unavailable to him, as we witness in the subsequent episode in which Jung first became fully conscious of the two personalities as separate persons—a process that brought him to the "disappointing realisation that now, at any rate, I was nothing but the little schoolboy who

… had to behave according to his age. The other person must be sheer nonsense." (Jung, 1989, p. 35)

Psychologically, Jung's centre of gravity seems to have shifted in the direction of a conscious (albeit reluctant) identification with personality No. 1. As he points out, for all the enticing profundity of "the sphere of the 'old man,' who belonged to the centuries," it was simply not enough (Jung, 1989, p. 48); what Jung required at this point was an "active and comprehending ego." (Jung, 1989, p. 68) Later still, Jung describes how the "No. 2 personality became more and more doubtful and distasteful to me, and I could no longer hide this fact from myself. I tried to extinguish No. 2, but could not succeed in that either." (Jung, 1989, p. 74)

Jung experienced a growing need to live "in the here and now." Although No. 2 offered him a sense of transcendence, its "passivity" left him feeling "incapable of moving so much as a pebble upon the earth." Now there was nothing for it but to "wait and see what would happen." For the moment he was "caught in an insoluble conflict." (Jung, 1989, p. 75)

In the 1931 essay, "The Stages of Life," Jung offers a psychological description of the "inner division within oneself" that can occur in the psyche of a young person:

> [It] arises when, side by side with the series of ego-contents, a second series of equal intensity comes into being. This second series, because of its energy value, has a functional significance equal to that of the ego-complex; we might call it another, second ego which can on occasion even wrest the leadership from the first. This produces the division with oneself, the state that betokens a problem. (Jung, 1931b, para. 757)

Jung goes on to point out that the common-sense solution to this problem would be to identify with one of the two ego-states and reject the other. However, Jung continues,

> Whoever protects himself against what is new and strange and regresses to the past falls into the same neurotic condition as the man who identifies himself with the new and runs away from

the past. The only difference is that the one has estranged himself from the past and the other from the future. In principle both are doing the same thing: they are reinforcing their narrow range of consciousness instead of shattering it in the tension of opposites and building up a state of wider and higher consciousness. (Jung, 1931b, para. 767)

Jung's emphasis here is upon the broadening of consciousness, a process which can occur only when there is neither a chronic alternation of the two ego-perspectives nor a one-sided repression of one by the other. Each needs to be brought into contact with the other in consciousness—a process which although it inevitably constellates an experience of tension and conflict, is, Jung implies, the only way to further the process of individuation.

Something very similar is detailed in Jung's *MDR* account of his attempts to settle his identity within the domain of each of the two personalities in alternation, and his ultimate realisation that he owed allegiance to *both* personalities, even though this also meant negotiating the conflicts that would inevitably arise between the two.

On rare occasions, Jung glimpsed what it might be like to move beyond the conflict between the two personalities and achieve a more harmonious correlation. Here, for example, Jung describes the feeling that accompanied his important decision to pursue a career in psychiatry— and thereby fulfil the requirements of both personalities:

It was as though two rivers had united and in one grand torrent were bearing me inexorably toward distant goals. This confident feeling that I was a "united double nature" carried me as if on a magical wave through the examination, in which I came out at the top. (Jung, 1989, 109)

An earlier example is perhaps more revealing. Jung was confused and doubtful about the direction his academic studies should follow, but then two dreams "removed all ... doubts" and decided him "overwhelmingly in favor of science" (Jung, 1989, p. 85). This decision required the cooperation of both personalities, since, on the one hand, as Jung puts it elsewhere, "there was no doubt in my mind that No. 2 had something to do with the creation of dreams," (Jung, 1989, p. 89) while on the other, "Science met, to a very large extent, the needs of No. 1 personality." (Jung, 1989, p. 72) By utilising insights gained from dreams (personality No. 2) to guide his path toward a scientific goal (personality No. 1), Jung revealed to himself (and to his readers) the creative potential of the dynamic between them.

When both personalities engage in this way, what is achieved is what we might articulate metaphorically as *binocular* vision. To bring together two different perspectives, each of which possesses the monocular vision of a single eye, provides a more comprehensive, three-dimensional vision that transcends the limited possibilities offered by each of the original single perspectives.

We can see another example of this binocularity in the approach to nature that Jung was developing at this time. Through the lens of personality No. 2, Jung viewed nature as the numinous "God's world." However, through the No. 1 lens of scientific curiosity (newly stimulated by his academic studies) Jung gained a very different perspective. Jung's goal was to "get to know nature, the world in which we live, and the things around us," (Jung, 1989, p. 85) and that now involved a binocular approach that on one level enlisted the extraverted use of instrumental reason (nature as object), and on another level evoked the deeper and darker kind of understanding that for Jung was always constellated by subjective interiority. By bringing together these two conflicting tendencies, Jung was able to gain a new breadth of vision that added up to considerably more than either could offer in isolation.

## The Storm Lantern Dream

According to *MDR*, it was another dream that clarified the respective roles that No. 1 and No. 2 were to play within Jung's life:

> It was night in some unknown place, and I was making slow and painful headway against a mighty wind. Dense fog was flying along everywhere. I had my hands cupped around a tiny light which threatened to go out at any moment. Everything depended on my keeping this little light alive. Suddenly I had

21

the feeling that something was coming up behind me. I looked back, and saw a gigantic black figure following me. But at the same moment I was conscious, in spite of my terror, that I must keep my little light going through night and wind, regardless of all dangers. When I awoke I realized at once that the figure was a "specter of the Brocken," my own shadow on the swirling mists, brought into being by the little light I was carrying. I knew, too, that this little light was my consciousness, the only light I have. My own understanding is the sole treasure I possess, and the greatest. Though infinitely small and fragile in comparison with the powers of darkness, it is still a light, my only light. (pp. 87-88)

Jung interpreted the dream as offering him a profound insight into how he henceforth needed to regard the roles of the two personalities in his life:

Now I knew that No. 1 was the bearer of the light, and that No. 2 followed him like a shadow ... In the role of No. 1, I had to go forward into study, moneymaking, responsibilities, entangle- ments, confusions, errors, submissions, defeats ... I recognized clearly that my path led irrevocably outward, into the limitations and darkness of three-dimensionality. (Jung, 1989, p.88)

This dream clearly performed the kind of compensatory work that, according to Jung, dreams invariably perform, in that it made Jung aware of things that had hitherto been unavailable to his conscious mind. However, what is particularly striking about this dream's imagery is the way it inverts the symbolic landscape we are used to finding in Jung's writings (and in Jungian literature) whereby the *inner* realm is invariably represented as the source of psychological illumination. In the dream, however, "the inner realm of light appears as a gigantic shadow," and, as Jung acknowledges, it was precisely this insight that "was not something I would have hit on of my own accord." (Jung, 1989, p. 89) As Jung tells us in *MDR*, dreams "are invariably seeking to express something that the ego does not know and does not understand." (Jung, 1925a, para. 189) What Jung's ego doesn't know here is that at this point he needs to recognise the crucial importance of this little light of consciousness (No. 1). The implication, then, is that what requires correction is Jung's conscious one-sidedness in the direction of personality No. 2. The compensatory character of the dream resides in the unexpected notion that for Jung at this time, it was personality No. 1 that brought light, and personality No. 2 shadow.

In *MDR* Jung tells us that he took the dream to be informing him that the path of individuation required him to submit to a future that he found consciously antipathetic. This was the No. 1 dimension of "study, money-making, responsibilities, entanglements, confusions, errors, submissions, defeats." (Jung, 1989, p.88)

We might see this as Jung's reluctant acceptance of a developmental need to tick off a series of first-half-of-life achievements before moving into a second-half-of-life individuation process. This would be, however, to diminish its importance. The crucial point, as Jung understood it, was that the dream encouraged him to achieve binocularity by bringing the outer-facing world of work and relationship (No. 1) into conscious relation with the inner "God's world" of No. 2, a dimension that until now he had been working hard to maintain as a radically separate compartment within his psyche.

The standard Jungian notion is that individuation is a process of transformation whereby the ego draws ever nearer to the numinous riches of personality No. 2 (Jung, 1951, para 44). However, this dream points to a context in which the deeper necessities of Jung's soul – the avoidance of one-sidedness - required a shift *away from* "God's world" toward man's world (personality No. 1).

The wider implication of the dream is that one-sidedness can show up either in the direction of personality No. 1 or in the direction of personality No. 2. For the psyche, both kinds of one-sidedness are equally toxic because they impede relationship between the two personalities and therefore individuation itself. It is highly significant that, in the dream, personality No. 2 is represented as the shadow of personality No. 1, an image that evokes a relationship of fundamental interdependence and complementarity.

In *MDR* Jung acknowledges this sense of interdependence with this reflection: "I must leave No. 2 behind me, that was clear. But under no circumstances ought I to deny him to myself or declare him invalid. That would have been a self-mutilation …" (Jung, 1989, p.88) In fact, the dream points to a deeper realisation: Neither personality *could* really be "denied," since each only exists as the shadow of the other. In the terms of Jung's mature psychology, what is expressed here is, in Mary Williams's words, "the indivisibility of the personal and Collective Unconscious" (Williams, 1963); the personal (No. 1) is meaningless in the absence of the archetypal (No. 2), and conversely, the archetypal is meaningless when cut off from the personal. I will return to and expand upon this crucial point in Chapter 6.

In Marie Louise von Franz's discussion of the storm lantern dream, she directly maps Jung's personality No. 1 onto his "own human ego" and No. 2 onto "the activated, and therefore, perceptible, unconscious." (von Franz, 1998, p. 38) By narrowing down the dynamic of the two personalities to a relationship between ego and unconscious, von Franz reveals an immunity to the depth, richness, and novelty of what Jung is actually describing. No doubt the relationship Jung is seeking to sketch out in *MDR* can be conceptualised within the discourse of ego and unconscious, but ultimately this reductive articulation seems both doctrinaire and underpowered.

## A United Stream

The richness and complexity of what I am describing becomes evident in Jung's description in *MDR* of the sudden illumination he received at about this time when reading a psychiatric textbook by Richard von Krafft-Ebing. With great excitement he realised that psychiatry might provide the place in which "the two currents of my interest could flow together and in a united stream dig their own bed," (Jung, 1989, p. 109) an image that clearly evokes the two personalities and the need to live a life in which both could somehow coexist.

Jung's excitement seems to have derived from the powerful insight that in psychiatry he had discovered an arena in which he might empirically explore both "biological and spiritual facts": "Here at last was the place where the collision of nature and spirit became a reality." (Jung, 1989, p. 109)

Jung's subsequent comment further deepens our understanding of this important event. He points out that Kraft-Ebbing's textbook stimulated this insight because it is in part the subjective confession of the author. With his specific prejudice, with the totality of his being, he stands behind the objectivity of his experiences and responds to the "disease of the personality" with the whole of his own personality. (Jung, 1989, p.119)

In other words, the psychiatrist's "specific prejudice" (the limits intrinsic to any subjective approach, i.e. the "personal equation," [Jung 1921, paras. 9f]) is put into dynamic relation with "the objectivity of his experiences" (the limits intrinsic to any objective approach, i.e. the scientific perspective), and it is precisely the conjunction of the two that, in binocular fashion, offers the possibility of a response "with the whole…personality."

Within this context, Jung brings together two quite different oppositional pairings—that between the biological and the spiritual and that between the subjective and the objective. He thus indicates that what matters is not which particular opposites come into play, but the dynamic process by which they are brought together. His point is that these dynamic tensions—precisely the tensions we find between personality No. 1 and personality No. 2—constitute the primary motor within every dimension of his psychology.

Whether we are dealing with nature/spirit or subjective/objective or any of the numerous oppositional pairings that recur throughout Jung's writings, it is always the case that one of these opposite ideas or qualities will tend to be dominant and the other marginal. To use the imagery of his recent dream, one will tend to be seen as candle and the other, inevitably, as shadow. Under these circumstances, the psychological work required, as Jung sees it, consists in allowing what is shadowy, hidden, and marginal into awareness so that it can be brought into tension with the dominant quality, idea, or principle. This basic principle is neutral with regard to which specific ideas or qualities might be at any point dominant and which marginal. One could imagine different contexts in which either nature or spirit, for example, might be perceived as dominant or hidden, and the same goes for objective or subjective perspectives.

It should be remembered that this psychological process is not merely an abstract or theoretical exercise, since, as Jung insists, it involves the whole person. As he remarks later in *MDR*,

The opposites and the contradictions between them do not vanish . . . even when for a moment they yield before the impulse to action. They constantly threaten the unity of the personality, and entangle life again and again in their dichotomies." (Jung, 1989, p.346)

## Return to the Personal Myth...

The story of the two personalities in *MDR* describes a difficult negotiation between the claims of two mutually conflicting teloi, each of which seeks to find its place in the emergent unfolding of Jung's psychological life. The care with which Jung elucidates the twists and turns of the two personalities points to an awareness that these experiences are tracing out the first version of a process to which he would later give the name of individuation.

As we shall see, the theme of the two personalities continued to be the red thread that ran throughout Jung's developing psychology. In the following chapters, we will see Jung finding different ways to allow for this core dynamic within an increasingly complex psychological model.

His theory of the feeling-toned complex (1903-08) allowed for nonpathological multiplicity and hence a level of friction, and even conflict, within the normal psyche. The development of the technique of active imagination (1913-16) offered an arena within which dialogical relationships could emerge between the conscious ego (qua personality No. 1) and any number of inner others (qua personality No. 2). The transcendent function (1916) provided him with a dynamic explication of the creative and developmental process by which any meeting between conscious ego (No. 1) and inner (unconscious) other (No. 2) enables psychological movement (i.e., individuation). The theory of types (1921) exemplifies this process in action: In order to avoid psychic stasis and enable psychic movement, the dominant conscious typological identification (whatever it may be) (No. 1) needs to be brought into tension with the so-called inferior function (whatever it may be) (No. 2), so that the transcendent function may enable the (individuation) process to occur. Generally, neurosis gets defined by Jung as psychological one-sidedness, and this becomes generalised outward and applied to the wider collective, such that a narrowly rationalistic, positivistic, or materialistic culture is perceived as requiring a creative tension with energies, images, and forces that are (for example) irrational and spiritual. By contrast, in the case of a Christianity seen as one-sidedly spiritual, it is the material dimension that seeks inclusion. The flexibility of this approach is that it apportions no particular a priori values to either side of any binary: What is valuable can never be decided in advance because it always depends upon what quality or dimension is missing in the particular situation.

Finally, all of Jung's late alchemical works revolve around that question that finds its fullest expression in his chef d'oeuvre, *Mysterium Coniunctionis,* the subtitle of which speaks for itself: *An Inquiry into the Separation and Synthesis of Psychic Opposites in Alchemy* (Jung, 1955). However esoteric such a project may appear, on the psychological level that remains always Jung's primary concern it is clearly, intimately linked to the problem described in personal mythic form as that of the two personalities.

## … And its Problems

However, despite all the above, it seems to me important to also acknowledge the serious potential problems that arise in the context of any psychology so closely identified with a single person's personal myth. Some have found the whole idea of a psychology so intimately bound to the inner world of its creator nonsensical and have turned away with a shrug or, as we shall see in the next chapter, have joined Donald Winnicott in using it as a stick with which to pathologize Jung and his ideas (see Saban, 2016). However, if we wish to soberly evaluate Jung's psychology, it is important to acknowledge the problems that are uniquely provoked by a psychology grounded in the personal myth of its creator. It becomes particularly important to remain vigilant to the blind spots that will inevitably accompany such a psychology.

As is well known, Jung (like Freud) never underwent a thorough analysis. However impressive Jung's insight into his own psyche may appear to the outsider, it would be dangerously naive to assume that there were no blind spots in Jung's self-understanding. As Jung himself puts it, "In respect of one's own personality one's judgment is as a rule extraordinarily clouded." (Jung, 1921, para. 2) If the objective claims of Jung's psychology are coextensive with his subjective understanding of his personal myth, then it urgently behooves post-Jungians to exercise their freedom and ability to question or critique the quality or extent of that understanding.

Jung's concept of individuation is bound up with the correction of psychological one-sidedness, a problematic that I have argued can be traced back to Jung's own struggle with his two personalities. However, even if we acknowledge the psychological importance of the struggle to avoid one-sidedness, it does not follow that the particular *character* of that struggle as it showed up in Jung's life is equally significant. As we shall see, Jung's personal equation involved him in wrestling with a psychic undertow that drew him repeatedly toward the numinosity of personality No. 2 (the archetypal); as a result, Jung needed again and again to strenuously reassert the claims of personality No. 1 (the personal). The specific way this happened to play out within Jung's life should not be allowed to obscure the important fact that, as we have seen, the under-lying dynamic itself is fundamentally neutral, in that it never ascribes positive or negative valency to either domain. [5] Ultimately, the personal and the mythic coinhere, a notion articulated in Jung's psychology in a repeated emphasis (on a theoretical level) on the importance of bringing and keeping both realms together. On a fundamental level, they always already *are* together.

There is, however, a problematic tension between this intuition and the contrasting fact that throughout the development of his psychology, Jung's persistent pull toward No. 2 shows up again and again in a strongly reductive tendency to separate out and prioritise those images and experiences that align with personality No. 2 over and against the dimension of life that Jung identified with No. 1. I shall return to this problem in the later chapters of this book. What first needs to be convincingly shown is the way in which the dynamic between the two personalities played out within the development of Jung's psychology.

# ENDNOTES

[1] Much of the information of this sort to be found in *MDR* had been available to Jung's inner circle since the 1925 seminar (Jung, 1990). Readers acquainted only with Jung's published writings were unaware of the importance of the personal dimension until the posthumous publication of *MDR*.

[2] I hope it is obvious that I am not making the highly reductive argument that every concept in Jung's psychology is nothing but a result of a personal experience of Jung's.

[3] The term occurs in this sentence of the English translation: "Thus it is that I have now undertaken, in my eighty-third year, to tell my personal myth." It is a rendering by the English translators, Richard and Clara Winston, of this German passage: *"So habe ich es heute, in meinem dreiundachtzigsten Lebensjahr, unternommen, den Mythus meines Lebens zu erzählen."* The German phrase, *"den Mythus meines Lebens"* (literally, "the myth of my life") conveys something subtly different from the phrase "my personal myth," although precisely where the difference lies is hard to discern. Presumably, the translators chose to use the phrase "personal myth" because they wanted to particularly emphasise the personal dimension apparent in Jung's statement that this is *"den Mythus meines Lebens"* an emphasis he reiterates a little later: it is, he says, *"my* fable, *my* truth" (*mein Märchen, meine Wahrheit*). What we are to read is not just the *myth* of Jung's life, it is the myth of *Jung's* life. Hence, it is a myth, but it is also Jung's myth—his *personal* myth.

[4] Ernst Kris introduced the term to psychoanalytic literature in 1956 (Kris, 1956). However, Kris means by "personal myth" something quite different from Jung. Kris refers to the pathological phenomenon of a patient turning personal history into "a treasured possession to which the

patient is attached with a peculiar devotion." There may be a sense in which this is true of Jung, but it is not what Jung means by it.

The term crops up, not surprisingly, in post-Jungian literature, and especially in the writings of Susan Rowland. In various works over a 10-year period Rowland has put repeated emphasis upon the importance of the "personal myth" in Jung's writings. (See Rowland, 2002, 2003, 2011, 2005). As Petteri Pietikäinen has pointed out, the term "personal myth" possesses a paradoxical quality which resides in the fact that "it is one of the few basic characteristics of myth that it is an anonymous text, without a known author and therefore irreducible to an individual." (Pietikäinen, 1999, p. 237) For Rowland, its critical importance resides in this dual or ambiguous dimension; this is because "personal myth" possesses, for her, a crucial function as a bridging term between understanding that derives from individual experience and under-standing that relates to the conceptual, and particularly, in Jung's case, the universalising tendency toward Grand Narrative.

In this paper, I want to stay with what I see as the richness of this paradoxical concept, though my arguments and my intentions differ from those of Rowland, without, I hope, being in conflict with them

[5] For example: "Hence it is essential for progression… that impulse and counter-impulse, positive and negative, should reach a state of regular interaction and mutual influence" (Jung, 1928a, para. 61).

# CHAPTER 2
# Jung and the Dissociated Psyche

As we have seen, in *MDR* Jung introduces his discussion of the two personalities with a statement that has important implications regarding the particular model of the psyche that he developed in Analytical Psychology:

> The play and counterplay between personalities No. 1 and No. 2, which has run through my whole life, has nothing to do with a 'split' or dissociation in the ordinary medical sense. On the contrary, it is played out in every individual. (Jung, 1989, p. 45)

Here, Jung makes a strong claim about the nonpathological dissociability of the psyche. The normal psyche, he tells us, is neither simple nor unitary but is both complex and multiple. In this chapter, I argue that what Jung says about the two personalities is in every respect consistent with the central thread of his mature psychology—the psychology of the collected works. I also want to argue that from a very early point in the development of that psychology, Jung was making theoretical choices that stemmed from the insights gained from his experience of the two personalities.

What Jung learned from this experience was, first, that psychological development—individuation—required a mechanism whereby one-sidedness could be corrected, and second, that it would require a psychological model sufficiently flexible to allow for the possibility of intrapsychic conflict between different autonomous forces. Only this kind of model could allow for the kind of quasi-dialectical movement out of oppositional conflict that, in the dynamic of the two personalities, led toward a third, more balanced, position.

As it happens, at precisely the time that Jung was arriving at intellectual maturity, various psychological models were available to him that offered precisely these possibilities. In this chapter, I want to examine those models that might have influenced Jung during the crucial period 1900-14. In this way, I hope to be able to follow, as a kind of red thread, the ways in which the dynamic of the two personalities shaped Jung's psychological choices during that period.

An issue that would become crucial to the model Jung was eventually to develop was that of dissociation. This topic was hotly debated in the field of psychiatry during the early period of Jung's development, although, as we will see, the subsequent rise to dominance of Freud's psychoanalysis meant that it was later to become obscured, if not erased.

Three identifiably different theoretical approaches to the question of dissociation were in operation in 1900. The first was that of Frederic Myers (English) (followed more or less closely by his friends and colleagues, William James [American] and Theodor Flournoy [Swiss]). The second was that of Pierre Janet and the "French school." The third was that of Sigmund Freud.[1]

Because Jung was a friend and colleague of Freud's during the period 1904-10 and became an active supporter of the psychoanalytic movement, many commentators have assumed that during that period Jung fully accepted Freud's model of the psyche (e.g., Kerr, 1993). I will argue here that this was never the case and that, in fact, Jung's understanding of the psyche differed markedly from the psychoanalytic model.[2] Others have suggested that the crucial influence upon Jung was Pierre Janet's model (e.g., Haule, 1984). I will try to show here that there are significant differences between Jung's position and that of Janet. My basic argument is that the approach that is closest to Jung's is that of Myers. I should point out that, although Jung was certainly influenced by the ideas of all these men, his mature psychology draws on and moves beyond these traditions.

I want to focus here on the ways in which Jung's early experiences of the two personalities might have rendered certain psychological ideas and models more attractive to him than others. This line of enquiry will also shed some light on why post-Jungian attempts to merge Jung's ideas with those of psychoanalysis tend to become mired in intractable difficulties. As we shall see, these attempts at merger pay too little notice (and frequently none at all) to important differences between the models of the psyche that underpin the two psychologies.

## Winnicott's Review of *MDR*

In 1964, the renowned English pediatrician and psychoanalyst Donald Winnicott published (in the *International Journal of Psychoanalysis*) a review of the 1963 English translation of Jung's memoir, *Memories Dreams Reflections*, (Winnicott, 1992). Jung had died in 1961, but he had left a co-written autobiography to be published after his death. Winnicott's review is highly interesting for all kinds of reasons, but I want to focus here upon what it tells us about a *psychoanalytic* response to Jung, and specifically to Jung's account of his two personalities.

In *MDR*, as we have seen, Jung insists that the "play and counterplay" between his two inner personalities should not be taken as pathological, on the grounds that such a dynamic is psychologically normal. In Winnicott's review, Jung's claim is simply ignored. To Winnicott, it was patently obvious that Jung's account of his early years pointed to serious pathology. Indeed, he retrospectively diagnoses him with a "childhood schizophrenia." (Winnicott, 1992, p.320) Winnicott takes it for granted that a healthy psyche is necessarily *unitary* (or as he describes it a "unit psyche"). He also assumes that the sole function of the unconscious is to serve as a location in which to deposit whatever the "unit psyche" needs to repress. This leads him to make this kind of judgment:

> Whatever Freud was, he had a unit personality, with a place in
> him for his unconscious. Jung was different. It is not possible for
> a split personality to have an unconscious, because there is no
> place for it to be. Like our florid schizophrenic patients … Jung
> knew truths that are unavailable to most men and women. But
> he spent his life looking for a place to keep his inner psychic

reality, although the task was indeed an impossible one. (Winnicott, 1992, p.324)

Winnicott can see that Jung's personal psychology differed from Freud's. He can also see that there are fundamental differences between Jungian psychology and Freudian psychology.[3] He rightly interprets the gulf between them as grounded in a fundamental disagreement about the nature and function of the unconscious. For Winnicott (and for Winnicott's Freud), the unconscious is primarily "a place" for what gets repressed, while for Jung the unconscious is (among other things) an arena for dissociated alter-personalities. As Winnicott emphasises:

> [T]he psychoanalyst would sacrifice essential values were he to give up Freud's various meanings for the word unconscious, including the concept of the repressed unconscious. It is not possible to conceive of a repressed unconscious with a split mind; instead what is found is dissociation. (Winnicott, 1992, p.325)

Winnicott doesn't seem to be able to entertain the notion that Jung is propounding a model of the psyche that is radically different from the model Winnicott assumes to be self-evidently correct. For Winnicott, Jung's words are merely symptomatic of his "childhood schizophrenia." It follows that Jung's account of his childhood in *MDR* is of interest only to the extent that it may help "those with healthy unit personalities" to achieve empathy with "those [like Jung] whose divided selves give them constant trouble." (Winnicott, 1992, pp 327-8) Its sole virtue, in other words, is that it offers a rare insider perspective on a psyche that has suffered from, and to a certain extent healed itself of, psychotic illness. One way to regard Winnicott's review would be to take it as an example of the long and dishonorable psychoanalytic practice of using psychiatric diagnoses in order to attack its opponents, a practice that, in Jung's case, began with Freud himself. However, it seems more likely that Winnicott's assumptions are a by-product of the fact that, by 1964, the psychoanalytic understanding of the psyche (for all its undoubted twists, turns and re-inventions during this period) had held a dominant position within therapeutic circles for forty years. Perhaps this cultural hegemony made it difficult for Winnicott to imagine what an alternative model might look like.

In fact, psychoanalysis achieved dominance remarkably quickly. Eminent American psychiatrist (and expert on dissociation) Morton Prince summed up the situation in this way: "[By 1929] Freudian psychology had flooded the field like a full rising tide and the rest of us were left submerged like clams buried in the sands at low water." (quoted in Borch-Jacobsen and Shamdasani, 2011, p. 300)[4]. Although between 1900 and 1918 Freud appears to have considered alternative models of the psyche to be sufficiently threatening to fight them tooth and nail, by the 1960s alternatives to psychoanalysis were to be remembered, to the extent that they were recalled at all, as intellectual curiosities.

As it happens, Winnicott's approach continues to be accepted as more or less authoritative, not only by psychoanalysts, but by more recent Jungian writers (e.g. Satinover 1985, Meredith-Owen 2011). In what follows I shall attempt to explain how it is that in many Jungian circles a psychoanalytic approach continues to dominate the discourse. I shall return to Winnicott and his relationship to Jung at a later point.

## The Dissociationist Tradition

The notion that conflict can and does occur within the human psyche is obviously neither new nor original. Nonetheless, it achieved a novel articulation with the emergence of the idea of the dynamic unconscious. First emerging as a philosophical idea in the writings of the German idealists, it gained traction in the medical arena throughout the 19th century and eventually became dominant within the field of dynamic psychiatry (see Ellenberger, 2008, ffytche, 2012).

However, the ways in which this inner conflict was conceptualised took hugely varied forms. As we have seen, it is popularly assumed that Jung's Analytical Psychology is merely a heretical offshoot of Freudian psychoanalysis, which, as I have pointed out, dominated the field for much of the 20th century. In fact, this assumption underlies various post-Jungian attempts (notably those of Michael Fordham and the London school of Jungians) to synthesize Jung's psychology with concepts deriving from post-Freudian and particularly object relations theories.

However, with the publication of Henri F. Ellenberger's ground-breaking *The Discovery of the Unconscious* (Ellenberger, 1970), the assumption that Jung's psychological ideas were derivative of Freud's became increasingly untenable. Ellenberger pointed out that around the year 1900 psychoanalysis represented only one of numerous thriving alternative psychological models, which articulated versions of the unconscious (or, as it was also known the subconscious) that varied in significant ways. Ellenberger showed that Jung's psychology was heavily indebted to figures whose ideas were quite foreign to that of Freud and psychoanalysis, such as Pierre Janet in France, Frederic Myers in England, William James in the United States and Theodor Flournoy in Switzerland. These psychologists were elaborating models of the psyche and of psychic life that, for all their variations, agreed in an emphasis upon the fundamental *dissociability* of the psyche.

When Jung wrote in *MDR* that dissociation is "played out in every individual," he was a very old man. However, one can trace comparable ideas in Jung's work at least as far back as his doctoral dissertation, *On the psychology and pathology of so-called occult phenomena,* (Jung, 1902). Jung's thesis was both an account and an analysis of a series of séances conducted through a medium. As we now know, the medium in question was his own cousin Helly Preiswerk, who was 15 years old at the time of the seances. In the dissertation, Jung identified the various figures conjured up by the unconscious of his cousin as split-off aspects of her psyche. As Jung put it, the teenager led "a real 'double life' with two personalities existing side by side or in succession, each continually striving for mastery." (Jung, 1902, para. 44) His tentative conclusion was that such a development is not necessarily pathological. In fact, he suggested, a psychological arrangement of this kind may even point forward to future possibilities, since, as he put it, it is "conceivable that the phenomena of double consciousness are simply new character formations, or attempts of the future personality to break through." (Jung, 1902, para. 136)[5]

Not only were these ideas of Jung's entirely consistent with the psychology he was later to develop, they were also consistent with ideas to be found in the works of fellow Swiss Théodore Flournoy whose masterwork, *From India to the Planet Mars* (Flournoy, 2015) had been published in 1900. Flournoy had spent years working with Hélène Smith, a talented medium who, in her trance, appeared to be able to reenter various past lives, including those of, among others, Marie Antoinette, an Indian princess, Simandini, and a regular visitor to Mars. Flournoy presented Smith as a case of multiple personality, but of a nonpathological type. Flournoy's case lent weight to something his friend and colleague William James had previously suggested: "Mediumistic possession in all its grades seems to form a perfectly natural special type of alternate personality." (James, 1891, p. 393) Since the medium returned to healthy consciousness after the séance, it was apparent that certain kinds or levels of multiple personality could occur in the nonpathological psyche. At the very least, it would seem that a level of dissociation could be consistent with psychological normality.

Even some of those who argued most vigorously for the psychic reality of dissociation found this idea hard to swallow. Pierre Janet, for example, argued that although the medium was not necessarily a hysteric, she was definitely a pathological type. For Janet, the symptoms of dissociation always indicated some kind of pathology since a healthy consciousness was necessarily unitary, and therefore unconscious or subconscious processes simply could not occur in healthy people (Wright, 1997). Janet's thorough and detailed case histories showed him utilising hypnosis in order to trace his patients' symptoms back to a traumatic event that had been forgotten by the primary conscious personality. The trauma had, in effect, split the psyche into two (or more) personalities, each of which possessed some kind of autonomous consciousness. Through hypnosis, dreams, or automatic writing, Janet gained access to these "subconscious" personalities and thereby achieved the therapeutic goal of helping the patient regain the unity of consciousness that was proper to a healthy psyche.

For Flournoy and his colleagues Myers and James, Janet's carefully observed data was invaluable since it provided a plentiful supply of evidence for psychic dissociation. However, when it came to hypothesising about what they regarded as the positive, productive, and creative aspect of a multiple psyche, Flournoy and his colleagues found themselves quite as much in disagreement with Janet as they were, for different reasons, with Freud.

Along with Frederic Myers, Edmund Gurney and William James, Flournoy was an active member of the Society for Psychical Research, a British organisation that had been set up (in 1882) to conduct scientific investigations into the claims of spiritualism. The SPR rapidly extended its experiments and researches into the related fields of telepathy (a word first coined by Myers in 1882 [Myers, 1882, p. 147]), hauntings, clairvoyance, and precognitive dreams. Myers was probably the first to suggest that a separate state of consciousness could exist simultaneously alongside normal consciousness. This notion emerged from his extensive research into the phenomenon of automatic writing. As early as 1885 he coined the term "secondary self," (Myers, 1885, p. 27) a term later taken up by Janet. When, in 1886, Janet's experiments succeeded in showing that hysterics possessed secondary selves, Myers' colleague Edmund Gurney went further and did the same with "normal healthy subjects" who, using the planchette, found themselves producing automatic writing (i.e., producing written words without consciously writing) (Gurney, 1887, pp. 292–293). William James confidently stated that what these experiments had demonstrated was "the simultaneous existence of two different strata of consciousness, ignorant of each other, in the same person." (James, 1892, p. 688)

Multiplicity of personality was not in itself a new phenomenon. The rise of mesmerism in the late 18th century and its evolution into hypnotic trance in the work of Jacques François de Chastenet de Puységur, Antoine Despine, Eugène Azam and others, had revealed numerous cases that were characterised by some kind of splitting of the personality (Crabtree, 1993; Ellenberger, 1970). Perhaps the most famous of these was the case of Felida X, described by Azam in the 1860s. However, in these cases, the multiple selves tended to reveal themselves in chronological alternation (Taves, 2003, p. 307). What was new in the work of Myers, Gurney, and Janet was the co-presence of secondary selves acting simultaneously with the primary self (or ego).

It was precisely because Frederic Myers was positioned outside the scientific establishment during an era when positivism was in the ascendant that he was able to move beyond the limitations of a strictly experimental psychology (such as that of Wilhelm Wundt), and take the step of combining the clinical accounts of Janet and his colleagues with the results the SPR experimenters were carefully accumulating. This enabled him to construct a coherent, not to say grand, theory and model of the psyche. As it happens, Myers' personal aim was to seek evidence for human immortality. Nonetheless, as William James pointed out after Myers's death in 1900, "[Myers writings] have a value for Science entirely independent of the light they shed upon that problem." (James, 1901, p. 14)[6]

Myers rejected the notion that consciousness is unitary, and instead he suggested that the psyche has a "composite ... character." (Myers, 1903a, p. 9) For Myers, the ordinary, everyday "supraliminal" self "does not comprise the whole of the consciousness or of the faculty within us," since, below the threshold of normal consciousness there exist "subliminal Selves." (Myers, 1903a, p.14) The unity of the psyche is therefore "federative and unstable." (Myers, 1903a, p.16) This emphasis upon the "disintegrative" aspect of psyche should nonetheless be kept in tension with Myers's equally emphatic vision of the self as "profoundly unitary." (Myers, 1903a, p.34) While much of this is consistent with Janet's findings, Myers goes much further than Janet. He suggests, for example, that a measure of dissociation is to be found in the normal psyche and insists moreover that "the normal or primary self" (i.e. the ego) "is not necessarily superior in any other respect to the latent personalities [or subliminal selves] which lie alongside it." (Myers, 1888, p. 387). These subliminal selves can and do gain access to wider ranges of information and faculty than the ego:

I hold … that this subliminal consciousness … may embrace a far wider range both of physiological and of psychical activity than is open to our supraliminal consciousness. … The spectrum of consciousness, if I may so call it, is in the subliminal self indefinitely extended at both ends. (Myers, 1891, pp. 305-306)

Myers here uses a simile that may seem familiar to readers of Jung. In Jung's 1947 paper *On the Nature of the Psyche*, he compares the psyche to the colour spectrum, assigning its instinctual dimension to the infrared end and the archetypal, or "mystical," dimension to the ultraviolet end (Jung, 1947, para. 384 and paras. 414ff).[7]

Although Myers's meaning here is not exactly the same as Jung's, there are striking similarities between the two passages. We can hear pre-echoes of Jung's idea that the psyche is self-regulating and of Jung's characterisation of the unconscious as psychic treasure house:

Beyond the inferior or physiological end of that spectrum, we ought to find traces of a beneficent power over physiological processes which are not within the control of the supraliminal will. Coincidently with that spectrum we ought to find traces of a completer than the supraliminal memory, of a keener than the supraliminal sense-perfection, of a sounder than the supra-liminal judgment. And beyond the superior or psychical end of our metaphorical spectrum we ought to find traces of a knowledge subliminally acquired by methods unknown to the supraliminal self, and from sources to which that self has no access. (Myers, 1891 p.312)

Elsewhere, Myers uses a different metaphor to describe the relation of the supraliminal (ego) to the whole psyche:

Our supraliminal consciousness is but a floating island upon the 'abysmal deep' of the total individuality beneath it; and the waves which wash under one end of our narrow standing-place are continuous with the waves which wash under the other. (ibid. p.329)

Again, this pre-echoes a similar image in Jung:

[Ego consciousness] could easily be compared to an island in the ocean. Whereas the island is small and narrow, the ocean is immensely wide and deep and contains a life infinitely surpassing, in kind and degree, anything known on the island. … (Jung, 1937, para.141)

By the time he was writing his doctoral thesis, Jung had certainly read Myers's work, since Jung quotes there from one of Myers's articles in the Proceedings of the SPR (Jung, 1902, paras. 88ff, para 100). Jung had a well-documented and self-professed interest in the literature of psychical investigation, and so we shouldn't be surprised if he had some acquaintance with Myers's writings; we might indeed expect him to have read other articles by Myers from the same source, possibly including the articles on the subliminal self I have quoted above. As he references Myers's *Subliminal Consciousness* in a paper written 50 years later, my guess would be that Jung knew Myers's work reasonably well. [8]

What is certain is that Jung was directly influenced by both Flournoy and James. As Andreas Sommer emphasises, the psychology of James and Flournoy "cannot be understood without an appreciation of the considerable impact Myers' concept of the 'subliminal Self' had on both." (Sommer, 2011, p. 434) Therefore, as Sonu Shamdasani points out, even if Jung were not under the direct influence of Myers, "it would have been impossible for Jung to have been significantly influenced by Flournoy … without also taking on board fundamental aspects of the work of Myers." (Shamdasani, 2000, p. 462)

This influence can be seen in three crucial areas:

1. The "mythopoeic" faculty (Myers, 1903b, p. 5) of the subconscious, which "constantly produces fantasies, stories, poetic images, and other

spontaneous creations." (Crabtree, 2009, p. 356) This is the faculty responsible for dreams and visions, but also for the subpersonalities that are created and enacted in a mediumistic trance. This dimension of Myers's psychology was particularly developed by Flournoy in *From India to the Planet Mars* (Ellenberger 1970, pp 315-318), a work that, as we have seen, was very influential upon Jung's doctoral dissertation.

2. Alongside (and intimately related to) this mythopoeic faculty is Myers's (and Flournoy's) emphasis upon the *prospective* character of the unconscious/subliminal (Witzig, 1982, p. 138ff). Flournoy highlights this in his review of Jung's thesis:

> Altogether, Mr Jung thinks that, among those temperaments [natures] with an heredity and neurotic temperament like this subject, sleepwalking phenomena during the phase of puberty (facts of double consciousness, etc.) can have a teleological value: they express the transformations and new shapes of character, and represent the eruptions of the future personality across the obstacles which unfavourable circumstances oppose her normal development. (Quoted in Witzig, 1982, p. 138)

3. The (normal) psyche is dissociated: We possess, apart from our "supraliminal" ego consciousness, other consciousnesses, which show up in the form of mediumistic trance personalities, automatic writing, and (in pathological form) multiple personalities and hysterical subpersonalities.

In the work of Myers, Flournoy, and James, these ideas are inextricably intertwined. The same is true for Jung's psychology. Although Jung was undoubtedly also influenced in various ways by Pierre Janet,[9] Janet could not have signed up to any of these ideas because he placed a relentless emphasis on the *universally pathological nature of dissociation*. Jung's account of his two personalities would have indicated to Janet (as it did to Winnicott) only that Jung was suffering from serious psychological problems.

## Freud and Dissociation

When it comes to the question of dissociation, Jung's approach was as close to that of Myers's as it was distant from that of Freud. I am going to argue that this was true not only before Jung came under Freud's influence, but during and after the period of Jung's association with psychoanalysis.[10]

In 1912, Freud delivered a paper to the Society for Psychical Research titled *A Note on the Unconscious in Psycho-Analysis* (Freud, 1912). Myers had died young in 1900, but during his final 18 years, he had painstakingly built up within the Proceedings of the SPR a systematic conception of the psyche. James Keeley points out that Freud's paper—a paper that has the distinction of being his first systematic theorisation of the unconscious—was deliberately placed in the Proceedings of the SPR in order to put down a clear red line between his own version of the unconscious and that of Myers (Keeley, 2001). What is interesting is that Freud felt that this needed to be done. Even in 1912, Freud evidently saw Myers's subliminal self as a serious rival to Freud's own psychoanalytic conception of the psyche.

It had been in the SPR Proceedings that the work of Freud and his co-author Josef Breuer received its first acknowledgment in the English language. In 1894, Myers published a paper titled *The Mechanism of Hysteria*, which made up chapter 6 of his ongoing theoretical essay titled *The Subliminal Consciousness* (Myers, 1894). In that paper, Myers mentioned recently published work by Freud and Breuer (and specifically their *On the Psychical Mechanism of Hysterical Phenomena (Preliminary Communication)* (Freud, 1893). Myers characterised Freud and Breuer as providing clinical evidence to corroborate Myers's own ideas about the place of hysteria on his psychic spectrum. As he says, "I could not wish for a more emphatic support, from wide clinical experience, of the view of hysteria to which my own observations on different branches of automatism had already, by mere analogical reasoning, directed my thought." (Myers, 1894, pp. 14-15) He went on to offer some helpful criticism of Freud's and Breuer's approach:

What I would fain *add* to the exposition of Drs. Breuer and Freud the reader may have already divined. That extraordinary potency of subliminal action, which they frankly present as insoluble by pure physiology, is part and parcel of my scheme of man; and its occasional appearance in this disordered form is to me but the natural concomitant of its habitual and inevitable residence within us; in readiness—if we can contrive to summon it—to subserve our highest needs. (Myers, 1894, p.15)

Myers, in yet another pre-echo of Jung's later comments, sees Freud's and Breuer's approach as, on the one hand, too narrowly pathological and, on the other, not sufficiently teleological. Myers is also at pains to establish his priority (alongside Edward Gurney and Pierre Janet) with regard to the conception of what he describes as "stratified consciousness" and to imply thereby that the role of Freud's and Breuer's work is to merely offer support to what constitutes an already established body of work. At this stage, Myers clearly sees no great conflict between his own psychic model and that of Freud and Breuer.

In fact, for the contemporary reader, it would have been difficult to differentiate the approach to be found in Freud's and Breuer's 1893's *Preliminary Communication* from that of Myers. In that paper, for example, Freud and Breuer make this observation:

*The longer we have been occupied with these phenomena, the more we have become convinced that the splitting of consciousness which is so striking in the well-known classical cases under the form of* 'double conscience' ['dual consciousness'] *is present to a rudimentary degree in every hysteria, and that a tendency to such a dissociation, and with it the emergence of abnormal states of consciousness (which we shall bring together under the term* 'hypnoid') *is the basic phenomenon of this neurosis. In these views* we concur with Binet and the two Janets. (Freud, 1893, p. 12 Italics in the original)

We can assume that it was Breuer who wrote this particular passage, since, although Freud was willing to put his name to the paper, he was, even in 1893, already harbouring doubts about dissociation and beginning to develop his repression model. When it comes to the issue of dissociation, therefore, as Phil Mollon has remarked, "There is a paradox in the origin of psychoanalysis." (Mollon, 2011, p. 9) In the ur-case of the talking cure, that of Anna O, not only do we find prominently dissociative symptomatology, but also the terminology of Janetian dissociationism. What is often held to be the original psychoanalytic case therefore fails to fit within the psychological model generally accepted as Freudian. As Mollon points out, "The division between conscious and unconscious mind, and a process of 'repression,' which banishes unwanted contents of the mind to the unconscious, does not accommodate dissociation of the mind into alternate states of consciousness." (Mollon, 2011, p. 9) Ian Hacking, a philosopher who has written extensively about the phenomenon of multiple personality, agrees: "Repression and Dissociation were two opposed ideas, with roots in different traditions, and using distinct models of the mind." (Hacking, 1997, p. 117)

However, in the *Preliminary Communication*, Freud had not yet distanced himself from Breuer's dissociation model of the psyche. It was a year later that Freud's new theory of repression was to be revealed in 1894's *The Neuro-Psychoses of Defence* (Freud, 1894). By the time *Studies on Hysteria* was published in 1895, Freud was, as Philip Bromberg puts it, "for the most part openly contemptuous about the possible usefulness of theorizing about dissociation, hypnoid phenomena, or states of consciousness." (Bromberg, 1996, p. 271)

Seventeen years of psychoanalytic theorising divide these events from 1912's *A Note on the Unconscious*, years in which Freud had mapped out his evolving model of the psyche in several publications, (not least 1900's *Interpretation of Dreams*). However, in the 1912 paper, Freud evidently still felt the need to put blue water between his model and that of Myers (and also that of Janet, with whom, in the intervening years Freud had developed a bitter rivalry [See Perry and Laurence, 1984]). Keeley describes Freud's SPR paper as a "corrective manifesto for psychoanalysis," sent "into the heart of this rival school." (Keeley, 2001, p. 776)

The conflict between Freud's approach and that of Myers and Janet concerned the nature of the unconscious. Although, Freud argues, unconscious ideas can produce disturbing effects on the behaviour of the subject (e.g., parapraxes), these ideas are by definition absent from consciousness. It therefore makes no sense to suggest that they could possess consciousness of their own. According to Freud, contents that possess an instinctive, infantile, unreasoning, or predominantly sexual character are unacceptable to the conscious self and are therefore repressed into the unconscious. As Jung later put it, "[Freud] saw the unconscious as a sort of storeroom where all the discarded things of consciousness were heaped up and left." (Jung, 1987, p.339) As Jung never tired of reminding his readers, this constituted a major difference between his own way of seeing the unconscious and that of Freud.

For Jung, on the other hand, the unconscious was, as he put it, "a matrix, a sort of basis of consciousness, possessing a creative nature and capable of autonomous acts, autonomous intrusions into the consciousness." For Jung, the unconscious is therefore "a real fact, an autonomous factor that was capable of independent action." (Jung, 1987, p.339) These ideas of Jung are recognisably in the tradition of Myers, for whom the unconscious (or as he described it, the subliminal) was not only the matrix for potential future development, but also an arena in which autonomous coconscious 'personalities' could, under certain circumstances, be in communication with normal consciousness. The nature of Freud's opposition to Myers's conception of the (subliminal) unconscious therefore clarifies the ways in which the psychoanalytic unconscious differs from Jung's (creative and multiple) unconscious.

In the SPR paper, Freud suggests that instead of talking about a "splitting of consciousness," as in the famous case of dual consciousness described by Azam (the case of Felida X) it would make most sense to say that we are dealing with a "shifting of consciousness," ("Wandern des Bewußtseins") where that function simply oscillates between two different psychical complexes "which become conscious and unconscious in alternation." (Freud, 1912, p. 263) As Adam Crabtree points out, Freud thereby signally fails to explain "those numerous cases in which two apparent intelligences communicate simultaneously," (Crabtree, 2009, p. 329) cases which made up the bulk of Myers's, James's and Janet's examples of automatism and which Morton Prince later described in terms of "co-consciousness." (Prince, 1907)

In the years after his split with Jung, Freud continued to adjust and develop his approach to the relation of conscious and unconscious. In his later topology of the psyche, as found in, for example, *The Ego and the Id* (Freud, 1923), Freud goes beyond the basic conscious/unconscious model and acknowledges conflict among various psychic parts: ego, id, and superego. Nonetheless, even here Freud seems keen to emphasise that unconscious impulses that are in conflict with the conscious ego can never attain to any consciousness of their own. It is the ego's resistance to the unconscious impulse that, as it were, brings it to consciousness (Freud, 1923, p.22). What is clear is that, even when Freud's later model appears to move in the direction of a multiplicity of psychic parts, he adamantly refuses to allow for any consciousness outside the ego. In his last years, he made a renewed attempt at the topic with his work on what he called the splitting (*Spaltung*) of the ego (Freud, 1938). With the concept of the split ego, Freud finally made room for some of the phenomena that, in an attempt to distance his psychology from that of the dissociationists, he had hitherto ruled out. Like his old rival Janet, Freud never ceased to assume that the splitting of the ego should be seen as a pathological development.

## Jung

As we have seen, Jung's 1902 doctoral dissertation closely paralleled Théodore Flournoy's *From India to the Planet Mars* (Flournoy, 1900), not only in its form but more importantly in its theoretical intentions and assumptions. Jung cites not only Myers, Flournoy, James and Janet but many other dissociationist theoreticians, including Théodule-Armand Ribot, Charles Richet, Morton Prince, and Alfred Binet. Although at this point Jung had yet to meet Freud, he refers in several places to his writings.

Here, for example, Jung sounds a Janetian tone in his embrace of dissociation as an explanatory principle and remains agnostic with regard to Freud's "repression" hypothesis:

> It was probably a dissociation from the already existing personality, and this split-off part seized upon the nearest available material for its expression, namely the associations concerning myself. Whether this offers a parallel to the results of Freud's dream investigations must remain unanswered, for we have no means of judging how far the emotion in question may be considered 'repressed.' (Jung, 1902 par. 97)

Jung's 1905-07 writings on the word association experiment (Jung, 1973a) contain numerous approving mentions of Freud, as we might expect from a period in which Jung's friendship with Freud and his interest in psychoanalysis flourished, and accordingly we find far fewer references to the French and Anglo-Saxon dissociationists than we found in Jung's dissertation. What is certainly the case is that Jung wishes his readers (and above all Freud himself) to consider him a devotee of psychoanalysis.

When Freud came to read Jung's *Association Studies*, he was delighted to find repeated attempts by Jung to argue for the correctness of the psychoanalytic approach. He wrote to Jung, "'Psychoanalysis and Association Experiments,' pleased me most, because in it you argue on the strength of your own experience that everything I have said about the hitherto unexplored fields of our discipline is true." (Freud and Jung, 1977, p. 3)

For the moment, the abundant good will that characterised the early stages of the relationship between Jung and Freud seems to have enabled both men to ignore difficult areas of potential conflict, and in this way incompatibilities of theory were rendered all but invisible. The Freud/Jung correspondence makes it clear that as soon as Jung committed himself to the psychoanalytic cause, and especially after he had been anointed "crown prince," the primary focus for both men became the battle against the enemies of psychoanalysis. In effect, Freud and Jung were bonded by the powerful dynamic of the war mentality that powered this "us against them" conflict. This bond was cemented by the evident personal warmth of the relationship between the two men (to be examined in the next chapter). One can only assume that all these factors encouraged Freud to disregard the discrepancies between their respective psychological models, or at least to postpone any reckoning until much later. As Freud wrote in his second letter to Jung, "I venture to hope that in the course of the years you will come much closer to me than you now think possible." (Freud and Jung, 1977, p.5)

In the early stages of the development of depth psychology, not surprisingly, the focus was primarily upon those ideas that were shared rather than on the differences between them. During his time at the Burghölzli, therefore, Jung was probably not fully aware of the theoretical incompatibilities between his psychological perspective and that of Freud. Eugen Bleuler, for example, Jung's boss at the Burghölzli, maintained an eclectic approach to the various theoretical approaches available at the time. Although Bleuler initiated and encouraged Jung's enthusiasm for Freud's ideas and showed an interest of his own (Dalzell, 2007), he resisted an *exclusive* adherence to psychoanalytic ideas, continuing to support ideas associated with both Myers' subliminal consciousness and Janet's subconscious.[11] Such tolerance was to become difficult to maintain in the face of increasingly insistent calls from the psychoanalytic community to conform to Freud's ideas, and indeed it was Bleuler's resistance to what he experienced as unpalatable dogmatism that led ultimately to a break between the two men and to a cooling of Bleuler's relationship with Jung (Makari, 2009, p.250ff).

As Patrick Vandermeersch has conclusively shown, Jung's understanding of psychoanalytic concepts such as repression continued to differ in important ways from that of Freud (Vandermeersch, 1991, p.84ff). As John Ryan Haule also notes, "The careful reader discovers only the loosest connection between [Jung's Word Association studies] and the contemporary works of Freud." (Haule, 1984, p. 648) One important difference, as many have commented, concerns the role of sexuality. For example, as Haule points out, in Jung's work, "there is nothing to indicate that sexuality determines all complexes or lurks 'latently' behind the 'manifest' responses of the patient. Rather Jung takes the responses quite literally." (Haule, 1984, p. 648) However, the theoretical differences between the two psychologists by no means end with the issue of sexuality.

Both Jung and Freud agreed in recognising that unconscious contents have the potential to disrupt and disturb ego consciousness, and from this point of view, Jung's complexes seem broadly coextensive with Freud's parapraxes and were presumably taken as such by Freud.

However, there was a crucial disagreement when it came to the question of repression and the autonomy of the unconscious. Jung insists, in a preface to his 1935 edition of *The Relations between the Ego and the Unconscious* that the factor that "distinguishes [his] views so radically from those of Freud" was the "idea of the independence of the unconscious"— and this idea, he adds, had first come to him "as far back as 1902, when I was engaged in studying the psychic history of a young girl somnambulist." [i.e. Helene Preiswerk] (Jung, 1935a, p.123) This notion of an autonomous unconscious was utterly incompatible with Freud's repression model.

From the vantage point of old age, Jung's story was that Freud's exclusive insistence on the mechanism of repression provided an early bone of contention between the two men. Jung was interviewed in 1957 by Richard Evans, and during a discussion of the word association experiments, he claimed,

> That was my first point of difference with Freud. I said there were cases in my observation where there was no repression from above, but the thing itself is true. Those contents that became unconscious had withdrawn all by themselves, they were not repressed. On the contrary, they have a certain autonomy. I discovered the concept of autonomy because these contents that disappear have the power to move independently of my will. (Jung, 1987, p. 283)

As Shamdasani remarks,

It is somewhat ironic that Jung cites as his first divergence from Freud, the issue over which the supposed similarity between his association experiments and psychoanalysis was made, and through which the former was supposed to provide experimental confirmation of the latter (Shamdasani, 1998, pp. 120–121).

## Complex and Personification

Jung seems to have been drawn to the idea of the complex precisely because it enabled him to articulate a psychological model that, as Haule puts it, could account for the existence "of multiple, simultaneously active, subpersonalities." (Haule, 1984, p. 648) Complexes could, under certain circumstances, momentarily possess the subject in ways that paralleled, in a rather less dramatic form, the behaviour of the *alters* of multiple personality, or the trance personae of the medium. Of course, from Jung's point of view, they also paralleled the behaviour of his two personalities.

In later years, Jung often emphasised the core importance of his early work on complexes. In a 1934 paper reviewing the complex theory, for example, he clarified the link between his writings on complexes and the work of Janet, Prince and the dissociationists by pointing out that "fundamentally there is no difference in principle between a fragmentary personality and a complex." (Jung, 1934b par. 202) "The existence of complexes" as Jung puts it, "throws serious doubt on the naïve assumption of the unity of consciousness…" (Jung, 1934b par. 200)

In 1936's *Psychological Factors Determining Human Behaviour* (Jung, 1936a), Jung discussed complexes in a paragraph devoted to "the psyche's tendency to split," which he describes as "fundamentally … a normal phenomenon." (Jung, 1936a, par. 253) When he goes on to characterise complexes as behaving "like independent beings" and to equate them with "the voices heard by the insane," Jung reminds us of his early affiliation with the dissociationists. Later, he directly evokes the Myersian tradition by pointing out that they can "take on a personal ego-character like that of the spirits who manifest themselves through automatic writing and similar techniques." (Jung, 1936a, par. 253)

By drawing attention to the personified form in which complexes show up, Jung is glancing back to Flournoy, who had in 1901 described the subliminal mind as possessing an "imaginative process of foreign personification." (Flournoy, 1901) In fact, the process of personification was to take on a crucial importance in Jung's mature psychology. "[T]he unconscious spontaneously personifies," (Jung, 1939, para. 514) he insists, and he emphasises that this is not an action of the ego: "It is not we who personify [unconscious figures]; they have a personal nature from the very beginning." (Jung 1929, para. 62)

It was this emphasis upon psychic personification that led Jung to develop a psychological taxonomy that resembled a virtual Dramatis Personae (shadow, anima, animus, puer, senex, wise old man, etc.). He makes a point of using overtly theatrical terms to describe the personifications that occur in dreams and active imaginations (Jung, 1955 par. 706 and 753, 1945 pars. 561ff) and portrays "the transformation process of the unconscious psyche" as a "drame intérieur." (Jung, 1935a, p.123)

Indeed, the "possibility of change and differentiation" (Jung 1936a par. 255) that is so essential for psychotherapeutic work is itself, Jung claims, bound up with the dissociability of the psyche. The normal psyche's ability to become aware of its own multiplicity is precisely what gives it the capacity to self-regulate: the inner division is what enables us to first see, and then correct one-sidedness. For Jung, this is the dynamic that powers the process of individuation.

We can see this process most clearly in Jung's so-called confrontation with the unconscious, in which he encountered the autonomous figures of the objective psyche. These are the encounters that Jung recounts in *The Red Book*. According to *MDR*, Jung learned a crucial lesson from these encounters: "There is something in me which can say things that I do not know and do not intend, things which may even be directed against me." (Jung, 1989, p. 183) What necessitated this painful process of correction is clear from the context—the one-sidedness of Jung's ego perspective: "Whenever the outlines of a new personification appeared, I [ego] felt it almost as a personal defeat." (Jung, 1989, p. 183) This process is entirely consistent with the insights Jung had gained from his struggle with the two personalities; as we shall see, it represented a further development of the logic of opposites that had emerged from Jung's early experiences.

As I have pointed out, Jung's psychological ideas, and the techniques he subsequently developed, invariably emerged from his personal experiences. This is certainly the case here. Jung's original experience of inner division fed directly into the theoretical notion that the psyche universally manifests in multiple, personified form. His experience of conscious engagement with personality No. 2 fed into his therapeutic suggestion that the ego needs to engage in a reciprocal process of shaping hitherto inchoate unconscious events through an imaginative process of personification:

> The essential thing is to differentiate oneself from these unconscious contents by personifying them, and at the same time to bring them into relationship with consciousness. That is the technique for stripping them of their power. It is not too difficult to personify them, as they always possess a certain degree of autonomy, a separate identity of their own. Their autonomy is a most uncomfortable thing to reconcile oneself to, and yet the very fact that the unconscious presents itself in that way gives us the best means of handling it (ibid. p. 187).

As Craig Stephenson notes, the aim here is for the ego-complex to be able to "experience the autonomy of the unconscious complex as a splinter psyche and eventually reconcile itself to the contradictions inherent in psychic reality through a personified confrontation and meeting." (Stephenson, 2009, p. 166). However one-sided the ego may be, Jung implies, so long as it possesses sufficient awareness and sufficient humility, it can seek out a dialogical encounter with its own other, and this process will body forth the contradictions that are inherent to the psyche. When Jung talks, in often rather abstract terms, about the meeting of opposites, this is the experiential process he is referring to. These, often conflictual, encounters are brought about by a reciprocal engagement between ego and unconscious. The willing ego, possessed of the requisite "negative capability," will partly find and partly create those persons of the unconscious who are also, in a sense, seeking out the opportunity to be encountered.[12]

In this chapter, we have explored the important role of this engagement with the inner other in the development of Jung's ideas. We have also characterised this encounter between conscious ego and autonomous unconscious in terms of a meeting between personality No. 1 and personality No. 2. However, it is also the case that this *intrapsychic* relational process was accompanied in the period we have been looking at by important interpersonal relationships. Jung's conscious ego (No. 1) was in this period also constantly confronted by the *outer* world, and particularly in the form of highly significant relational connections with outer others (colleagues, friends, family, patients and lovers). Given this, it seems reasonable to ask to what extent the encounter between personality No. 1 and personality No. 2 might also have played out in the outer arena. In the next chapter, I would like to explore this possibility within the specific relational dynamics of Jung's highly numinous encounter with Freud.

[1] Those who have dealt with this topic tend to generally make a strong distinction between "dissociationist" psychologies and repression-based psychologies, thus lumping Janet's psychology together with Myers's. The problem with this is that it obscures important differences between the ideas of these two important figures, and it also blurs important shifts within Freud's ideas at various stages with regard to psychic splitting. I therefore here treat the ideas of Myers and those of Janet as separate approaches. I also want to try to give due weight to the ambiguities of Freud's position and the difficulties he had in transcending them.

[2] This point is not original. My work here depends upon the careful and persuasive scholarship of, for example, Ellenberger (1970), Taylor (1998, 1996, 1986, 1980), Shamdasani (2003, 2002, 2000, 1998, 1994, 1993), and Haule (1984, 1983). The fact that many Jungian writers continue to ignore this work, and what it might mean, especially in terms of its clinical implications for Analytical Psychology, encourages me to reemphasise its importance.

[3] There are, as we will see, serious questions to be asked with regard to the accuracy of Winnicott's representation of Freud's position.

[4] Morton Prince was the writer of the classic *The Dissociation of a Personality* (Prince, 1905).

[5] William Goodheart has suggested that Jung embraced the notion of the dissociation of autonomous complexes (and simultaneously rejected Freud's repression theory) as an attempt to defend himself against the erotic difficulties he was experiencing in his relationship with Preiswerk (Goodheart, 1984). As John Haule argues, such an argument stumbles over evidence of Jung's long-standing and consistent affiliations with

the dissociationist tradition. Haule also makes the excellent point that "there is nothing intrinsic to the concept of complex which would wall it off from the outside world" (Haule, 1985, p. 177). In other words, there is no conflict between accepting a dissociation-based psychic model and recognising the crucial importance of the interactional field. Indeed, in Jung's later psychology of the transference he fruitfully brings both these notions together. Nonetheless, Goodheart's wider thesis, that Jung was particularly attracted to the notion of an autonomous psyche that operates independently of relational (social/political) considerations (i.e. No. 2) because of his difficulties with the outer-facing dimensions of the psyche (i.e. No. 1), is much more credible, as I go on to argue in the later chapters of this book.

[6] Myers's theory was shaped in a series of articles in the Proceedings of the SPR published between 1884 and his death in 1900 but is to be found in its most complete form in the posthumously published two-volume *Human Personality and Its Survival of Bodily Death* (Myers, 1903a, 1903b).

[7] This paper, which contains a section titled "The dissociability of the psyche," also contains a footnote devoted by Jung to William James's phrase "fringe of consciousness," a term which, as Jung acknowledges, James himself "identifies with the 'subliminal consciousness' of F. W. H. Myers." Jung goes on to point the reader to the precise article of Myers that contains the spectrum reference I have quoted above, though he does not acknowledge Myers's use of the metaphor. (Jung, 1947, par. 383 n.47)

[8] There are also numerous possible common sources, such as romantic thinkers like Carl Gustav Carus (1789-1869). In Myers's case, this Romantic influence would have arrived via his profound knowledge of the English romantic poets, especially Wordsworth and Coleridge.

[9] Jung studied in Paris with Janet during the winter semester of 1902-03.

[10] It goes beyond the remit of this work to make a detailed case for the further thesis that later developments in psychoanalytic theory sustained and deepened that difference. However, as my comments on Winnicott tend to show, such an argument is at the very least plausible.

Nonetheless, it is also arguable that, as has undoubtedly been the case in other unrelated areas, such as countertransference, both Freud himself and post-Freudians have belatedly found a way toward theoretical positions that seem to echo Jung's position, (without, of course, acknowledgment of Jung's priority). Some have even argued that in the Freud-Jung relationship the influence was not all one-way (Kerslake, 2007, p. 101) and that the impact of Jung's ideas on Freud was long-lasting. In this case, ideas about the division of the ego that we find in late Freud (Freud, 1938) get taken up by other psychoanalysts. As Brenner puts it:

> Given the evolution of Freud's theorizing over time, he invoked the concept of splitting to describe a dividedness of consciousness, between the id and the ego, the ego and the superego, and within the ego itself. It fell upon his followers to apply this mechanism to virtually all of their own models of the mind, such as the normative split in the ego between observing and participating ego ... splitting in object relations theory ... and the vertical split in self psychology... (Brenner, 2009, p. 14).

In this way, it became possible for Freud's successors (e.g., Klein and Kohut) to allow for phenomena which, as we have seen, the repression theory of the period during which Jung worked with Freud simply rendered invisible.

[11] For example, in "Consciousness and Association" (Bleuler, 1918), Bleuler's contribution to the Jung-edited volume, *Studies in Word Association*, he writes, "If we use the experiments ... of thoughtreading, of the planchette (unconscious writing), and of table-rapping, we find ... remarkable unconscious activities. ... Automatic writing, in particular, deserves more attention from psychologists than it has received." (Bleuler, 1918, p.275).

[12] Shamdasani suggests that when developing the techniques that would later become known as active imagination, Jung probably drew on sources like Loyola and Swedenborg, and contemporary figures like Silberer and Staudenmaier (Shamdasani, 2009, p. 200). What seems also

likely is that it was the fertile meeting between these influences and his own early experience of the two personalities that enabled such experiments to be imagined. As we have seen, Jung's willingness to entertain the possibility of subconscious and subliminal selves derived from his extensive readings in James, Myers and Flournoy, but it also drew on his own experience of inner conflict, played out via auto-nomous and personified complexes.

# CHAPTER 3
# Secrets and Lies

"[I]t is a joy to be hidden but a disaster not to be found."
(Winnicott, 1990, p.186)

In the previous chapter, I focused upon psychological theory, and specifically upon the theoretical gulf between Jung and Freud, which, despite appearances, persisted throughout the period of their closest collaboration. In this chapter, I want to look more closely at the *personal* dimension of the Freud/Jung relationship. What I want to argue is that in order to fully grasp the significance of this important friendship to Jung, we need to take into account Jung's early experiences as recounted in *MDR*.

## Jung's Secret

The word "secret" (*Geheimnis*) peppers the initial sections of *MDR*. In the first chapter, which contains an account of Jung's earliest years, the word appears in the specific context of certain highly significant dreams, games, activities, and experiences. These include Jung's underground phallus dream ("Through this childhood dream I was initiated into the secrets of the earth" [Jung, 1989, p.15]), the affinity of that dream to Oriental god images ("It was a secret I must never betray" [Jung, 1989, p.17]), the stone on which Jung sat wondering if he was stone or sitter ("there was no doubt whatsoever that this stone stood in some secret relationship to me" [Jung, 1989, p.20]), the carved manikin Jung hid in the attic ("All this was a great secret. ... No one could discover my secret and destroy it" [Jung, 1989, p.21]) and the scrolls Jung hid in the manikin's box ("written … in a secret language of my own invention" [Jung, 1989, p.21]). This is by no means an exhaustive list. In the same chapter, Jung devotes an extended passage to the significance of the secret:

> This possession of a secret had a very powerful formative influence on my character; I consider it the essential factor of my boyhood. Similarly, I never told anyone about the dream of the phallus; and the Jesuit, too, belonged to that mysterious realm which I knew I must not talk about. The little wooden figure with the stone was a first attempt, still unconscious and childish, to give shape to the secret. I was always absorbed by it and had the feeling I ought to fathom it; and yet I did not know what it was I was trying to express. I always hoped I might be able to find something perhaps in nature that would give me the clue and show me where or what the secret was. At that time my interest in plants, animals, and stones grew. I was constantly on the lookout for something mysterious. Consciously, I was religious in the Christian sense, though always with the reservation: "But it is not so certain as all that!" or, "What about that thing under the ground?" And when religious teachings were pumped into me and I was told, "This is beautiful and this is good" I would think to myself: "Yes, but there is something else, something very secret that people don't know about. (Jung, 1989, p. 22)

For Jung, the secret seems to have possessed an ineffable quality. Of course, Jung's secret experiences (underground phallus dream, manikin, stone, fire, Basel cathedral vision) could have been put into words, and yet the particular quality that the secret possessed for Jung seems to have remained inaccessible and mysterious. As he put it, the secret evoked "a feeling of curious and fascinating darkness." (Jung, 1989, p.20) The carved manikin, and by implication all the other numinous experiences from this time, were merely attempts "still unconscious and childish, to give shape to the secret." (Jung, 1989, p.22) Later he says he hoped in vain that nature would "give [him] the clue and show [him] where or what the secret was."

(Jung, 1989, p.22) The essence of the secret, he implies, always transcended these actual objects and events and remained ultimately unknowable.

This quality contributed, of course, to Jung's enormous difficulty in conveying the secret to others. But the problem went much further than this. For Jung, even the thought of attempting to communicate the secret overwhelmed him with a powerful feeling of dread. Jung was haunted by the fear that any betrayal of the secret could be literally fatal. He remembers thinking that these secrets "must never be betrayed, for the safety of my life depended on it." (Jung, 1989, p.22)

Strictly speaking, it was, of course, impossible for Jung to betray a secret that was, as we have seen, inaccessible to himself. However, as we will see, for Jung even the idea of attempting to translate the secret into superficial or clumsy everyday language was experienced as a such profound betrayal that it held the capacity to undo the cohesion of his own inner identity—an identity that increasingly depended upon the possession of the secret.

As a result, Jung's secret left him feeling intensely isolated. He tells us that "it induced in me an almost unendurable loneliness." (Jung, 1989, p.41) This, in turn, brought up a compensatory need to communicate the secret: "[M]ore than ever I wanted someone to talk with." (Jung, 1989, p.63) However, this need to communicate was tempered by another need: to ensure his safety. Before feeling able to speak, Jung needed to first "find out whether other people had undergone similar experiences." (Jung, 1989, p.41) He was left in a state of acute inner conflict: He had to speak but could not.

Jung's sense of alienation intensified: Even if he had been able to overcome his aversion to talking about the secret, he was nonetheless incapable of doing it justice. Somehow, it would remain incomprehensible or unacceptable, because something about the secret was radically foreign to the world in which such communication could occur.

Jung dreaded what he imagined to be the destructive incomprehension of others: He tells us, for example, that he didn't speak to his mother about the book of Oriental gods because he "knew that she would reject my 'revelation' with horror, and I did not want to expose myself to any such injury." (Jung, 1989, p.17) Later, Jung described himself sensing "in others an estrangement, a distrust, an apprehension which robbed me of speech." (Jung, 1989, p.63) Later still, he identified the world of the secret with his No. 2 personality, which "felt that any conceivable expression of himself would be like a stone thrown over the edge of the world, dropping soundlessly into infinite night." (Jung, 1989, p.87)

In *MDR*, Jung tells us that on first encountering Nietzsche he recognised the philosopher's story as terrifyingly familiar: "at least in regard to the 'secret' which had isolated him from his environment. Perhaps who knows? he had had inner experiences, insights which he had unfortunately attempted to talk about, and had found that no one understood him." (Jung, 1989, p.102) Jung's attempts to speak about these matters with his father were fruitless. He "dared not and could not reveal" his "great secret" to his father, who he knew was incapable "of understanding the direct experience of God." (Jung, 1989, p.93) Feeling increasingly isolated, Jung wanted to share who he really was—his innermost private identity—with others, but he didn't know how to do so. Crippled by dread, he was unable to trust the world as a safe place to receive his attempts to communicate the secret.

This situation sheds a great deal of light on Jung's later tendency to compartmentalize by erecting a barrier between the dimension of the secret (inner world) and that of the outer world. Although, as we have seen, the logic of the two personalities meant that psychic health and the avoidance of one-sidedness depended upon enabling both dimensions to enrich each other, Jung's early experience of the secret made it particularly difficult for him to bring together the two personalities in situations that specifically constellated his dread of betraying the secret. This secret-complex seems at times to have blinded Jung to the psychological necessity to communicate, however clumsily, his own highly vulnerable inner world to others.

In effect, for Jung to live isolated with the secret meant living solely as the inner-facing, unrelational, personality No. 2. At times, Jung seems to have become aware that the one-sidedness of such a life would make it cripplingly neurotic. When, as a child, his fainting fits kept him away from school, he was able "to plunge into the world of the mysterious," while "growing more and more away from the world." (Jung, 1989, pp. 30-1) For all its allure, however, Jung soon realised that this arrangement was psychologically unhealthy: "That was when I learned what a neurosis is."

(Jung, 1989, p. 32) Consequently, he made a conscious effort to correct the situation by reengaging with school and a life in which he related to others. Ultimately, the lesson learned was that he could not thrive when he inhabited either personality alone. He needed a life that made space for both the inner-facing personality No. 2 and the outward-looking personality No. 1. In this context, that had to mean finding a way to communicate his secret to another person.

However, at other times, the dread that had accompanied Jung's experience of the secret seems to have overridden this awareness. In *MDR*, Jung goes so far as to boast about his ability to remain silent about the secret, providing a rationalization of this tendency toward one-sided isolation:

> My one great achievement during those years was that I resisted the temptation to talk about [the secret] with anyone. Thus the pattern of my relationship to the world was already prefigured: today as then I am a solitary, because I know things and must hint at things which other people do not know, and usually do not even want to know. (Jung, 1989, pp. 41-2)

There seems to be a problematic contradiction here. On the one hand, Jung seeks to convince us that his own individuation process required an experience of creative connection between personality No. 1 and personality No. 2, and that such a process holds outer and inner engagement as equally valuable. On the other hand, he also seems to want to argue that his inner life should take psychological priority over the outer life of relationship. In *MDR*'s "Late thoughts" he amplifies this idea:

> There is no better means of intensifying the treasured feeling of individuality than the possession of a secret which the individual is pledged to guard... Like the initiate of a secret society who has broken free from the undifferentiated collectivity, the individual on his lonely path needs a secret which for various reasons he may not or cannot reveal. Such a secret reinforces him in the isolation of his individual aims... Only a secret which the individual cannot betray - one which he fears to give away,

or which he cannot formulate in words, and which therefore
seems to belong to the category of crazy ideas can prevent the
otherwise inevitable retrogression [into neurosis]. (Jung, 1989,
pp. 342-4)

Jung here develops a quasi-heroic justification for his own decision to
follow what he represents as an isolated path. Jung's individual preference
thus becomes inflated into a general dictum on individuation and the
avoidance of neurosis. However, looked at more closely, the passage seems
increasingly confused. First, Jung identifies "the treasured feeling of
individuality" with a state of lonely isolation, implicitly identifying it with a
state of separation from society and one's fellow man. This idea seems to
conflict with Jung's claims elsewhere that individuation brings us into
closer relation to others. Second, Jung puts forward two related reasons
why this individuated person should not communicate his "secret": a) fear
and b) inarticulacy—an inarticulacy stemming from the assumption that
anyone hearing the secret would dismiss it as a "crazy idea." Since, as we
know, Jung (aware of Nietzsche's example) is terrified of his ideas being
seen as crazy, this, in effect, reduces the second category to the first.

Jung seems to be telling us that the one way to avoid neurosis is to
have a secret that one is frightened of expressing. This bizarre idea only
makes psychological sense if we understand it in the light of the early
chapters of *MDR*. There it was precisely Jung's own secret that he could
"not betray," that he "fear[ed] to give away," that he could not "formulate in
words and which therefore seems to belong to the category of crazy ideas."
In effect, Jung is retrospectively justifying the defensive fearfulness of his
childhood, by transforming it into a universal prophylactic against
neurosis! At root, there is a fundamental confusion here between two very
different ideas about individuation: The first seeks acceptance of a
dimension that is ultimately ungraspable and inexpressible. The second
requires the literal possession of a secret that must never be expressed.

It is important at this point to note that Jung's emphatic embrace of
secret-keeping as a recipe for psychic health is not necessarily his last word
on the topic. As is often the case, elsewhere in Jung's writings we can find
contrasting passages that imply at the very least some ambivalence with

regard to this question. For example, elsewhere in *MDR*, Jung reflects upon the nature of the psychotherapeutic process:

> In many cases in psychiatry, the patient who comes to us has a story that is not told, and which as a rule no one knows of. To my mind, therapy only really begins after the investigation of that wholly personal story. It is the patient's secret, the rock against which he is shattered. If I know his secret story, I have a key to the treatment. The doctor's task is to find out how to gain that knowledge. ... In therapy the problem is always the whole person, never the symptom alone. We must ask questions which challenge the whole personality. (Jung, 1989, p. 117)

The suggestion here is that the therapeutic process enacts a meeting between therapist and patient within the dimension of the secret and that it is only the speaking and the hearing of that secret that can release the patient from neurosis—a release that Jung evocatively equates to a shattering against "the rock" of the secret. In Chapter 6, we will look more closely at the ways in which Jung's ideas about the therapeutic relationship sometimes contrast with other aspects of his psychology.

As Jung's writings elsewhere make clear, there is no contradiction between 1) accepting that "the secret" is an unknowable and inexpressible dimension of the psyche and 2) wishing to shape and communicate such an experience with others. Throughout *MDR*, Jung's insistence upon the importance of the secret is accompanied by a simultaneous attempt to communicate that secret. Not only is the secret conveyed in the form of the childhood experiences about which Jung has, he says, rarely or never spoken, but, more importantly, the essence of the secret is evoked in Jung's eloquent and lengthy description of the highly personal and intimate feelings and ideas that made up his No. 2 personality, and his experience of what he calls "God's world." (Jung, 1989, p. 66) In fact, one could argue that every word of Jung's mature psychology is a (more or less successful) attempt to relate this "secret" to the "outer" world, and, I would add, thereby bring personality No. 1 into contact with personality No. 2.

What *MDR* does convey is the highly personal significance of the secret for Jung. Given the close relationship between Jung's No. 2

personality and the realm of the secret, and the energy, numinosity, and autonomy that both seem to share, Jung's complexed, and perhaps neurotic, attitude to the secret seems to point to a similarly unbalanced approach with regard to personality No. 2.

In the case of "the secret," there are, I believe, three quite different notions that seem at times confused in Jung's writings.[1] These are

1. The notion that psychology necessarily confronts a reality that is ultimately conceptually ungraspable and thereby deals with an unknowable mystery that *cannot* be fully conceptualised (i.e., the unconscious).

2. The notion that there is an aspect of the human personality that must and will always remain ultimately hidden and is therefore ultimately unreachable even through psychoanalytic means.[2]

3. The notion that there exists a given set of facts and ideas and understandings that can be known but must or should not be openly spoken about.

The third of these notions is highly problematic because it leads directly toward the idea of psychology as an esoteric—even cultlike—discipline.

## Jung and Freud

One way to approach the crisis that brought about Jung's confrontation with the unconscious, the writing of *The Red Book,* and the creation of Analytical Psychology is to see it as an entantiodromic shift within Jung whereby a period of relative emptiness and barrenness, permeated by superficial outer encounters, was superseded by a rich and soulful period characterised by solitude and inner work. It follows from this argument that the period of collaboration with Freud was, by comparison, sterile and shallow.

This is a rendering of events that is given some rhetorical force within the early sections of *The Red Book* and has subsequently been given added emphasis by Shamdasani (See, for example, Shamdasani and Beebe, 2010). If we translate this narrative into the language of the two personalities, the argument would be that, in order for Jung to give birth to Analytical

Psychology as we know it, an entantiodromic swing across from No. 1 to No. 2 was required.

Shamdasani has suggested that Jung ended a period of reflective self-analysis when he married Emma in 1902 on the grounds that at this point he ceased writing in the private diary/notebook in which he had been jotting down his private thoughts since adolescence. Shamdasani sees great significance in the fact that he restarted this practice in 1913, after an 11-year break, with the first entries in the Black books (Shamdasani, 2009, p. 196; Shamdasani and Beebe, 2010, pp. 428–429). However, although this does indicate a shift in the direction of increased introspection, it seems to me that we should be wary of attaching too much importance to it.

According to *MDR*, Jung's psychiatric work provided him with a vessel within which he could pursue both inner (No. 2) and outer (No. 1) interests, thus constellating the "confident feeling that [he] was a 'united double nature.'" (Jung, 1989, p. 109) I would also argue that it was precisely because both personalities seemed to be working in tandem that Jung was able, during his Burghölzli years, to concentrate his energies upon clinical and experimental work that expressed both sides of his personality. However, during this same period, Jung, who had experienced a lonely and isolated childhood, also found himself entering into relationships with both men and women that hinted at the possibility of cooperation, love, and friendship, and perhaps most significantly seemed to offer Jung an opportunity to experience a meeting between personalities 1 and 2.

The question that needs asking is whether Jung was proactively engaging with the interests and concerns associated with personality No. 2 during the 11 years between 1902 and 1913, or whether, as Shamdasani suggests, they remained mostly unexplored and unexpressed in this period.

What I intend to argue here is that, in the period 1906-12 (the period depicted above as sterile and soulless), Jung in fact made several serious attempts, in the arena of his *outer* relationships, to communicate those ideas, feelings, and motifs that he places into the category of "the secret" and which, as we have seen, constitute aspects of his No. 2 personality. Of these attempts, the most important occurred within the context of his relationship with Freud.

By paying close attention to the secret in the context of that relationship—and especially in its catastrophic ending—we will explore the plausibility of this alternative narrative. According to this version of events, it was the traumatic failure of Jung's sincere attempts to establish dialogue in the outer world (i.e., through his relationship with Freud) that constellated such an abrupt shift in the direction of *intrapsychic* dialogue. Looked at from this perspective, Jung's encounter with Freud represented a genuine attempt, via the medium of outer relationship, to bring personality No. 1 together with personality No. 2. It was the failure of this attempt that impelled Jung to retreat into an inner world within which the crucial dialogue between No. 1 and No. 2 could indeed take place—albeit solely on the intrapsychic level: between ego and unconscious.

## Jung's Love for Freud

Despite the fact that, as we saw in Chapter 2, Jung's approach to the psyche was closer that of Frederic Myers than it ever was with the psychoanalytic model, it is important also to acknowledge that Jung's most important personal and professional relationship during these years was his friendship with Sigmund Freud. As late as 1953, the numinosity of his relationship with Freud clearly remained undiminished for Jung. In conversation with Kurt Eissler, Jung, at 78, gushed,

> [I] loved Freud a great deal, admired and loved him so much. ... He could grasp all emotional states in others wonderfully. So, in that he was admirable! ... it goes to show, doesn't it, what bigness, what depth he had, you know?! ... it was a terrible disappointment to him that I turned away from him. And for me it was the same! ... So, for me, it [Jung's break with Freud] was a terrible loss... it would have been crazy, you know, to ever have wanted anything other than to work together with him! (quoted in Gale, 2015, p. 216 n.13)

With the exception of a handful of face-to-face meetings, the dialogue between Freud and Jung was mostly played out in the intimate yet detached form of an exchange of letters. During the years that elapsed between the first letters between Jung and Freud in 1906 and the eventual breakdown in their relationship in 1912, my suggestion is that Jung was proactively exploring and engaging his own personality No. 2 dimension via his bond with Freud.

Renos Papadopoulos has in several works explored this theme of Jung and the "other." (Papadopoulos, 1980, 1991, 2002) Papadopoulos has made the interesting suggestion that Jung's sense of connection with Freud relied partly upon the assumption that "the theme of the Other ... had the same 'inner' meaning for Freud as it had for himself." This assumption, Papadopoulos suggests, engendered in Jung a "special shiver of hope [which] must have activated hoards of expectations in Jung that Freud would assist him in solving their 'common' problematic." (Papadopoulos, 1980 p.248) The problematic in question was, I would argue, that of the two personalities.

Despite all the considerable professional and personal achievements of the period 1902-06, Jung remained disturbingly prone to the magnetic influence of his No. 2 personality. He describes in *MDR* how, even in his mid-30s, the world of the secret continued to exercise a powerful allure. Revisiting the stone on which he had sat as a child, wondering if he were the stone or the sitter, he reflected:

> I thought suddenly of my life in Zurich, and it seemed alien to me, like news from some remote world and time. This was frightening, for the world of my childhood in which I had just become absorbed was eternal, and I had been wrenched away from it and had fallen into a time that continued to roll onward, moving farther and farther away. The pull of that other world was so strong that I had to tear myself violently from the spot in order not to lose hold of my future. (Jung, 1989, p. 20)

Jung's susceptibility to the undercurrents of No. 2 and the dimension of the "secret" was, I would suggest, a significant factor in his attraction to the numinous promise of a relationship with Freud. In effect, this relationship offered Jung an opportunity to begin to shape and communicate that secret dimension that had seemed so impossible to speak about in his childhood and youth, but which, as we have seen, he privately yearned to convey to someone who might understand. Freud's insistence upon the importance of a scientific attitude in dealing with the depths of the psyche not only offered a plausibly respectable screen for Jung's hitherto unacceptable interests, but it also offered Jung a way to sustain and develop the binocular approach whereby No. 1 could be brought into play with No. 2.

Papadopoulos suggests that within this relationship, Freud's own unconscious needs paralleled those of Jung, such that Jung also became for Freud some kind of inner other. This idea is supported by Freud's biographer Elizabeth Roudinesco's observation that "the irrational part of [Freud] … would always lead him to defy the order of reason, whether through his interest in occult phenomena and telepathy or through his attraction to the most extravagant speculations." (Roudinesco, 2016, p. 40) We might even go so far as to describe "this irrational part of Freud" as a No. 2 personality. Like Jung's No. 2, this facet of Freud's personality was generally secreted from public view. When it came to his own interest in telepathy, for example, he ordered Ferenczi: "Let us keep absolute silence about it" (Freud and Ferenczi, 1993, p. 81). It is possible that the subterranean communication of Jung's "secret" was perhaps being met by a parallel "secret" within Freud, and that this was one of the factors that drew the two men together. Leonard Shengold suggests, "Freud found in Jung, as he had in [Wilhelm] Fliess, something he longed for—the promise of magic, which corresponded to something Freud mistrusted in his own personality and felt as a deficiency that would be supplied by another man." (Shengold, 1976, p. 669)

In terms of Jung's development, what we can identify is a novel, albeit tentative, attempt to engage with personality No. 2 through an *outer* relationship with an actual person. We can see an example of this when we look at the intimate nature of what Jung was communicating to Freud from early in their correspondence. In a 1986 paper, Herbert Lehmann draws attention to the particular significance of an admission Jung made to Freud in 1906. He confessed to Freud that in his book on dementia praecox (Jung, 1907) a dream he had represented as that of a patient, was in fact his own dream (Lehmann, 1986). The dream in question, as Lehmann convincingly shows, spoke in symbolic terms about the tension and conflict between two aspects of Jung's life: that aspect represented by wife and family (which, as we will see, Jung tended to associate with personality No. 1) and a problematically different aspect, which Lehmann persuasively argues was related to Jung's affair with Sabina Spielrein. In the next chapter, I explore the ways in which the relationship with Spielrein, like that with Freud, offered Jung the opportunity to engage with qualities and ideas that expressed aspects of personality No. 2. That Jung was willing to share the dream with Freud and indeed to request from him an interpretation clearly implies that even at this early stage of the friendship Jung "felt that he could 'let his No. 2 loose' upon Freud, because Freud 'knew and understood about such things.'" (Lehmann, 1986 p.203)

The relationship with Freud seems to have given Jung the confidence to reveal some highly personal and delicate areas of his life. In effect, Jung utilised Freud as a combination of friend, supervisor, and analyst. Although Jung did reveal (in the context of an admission of his own "religious" transference to Freud) an incident of childhood sexual abuse, he generally held off from touching directly upon the dimension of the "secret" that constituted his earliest and most powerful experiences of his No. 2. Nonetheless, the openness and vulnerability that characterise Jung's earliest letters to Freud demonstrate, as Lehmann puts it, "an extraordinary demonstration of trust on Jung's part." (Lehmann, 1986, 202) It is evident that Jung's openness evoked parallel feelings in Freud, and it was surely this sense of mutual frankness and intimacy that underpinned the significance of the relationship on both sides.

Peter Homans has described the Freud/Jung relationship as "a narcissistic transference." (Homans, 1995, p. 37)[3] He bases this conjecture on the assumption that both Freud and Jung shared a certain level of narcissistic personality organisation. The consequent transference between them was, Homans suggests, "fraught with the language of idealization and merger." (Homans, 1995, p. 41)[4] I think Homans is pointing to what I have described in other terms as Jung's secret-complex, and the powerful echo it seems to have found in Freud's personality. We might describe the problem as related to the difficulty both men had, though in very different ways, in relating their personality No. 1 to their personality No. 2.

## 1909—a Turning Point

For all the potential benefits of Jung's intimacy with Freud, it inevitably brought the older man into increasing proximity to those dimensions of Jung's life that, as we have seen, he had spent many years secreting from the "outer" world. Not surprisingly, Jung's ambivalence toward Freud intensified accordingly and eventually hardened into something much more destructive. As we will see, Jung's secrecy was to play a crucial role in the unraveling of the friendship.

The fault lines that lay behind the eventual collapse of the Freud/Jung relationship can be traced back to the earliest communications between the two men. However, tensions between them came into much sharper relief in the events of 1909. In March that year, Jung made his second visit to Freud's home in Vienna. Jung tells us in *MDR* that on this occasion he asked Freud for his opinions on precognition and parapsychology in general. Freud rejected the whole idea as "nonsensical." (Jung, 1989, p. 155) Angered by Freud's "materialistic prejudice," Jung tells us: "I had difficulty in checking the sharp retort on the tip of my tongue." (Jung, 1989, p. 155)

There are two aspects of this encounter that should be noted. First, Jung kept to himself (i.e., secreted) his emotional response to Freud. Second, given the fact that Freud emphatically instructed Jung on their first meeting in 1907 to stand fast against the "black tide of mud of occultism," (Jung, 1989, p. 150) it seems strangely naïve of Jung to expect any other reaction from Freud. Jung's level of affect seems therefore disproportionate. What it does indicate is a striking gap between Jung's projection onto Freud (as potential carrier of the "secret"?) and all that he consciously knew about the man, a gap that was painfully exposed when Jung was met by Freud's actual reaction.

However, the situation was more complex than this analysis allows. Given what we know about Freud's own No. 2, it seems at least possible that Freud's knee-jerk rationalism was a reaction that defended him not only against Jung but also against his own hidden secret (i.e., his fascination with the occult). If so, then we might see Jung's furious outrage as in fact directed at what he obscurely felt to be a double betrayal by Freud, in that it constituted a rejection of Freud's own No. 2 and a rejection of Jung's No. 2.

Jung's anger at Freud's rejection was, he tells us, experienced in the form of a "red-hot ... glowing vault" in his diaphragm (Jung, 1989, p. 150.), a reaction that we might see as a powerful somatic resurgence of the hidden (occult) aspects of Jung's No. 2. The inner "vault" in which Jung's No. 1 had attempted to bury these powerful feelings was beginning to disgorge its contents.

We might understand this event as an unconscious attempt by Jung to discover the limits of his relationship with Freud, and specifically the capacity of the friendship to safely contain the energies of the secret. For Jung, the mystery of the secret had by now become bound up with a conception of the unconscious that far exceeded the positivistic and materialistic limits of conventional psychological science. As we have seen, this put it into extreme tension with Freud's psychological model. Jung's ambivalence is acted out in an attempt to communicate this unknowable (occult) dimension within his relationship with Freud while simultaneously sabotaging that very attempt by forcing the issue into a form that Freud would be sure to reject.[5] Consciously or unconsciously, Jung seems to have been determined to test the relationship, if necessary, to destruction. In *MDR*, Jung tells us that the 1909 incident "aroused [Freud's] mistrust of me" (Jung, 1989, p. 156); under the circumstances, we can assume that any mistrust engendered was entirely mutual.

## Secrets, Dreams and Lies

These tensions between the two men seem to have escalated during the trip to America undertaken by Freud, Jung, and Ferenczi later the same year. Significantly, it was to be a secret that functioned as a final straw in Jung's alienation from Freud. Jung and Freud were, of course, in daily contact and whiled away the hours interpreting each other's dreams. Despite Freud's initial failure to offer any useful interpretations of his colleague's dreams, Jung was, he says, nonetheless keen to continue these dream sessions: "[T]hey meant a great deal to me, and I found our relationship exceedingly valuable. I regarded Freud as an older, more mature and experienced personality, and felt like a son in that respect." (Jung, 1989, p. 158)

All was to change, Jung tells us, when he requested some personal details from Freud to enable a fuller interpretation of one of Freud's dreams. Freud insisted upon keeping his own secrets, replying with "a look of the utmost suspicion ... 'But I cannot risk my authority!'" "At that moment," Jung comments, "he lost it altogether. That sentence burned itself into my memory; and in it the end of our relationship was already foreshadowed, Freud was placing personal authority above truth." (Jung, 1989, p. 158).[6]

This passage in *MDR* is immediately followed by another telling episode from the same trip. Jung was recounting to Freud the house dream that he later saw as foreshadowing the concept of the collective unconscious. Prompted by the image of the two skulls in a cave at the deepest level of the house, Freud pressed Jung to provide some plausible victims of a repressed murderous wish. At this point, Jung tells us, he knew perfectly well that such an approach completely missed the dream and its meaning, but, he says, "I would not have been able to present to Freud my own ideas on an interpretation of the dream *without encountering incomprehension and vehement resistance.*" (Jung, 1989, p. 160, my italics)

Jung's relatively ambivalent stance during his visit to Freud earlier that year had now hardened into a much more corrosive form of distrust. His decision at this point to his keep his new ideas from Freud marked a regressive shift. Jung's preemptive claim that had he tried to communicate his ideas to Freud, he would have met with "incomprehension and vehement resistance" find a striking parallel in the passages much earlier in *MDR* where he offers the reasons for his inability to communicate his childhood secret to others. For example, he had chosen not to communicate to his mother his feelings about the book of Oriental gods, because he "knew that she would reject my 'revelation' with horror, and I did not want to expose myself to any such injury." (Jung, 1989, p.17). I would suggest that at this critical point in his relationship with Freud, when the matter in hand—Jung's dream and its implications—touched on Jung's No. 2 personality, what became constellated was precisely the highly defensive, protective attitude that had been characteristic of Jung's childhood relation to the "secret." Jung's logic seems to have been: I cannot explain, and anyway what is the point of trying to explain; they will never understand.

## Father and Son

It seems likely that this highly defensive response in Jung was heightened by an additional factor. Both Jung and Freud (not to mention numerous commentators in the intervening years) have pointed to the importance of a father/son dynamic in the relationship between the two men. It is clear from the letters between them that Freud quite consciously regarded Jung as an idealized son and Jung reciprocated by responding to Freud as an idealized father (Freud and Jung 1977, p.122). As we have seen, Jung prefaced the section in which he describes the loss of his confidence in Freud by reminding us that he "felt like a son" to Freud (Jung, 1989, p. 158).

Hitherto, Freud had been, for Jung, positioned at the epicentre of the magic circle of personality No. 2, and he therefore took on the projection of benign and omniscient father. However, as 1909 proceeded, the gap between the projection and the reality started to become uncomfortably apparent to Jung. Not surprisingly, this disjunct evoked for Jung ominous echoes of the problematic relationship he had experienced with his real father.

In Chapter 1, I noted the importance of the so-called storm lantern dream to Jung's development. This dream indicated to him the need to relate to personality No. 2 as an autonomous figure, separate from his ego-complex. Significantly, the passages in *MDR* subsequent to the dream of the storm lantern focus upon the painful lack of emotional and intellectual intimacy within Jung's relationship to his father in the period leading up to his death (Jung, 1989, pp. 91-5). As we have seen, Jung's inability to communicate meaningfully with his father about the matters that were closest to his heart (i.e., the secret) was evidently hugely saddening and frustrating to him. In this case, the secret took the form of what Jung describes as "God's world." "[F]illed with secret meaning," this realm contained, "everything superhuman, dazzling light, the darkness of the abyss, the cold impassivity of infinite space and time, and the uncanny grotesqueness of the irrational world of chance." (Jung, 1989, p.72)

This was precisely the dimension that Jung looked to experience in the deepest mysteries of religion. He was therefore "profoundly disappointed" when his pastor father dismissed such matters in an offhand way. Discussions between father and son were "fruitless" and apparently "exasperated" both of them (Jung, 1989, p.93). In *MDR*, Jung remembers saying to himself: "There we have it; they know nothing about it and don't give it a thought. Then how can I talk about my secret?" (Jung, 1989, p.93) This remark is telling because it underlines yet again how difficult it was for Jung to risk attempting to communicate to another person the experiences, thoughts, and feelings associated with his No. 2 personality. For Jung, an insurmountable barrier stood between an inner secret realm of huge value and significance, and an outer world within which no meaningful communication of that realm could be made.

Jung's 1909 responses to Freud are strongly redolent of his earlier attitude to his father: "I saw … that he was completely helpless in dealing with certain kinds of dreams and had to take refuge in his doctrine. I realized that it was up to me to find out the real meaning of the dream." (Jung, 1989, p. 160)

The real significance of the quasi-paternal connection between Jung and Freud does not reside in the banal fact that Jung had a father complex, or even that his father complex had an Oedipal character. Far more important is Jung's secret-complex: Jung's dread had rendered him utterly incapable of communicating the secret to his father; now, yet again, it blocked his ability to communicate to Freud his most intimate and important ideas, feelings, and experiences. In his father's case, the block showed up as a fixed idea that his father (as representative of the outer, No. 1, world) *simply could not hear what he had to say*. Now, in 1909, despite Jung's near boundless admiration and love for Freud, the block returned with a vengeance.

## The Lie

Unwilling to explore the possible meaning of his dream in the company of his trusted mentor and quasi-analyst, Jung chose instead to lie. In *MDR*, Jung tells us that it was "plain" to him that the cave in his dream represented the "world of the primitive man within myself—a world which can scarcely be reached or illuminated by consciousness." (Jung, 1989, p. 160) Jung here points to precisely that aspect of the psyche that remains "secret" by virtue of being beyond conscious appropriation. However,

Jung's dream-cave also figures as a kind of crypt. It is a place in which he has secreted what matters most to him and a place which, according to the dream, he is now able to explore—but alone, and most certainly not with Freud! By refusing to communicate to Freud his own understanding of the dream, Jung is choosing to keep this insight as his own secret—hidden in the very crypt that he has just discovered, or perhaps rediscovered. Henceforth, Jung was back in touch with the inner secret, but it was a secret emphatically redefined by the fact of Jung's refusal to share it with the man with whom he had enjoyed the closest intimacy of his life.

Submitting to Freud's apparent need to find victims of a death-wish, Jung made a deliberate substitution: "'My wife and my sister-in-law'—after all, I had to name someone whose death was worth the wishing!" (Jung, 1989, pp. 159-60)

Jung offers us a series of increasingly unconvincing justifications for his lie:

> I did not then trust my own judgment, and wanted to hear Freud's opinion. I wanted to learn from him… I did not feel up to quarrelling with him, and I also feared that I might lose his friendship if I insisted on my own point of view. … I wanted to know what he would make of my answer, and what his reaction would be if I deceived him by saying something that suited his theories. (Jung, 1989, p.160)

In the manner of Freud's kettle "logic," the more reasons Jung gives us, the less persuasive they seem.[7] Having fed Freud the lie, Jung then claims to have felt justified when Freud produced precisely the interpretation that Jung expected, thus confirming his presupposition that Freud "was completely helpless in dealing with certain kinds of dreams and had to take refuge in his doctrine." Jung's defensive comments are redolent of a bad conscience, still clearly active more than 40 years after the event.

Both the lie and the subsequent withdrawal from the relationship with Freud take us back to Jung's primitive childhood dread of the consequences of betraying the "'secret." When Freud pressed the idea of the death-wish, Jung "felt violent resistance to any such interpretation" of a dream which, as Jung admits, "in particular was important to me." (Jung, 1989, p. 158-9) It is as if Freud had literally pushed his way into Jung's secret cave and, having poked around at the skulls, had forced a crudely reductive or positivistic interpretation on him, one that fatally conflicted with the numinosity that was evidently evoked by this dream (a numinosity that, unbeknown to Freud, echoed the "secret" experiences of Jung's childhood). In effect, Freud reactivated Jung's terror of betraying the secret. Jung's reaction seems characterised by the kind of defensive/aggressive grandiosity that often compensates deep-seated inferiority. For Jung to lie to Freud in these circumstances was, symbolically, to kill him, and thereby ironically, to fulfil Freud's own death-wish interpretation of the dream! The fateful consequence of this lie was that it permanently foreclosed any future possibility of relationship and mutuality of connection with Freud. Nothing of that sort could occur as long as Jung felt that "it would have been impossible for me to afford him any insight into my mental world. The gulf between it and his was too great." (Jung, 1989, p. 160) In effect, the lie locked him back into the solitary world of "the secret," the world he knew so well from his childhood.

## A Dream of Dis/enchantment

At this time, Freud and the world of psychoanalysis seem to have become emblematic for Jung of the tired and dried-up values he associated with a No. 1 that was severed from No. 2. Inevitably, this became apparent in Jung's tendency to experience Freud as a spectral echo of his own dead father. The feelings of outrage and betrayal that we can see played out in Jung's final letters to Freud were being powerfully constellated by what Jung experienced as Freud's relatively rapid journey from the numinous promise of No. 2 to the faded rationalism of the old paternal.

During the period in which he was writing *Wandlungen und Symbole der Libido*, the text that would bring about the final break with Freud, Jung had a dream, the significance of which is indicated by the fact that we have three published versions of it, first as written in the Black Books (quoted in the introduction to *The Red Book* by Shamdasani [Shamdasani, 2009, p. 198]), second in the 1925 seminar on Analytical Psychology (Jung, 1990, pp. 38-40) and third in *MDR* (Jung, 1989, pp. 186-189). I intend to concentrate here upon the earliest and least elaborated version:

> I was in a southern town, on a rising street with narrow half landings. It was twelve o'clock midday—bright sunshine. An old Austrian customs guard or someone similar passes by me, lost in thought. Someone says, 'that is one who cannot die. He died already 30-40 years ago, but has not yet managed to decompose.' I was very surprised. Here a striking figure came, a knight of powerful build, clad in yellowish armor. He looks solid and inscrutable and nothing impresses him. On his back he carries a red Maltese cross. He has continued to exist from the 12th century and daily between 12 and 1 o'clock midday he takes the same route. No one marvels at these two apparitions, but I was extremely surprised.
>
> I hold back my interpretive skills. As regards the old Austrian, Freud occurred to me; as regards the knight, I myself. Inside, a voice calls, 'It is all empty and disgusting.' I must bear it. (Shamdasani, 2009, p. 198)

Jung maps the image of the customs officer directly onto the real Freud, and the image of the knight onto the real Jung. What is striking here is that Jung offers no interpretation of the dream on the subjective level.

By the time of the 1925 seminar, this identification of the customs officer with Freud has become even more definite: "Suddenly I came upon a man, an old one, in the uniform of an Austrian customs official. It was Freud . . . obviously [the Austrian official] stood for the Freudian theory." (Jung, 1990, pp. 38-39)

When a dreamer uses the word "obviously" with regard to a dream interpretation, we should be on our guard. It tends to imply that the interpretation in question is strongly ego-syntonic and therefore probably also an attempt to fend off a complex. In 1925, Jung's Freud complex was evidently still strongly activated.

Thirty years later in *MDR*, Jung was still pinning the image of the customs official onto Freud: "As for the old customs official, his work had obviously brought him so little that was pleasurable and satisfactory that he took a sour view of the world. I could not refuse to see the analogy with Freud." (Jung, 1989, p.187)

In his 1916 *General Aspects of Dream Interpretation*. Jung describes how an objective interpretation can sometimes miss the mark (Jung, 1916b, paras. 511-514). Once, when interpreting a dream of his own, Jung tells us, he made an immediate association between a certain dream-figure and an actual person with whom Jung happened to be very angry, although in fact the dream-figure only superficially resembled this person. Eventually, Jung became unsatisfied with this interpretation, and subsequently realised that an interpretation on the subjective level—i.e., seeing the dream-figure as a shadow aspect of himself—was much more convincing, since such an interpretation, rather than reinforcing the conscious attitude, as Jung puts it, revealed "what sort of mistake I am making … [and] gives me an opportunity to correct my attitude." (Jung, 1916b, para.514)

If we return to Jung's customs official dream, we can see that Jung's insistence upon identifying this figure with Freud tells us merely that he consciously required the dream to be solely concerned with the split with Freud. The second figure, the knight, interpreted here as '"I myself,"' Jung amplifies in this way: It relates to "my own world, which had scarcely anything to do with Freud's," (Jung, 1989, p. 189) and he goes on to associate the figure with alchemy, Meister Eckhart, and the Grail—all three personal passions of Jung. He is thus making precisely the kind of binary oppositional differentiation (between Freud's world and Jung's world) that we would expect him to be consciously engaged in at a time when he was pulling away from Freud.

In the earliest Black Books version, the dream moves seamlessly from the customs official to the crusader. As a whole image, the dream highlights a dynamic and meaningful connection between these two sections, however divergent their tone or atmosphere may seem. In the two later versions, Jung distorts the image by compartmentalising the dream into two discrete units, and therefore deals with them as though they were two separate dreams. This attempt to radically segregate the two episodes is, I would suggest, itself symptomatic of a conscious desire to draw a line between the figure of the Austrian, and what it might mean, and the figure of the Crusader. It also reflects Jung's persistent tendency to put personality No. 1 and personality No. 2 in different compartments.

If we approach the dream on the subjective level, we can see these figures as two contrasting—even opposing—aspects of Jung's psyche, but it is important to remember that Jung's value-laden description of the Austrian as "fading," "shadowy," "prosaic," "elderly," "official," "sour," "melancholic," and "lost in thought" represents the attitude of Jung's ego to this figure; and when the Crusader is depicted as "numinous," "striking," "powerful," "unfathomable," and "full of meaning," these too are the judgments of the Jung-ego. So, when Jung awakes from the dream and immediately pins the figure of the Austrian onto Freud, and embraces the Crusader as himself, he is merely insisting upon an ego-syntonic interpretation that suits his conscious agenda. However, the deeper meaning of the dream—what Jung *does not know*—is contained not in either figure alone but in the relation between them.

Jung's dream seems to present a syzygy of two interlocking yet oppositional strands: the disenchanted, desiccated, senexlike aspect of No. 1 that Jung associated with his father and with Freud, and the thrillingly numinous puerlike No. 2. We can bring these two strands together by using what Patricia Berry describes as a "when-then" interpretation of the dream (Berry, 1978, p. 120). According to this perspective, the dream is indicating that *when* Jung rejects his No. 1 side as disenchanted and dessicated, *then* what arises is a renewed No. 2 that seems particularly and powerfully numinous. Jung's consequent rejection of Jewish psychoanalysis as overly rationalistic and reductive, and his embrace of a Christian (Aryan) mystical psychology felt to be deep and numinous, does violence to Jung's psychological need to keep both No. 1 and No. 2 together—despite the tensions between them. If so, then Jung's interpretation of the dream reveals him to be enthusiastically embracing the one-sidedness that the dream implicitly warns against.

The conclusion to Jung's account of the dream in *MDR* is highly significant: "My whole being was seeking for something still unknown which might confer meaning upon the banality of life." (Jung, 1989, p. 189)

Jung here insists upon a black-and-white perspective: The enchanted "something still unknown," which "might confer meaning" is posited as separate and in opposition to the disenchanted "banality of life" —i.e., the meaningless. Jung's interpretation clearly identifies Freud's psychology with the latter: the "all too familiar" and "all too human," the "black lees that spoiled the taste of life by showing only too plainly the ugliness and meaninglessness of human existence." (Jung, 1989, pp. 189-190)

Jung's ostensible argument is that the one-sidedness of Freud's psychology's leads it to overemphasise and even wallow in the disenchanted, seamy side of life, while his own, healthily balanced psychology regards such matters as uninteresting because they are commonplace. However, Jung's argument is undermined by the evident relish with which he himself lingers in "the human stable." Jung's choice of words ("banality," "black lees," "ugliness," "dung," the "mud of the commonplace") imply anything but a disinterested position of acceptance. Faced by the overwhelming banality and meaninglessness of life, Jung seems to be grasping for reenchantment and meaning. This sense of desolation is particularly evident in the postscript to the Black Books version of the dream (not reproduced in later versions): "Inside, a voice calls, 'It is all empty and disgusting.' I must bear it." (Shamdasani, 2009, p.198) Jung's apparent need to grasp at enchantment represents, as I will argue in Chapters 6 and 7, evidence of a one-sidedness that prioritises the numinous, personality No. 2 dimensions of psyche and life.

In its contemporary context, however, the dream succeeded in bringing to Jung's conscious attention his own overwhelming sense of disenchantment with Freud and, perhaps more importantly, with that Freudian aspect of Jung with which he had, for years, been aligning himself.

By the end, Freud, who had at first been only obscurely conscious of a disaffection of which Jung himself disclaimed any awareness, was mystified by what appeared to him as a treacherous volte-face and felt personally betrayed. Freud's old pattern was being replayed: Yet again, a friend had been revealed as an enemy. He bitterly rejected Jung as a mystic and an anti-Semite. Neither accusation was completely off-target but both missed the main point: Jung's increasingly autonomous and powerfully resurgent No. 2 was beginning to insist upon its own agenda, and Jung himself, having been hurt and disappointed in precisely those *external* relationships in which he had placed the hopes for expression (and possibly the redemption) of his No. 2, found himself turning *inward* for the next scene in his drama of self-discovery.

## Conclusion

In his review of *MDR*, Winnicott suggests that Jung's decision to lie to Freud about his house dream was "the nearest he came to a unit self. … When Jung deliberately lied to Freud he became a unit with a capacity to hide secrets instead of a split personality with no place for hiding anything." (Winnicott, 1992, p. 324) As I argued in Chapter 2, Winnicott is pathologising Jung's dissociative model of the psyche by applying a doctrinaire Freudian repression-based approach (see also Saban, 2016). My own opinion is that, far from marking a rare moment of psychological health, Jung's lie indicates a regression to the pathologically defended position of his childhood. Henceforth, there arose an unspoken but highly significant blockage in Jung's ability to trust others, and this blockage had the effect of reducing potential communication between personality No. 1 and personality No. 2. Henceforth, such communication was to occur solely on the intrapsychic level.

I shall argue that Jung's lie signals an important shift toward a new psychological status quo: On the inner level, the two personalities will be given the opportunity to engage with highly creative results. On the outer level, however, they will remain, for the most part, segregated and compartmentalised.

Jung's childhood reluctance to divulge his "secret" became a way of locking away and encrypting a crucial dimension of his inner life. With Jung's lie to Freud, this mechanism became reanimated. His old dread told him that in order to save his treasured secret, he needed to protect it from exposure to the vulgar air of normality. Otherwise, it would turn to dust.

This schism between the founders of the two most important traditions in depth psychology is bound up with a fact about its beginnings that, although well-known and indeed often remarked upon, remains striking. Neither Freud nor Jung ever subjected himself to an analysis of any depth or duration. For all their extraordinary creative achievements, the two men who made the greatest contributions to the creation of psychoanalysis, a therapy for which it is a cardinal principle that all those who practice it have themselves undergone it, never made themselves vulnerable in the ways they expected from their patients and trainees. We can perhaps see the dance that was played out through the Freud/Jung relationship as an interrupted foreplay to a mutual analysis that never happened. It is hard not to regret the fact that neither man seems to have been able to take the steps that might have allowed it to occur.

Instead, Jung took a backward step and underwent an inward shift. Jung was fond of the notion that in order to take a forward leap, it was sometimes necessary to first take a step back—*reculer pour mieux sauter*. If that leap was to be a leap into the outer world, then it never occurred, as henceforth he was to see individuation (and therefore the psycho-therapy designed to further individuation) as a transformative process that occurs and must occur *alone and in private*. If, as Jung suggests, "the individual on his lonely path [of individuation] needs a secret which for various reasons he may not or cannot reveal," (Jung, 1989, p. 343) then the work that is required has to be *inner* work: the private and lonely work whereby the individual acquaints himself with his own inner other and begins the process of conflict, negotiation, and dialogue that will lead him to the goal: the treasure of Self. This is most certainly a confrontation with the other, but a confrontation focused entirely upon the *inner* other, an inner other that is sharply and repeatedly differentiated from the *outer* other. Before going on to look at the implications of this for Jung's psychology, in the next chapter I want to look more closely at the contribution that Jung's outer relationships, and particularly those with women, made to both his own inner development and the development of his psychology.

# ENDNOTES

[1] The word *secret*, when it occurs in the English version of *MDR*, is always a translation of the German word *Geheimnis*. However, on occasion the translators have chosen to translate *Geheimnis* using the word *mystery* (and the related word *geheimnisvolle* as *mysterious)*. This evidently betrays an ambiguity in the German that is much less apparent in the English, since in the latter language the idea of a secret and the notion of a mystery tend to be quite clearly differentiated. It may be that this ambiguity has contributed to what I have described here as a confusion in Jung's approach.

[2] We might compare this idea with Winnicott's "each individual is an isolate, permanently non-communicating, permanently unknown, in fact unfound" —an idea that he puts into paradoxical though crucial conjunction with "although healthy persons communicate and enjoy communicating." (Winnicott, 1990, p. 187)

[3] Both transference and countertransference were concepts receiving a great deal of interest during the period of Jung's collaboration with Freud. Indeed, the first use of the latter term constituted one of many theoretical advances that were to come to fruition as a direct result of the interaction between the two men. The term "countertransference" was first used by Freud in a June 7, 1909, letter to Jung which addresses the problems that had developed with regard to Jung's relationship with Sabina Spielrein. (Freud and Jung, 1977, p. 231). This predates the first *published* use of the term in 1910s *The Future Prospects of Psycho-Analytic Therapy* (Freud, 1910, pp. 144–5). However, it should be pointed out that Freud's early use of the term countertransference referred merely to the analyst's projections onto the patient, which he considered to be uniformly a hindrance to the analytic process. Freud's ability to articulate

the relational complexities between analyst and patient was distorted by his relentless policy of reducing the interpersonal to the intrapsychic. This strategy, as Makari puts it, "allowed Freud to reduce the overwhelmingly complex problems of how two minds interacted and limit his exploration to the workings of one mind, the patient's." (Makari, 2009, p.33) Nonetheless, without Freud's notion of transference, Jung could never have gone on to develop the ideas that eventually saw light in his *Psychology of the Transference* (Jung, 1946).

4 A similar point is made from a psychoanalytic perspective in Loewald, 1977.

5 One wonders whether something of the same sort was behind Jung's extraordinary letter of February 11, 1910, in which he proposes that psychoanalysis become a new Dionysian/Christian religion (Freud & Jung 1977, p.293).

6 Jung's emphasis in *MDR* upon Freud's need for (and consequent loss of) "authority" is particularly interesting in the light of Jung's repeated use in *MDR* of the term "authority" (*Autorität*) when discussing his No. 2 personality. After recounting the experience of "happening to himself" that occurred immediately after the resolution of his fainting neurosis, Jung explains how he became newly aware of an inner "authority," (Jung, 1989, p. 33) and he goes on to make an "analogy between my feeling of authority and the feeling of value which the [secret pencil case in the attic] inspired in me ..." (Jung, 1989, p. 33). Later, Jung describes personality No. 2 as "important, a high authority" (Jung, 1989, p.34), and later again suggests that "I was afraid to wield that authority which my 'second personality' inspired in me." (Jung, 1989, p.43) His mother's No. 2 personality, too, is described as "a somber, imposing figure possessed of unassailable authority" (Jung, 1989, p.48) and as "wielding absolute authority." (Jung, 1989, p.51) In the light of what for Jung was evidently a close connection between the idea of "authority" and the world of No. 2, his emphasis upon Freud's absolute *loss* of authority on the trip to America seems particularly significant. It also perhaps points to the fact that Freud's loss was Jung's gain in that it ultimately enabled Jung to find a connection to his own authority—the authority of No. 2.

# Endnotes

There is a passage in *MDR* which, although not directly concerned with Jung's memories of Freud, seems relevant to this episode of Freud's "loss of authority":

> [I]n any thoroughgoing analysis the whole personality of both patient and doctor is called into play. There are many cases which the doctor cannot cure without committing himself. *When important matters are at stake, it makes all the difference whether the doctor sees himself as a part of the drama, or cloaks himself in his authority.* In the great crises of life, in the supreme moments when to be or not to be is the question, little tricks of suggestion do not help. Then the doctor's whole being is challenged. (Jung, 1989, pp.132-133 my italics)

Jung implies that an analyst who needs to hide behind his authority is incapable of taking his proper place in the dramatic process of dialogical mutuality and is therefore also incapable of engaging fully in a "thoroughgoing analysis." In effect, Freud stands accused by Jung of failing his patient (Jung), by insisting upon remaining aloof at a point when he most needed to commit his "whole being" to the therapeutic relationship.

[7] In the analysis of the dream of Irma's injection in Freud's *Interpretation of Dreams* (Freud, 1980), Freud refers to "kettle-logic," whereby multiple inconsistent arguments are marshalled to defend a point, e.g., (I) the kettle I'm returning to you is intact; (2) what is more, the holes were already in it when I borrowed it; and (3) besides, you never lent me a kettle.

# CHAPTER 4
# Erasure and Interiorisation

In his book *The Wounded Jung*, Robert C. Smith tells us that during Jung's "confrontation with the unconscious," "he withdrew from many outside activities. For a long period of time he neither wrote nor lectured." (Smith, 1997, p. 62) As Smith could easily have discovered by consulting the bibliographic volume of *the Collected Works* (Jung, 2014), Jung both wrote and lectured throughout the period he was composing *The Red Book*. However, this narrative—that in the wake of the split with Freud, Jung, rejected and abandoned, retreated into a state of complete solitude—is not Smith's but Jung's. In *MDR*, Jung seems to be particularly keen to convince his readers that his encounter with the unconscious was conducted not only entirely alone but also away from all the intellectual work he had been feverishly engaged in up to this point. He tells us, for example, that after writing *Wandlungen*, he "found [himself] utterly incapable of reading a scientific book. This went on for three years." (Jung 1989, p. 193) Given the steady output of publications and the lecturing commitments he continued to fulfill during this time, such a claim seems exaggerated to say the least.[1]

Another example of this kind of distortion occurs in Jung's description of his isolation during this period: "[a]fter the break with Freud, all my friends and acquaintances dropped away. ... Maeder and Riklin alone stuck by me. But I had foreseen my isolation and harboured no illusion about the reactions of my so-called friends." (Jung 1989, pp. 167–8) Jung's apparent desire to convince us that he was abandoned and alone would have been somewhat undermined had he acknowledged that the Zurich psychoanalytic group's decision in 1914 to resign *en masse* from the

International Psychoanalytic Association (and thereby support Jung) was almost unanimous—15 to 1 (Bair, 2004, 247).

It is necessary then to be wary of simply assuming that all Jung's statements about this episode in his life are factually, literally true. As we shall see, this is especially the case when it comes to his attempts to convey it as a period of complete introversion. In *MDR*, the 1925 Seminar, and *The Red Book*, Jung depicts his "confrontation with the unconscious" as an all-consuming, single-handed and solitary inner encounter with the collective unconscious, and many Jungian writers have simply taken Jung's account at face value. The particular attraction of this narrative seems to be that it echoes a heroic myth of descent into and triumphal return from the underworld (e.g., van der Post, 2002 passim; Stevens, 1999, pp. 177ff).[2] Marie Louise von Franz, for example, describes Jung as making a "journey into the beyond so that later he could render [the unfathomable contents of the unconscious] accessible to others in his work and in his books." (von Franz, 1998, p. 107) Jung himself goes so far as to identify his inner journey with Christ's death and resurrection: "No one knows what happened during the three days Christ was in Hell. I have experienced it." (Jung 2009, p. 243)

The focus of this chapter will be upon Jung's (and others') strong implication that the process of individuation is necessarily and exclusively an *inner* process requiring a state of complete solitude. *The Red Book*, for example, contains many passages like this: "I went into the inner death and saw that outer dying is better than inner death. And I decided to die outside and to live within. For that reason I turned away and sought the place of the inner life." (Jung, 2009, p. 267) The implication here is that Jung, and by extension anyone undergoing individuation, must cut himself off from outer life and relationships for the duration of the process. Von Franz describes Jung's life and work in this way: "The encounter of the single individual with his own god or daimon, his struggle with the overpowering emotions, affects, fantasies and creative inspirations and obstacles which come to light from within." (von Franz 1998, pp. 13-14) Even when the ultimate goal of such a process is represented as a fuller engagement with *outer* life and relationships, it is implied that such an outcome can only follow a sustained period of solitary inner work. It also follows from this that the work of the psychotherapist is to facilitate this inner process as it is undergone by the patient.

In the last chapter, I looked at Jung's attempts to enable, within the vessel of his relationship with Freud, an encounter between the (secret) dimension of his personality No. 2 and his (outer-looking) personality No. 1. In the aftermath of the break with Freud, Jung did, to a certain extent, turn away from his outward social life in order to focus more exclusively upon inner engagements with psyche. This led him to refigure his notion of self-development and eventually to articulate the primarily intrapsychic process of individuation.

In *The Red Book,* this shift is described as transformative, a transition of renewal from sterility to fertility. However, this particular narrative needs to be interrogated. As we have seen, Jung's difficulty in managing his relationship with Freud, (and, as we shall see, other relationships with women), probably triggered this renewed focus upon the intrapsychic realm of relationship. Nonetheless, however intractable these relationships may have been for Jung, it does not follow that they were sterile or unproductive or that they failed to provide an important, if not essential, stimulus within the co-context of Jung's psychological development and the development of his psychology. In fact, even during the period when, we are told, Jung experienced the most extreme solitude and isolation, it turns out that he was in fact continuing to further his psychological investigations via dialogical engagements undertaken via various outer relationships.

For reasons that we will go on to examine, Jung seems to have attempted to impose a radical separation between his inner relationships and his outer relationships, and to have prioritised the former and downplayed the latter. Inevitably, this prioritisation colours Jung's accounts of his own life history. However, if we want to avoid colluding in the one-sidedness of this narrative, we need to remain aware of two related facts. First, as we have seen and will continue to see, Jung's outer relationships played a far more important role than he is willing to acknowledge; and second, the narrative that prioritises inner over outer runs counter to the fundamental dynamic of Jung's psychology, whereby the one-sidedness of ego consciousness finds its correction through encounter with the unconscious which, as Jung points out, in his preface to a crucial text from the period we are discussing, "is not this thing or that; it is the Unknown as it immediately affects us." (Jung 1957, p. 68) Jung's point here is that we repeatedly encounter and are affected by the unknown not only in our inner life, but in our outer life, too. Indeed, in Jung's 1916 attempt to outline and conceptualise the process of active imagination (as he was simultaneously experiencing and recounting it in *The Red Book*), he drew specific attention to the crucial coimplication of outer and inner relationships—an insight he was later to articulate in this way: "[R]elationship to the self is at once relationship to our fellow man." (Jung, 1946, para. 445) As we shall see, this idea has important repercussions when it comes to what occurs in analysis, but it also has a crucial significance for the individuation process. In 1957, in conversation with E.A. Bennet on the subject of Freud's so-called self-analysis, Jung said, "It was nonsense to write, as Ernest Jones had done, that Freud conducted a personal analysis on himself. ... It was absolutely necessary in analysis to have another point of view, that of another person." (Bennet, 1985, p. 102) The implication is that whatever the quality of the inner work performed, outer relationships remain indispensable to psychological development.

## Intimate Relationships

The fact that Jung chose to portray his "confrontation with the unconscious" as an inward journey undertaken entirely alone is, of course, highly significant from a psychological point of view. However, it is also important to acknowledge the numerous ways in which the reality of the situation differed from this myth and, moreover, that these variations are at least as interesting, psychologically, as the myth itself. I have attempted to show, how, during the Burghölzli and psychoanalytic periods, the development of Jung's ideas was closely intertwined with his "outer" experiences, and that these outer experiences (particularly experiences of relationship with other individuals) were therefore at least as important as his "inner" experiences, or rather that it was the reciprocal dynamic *between* inner and outer that generated the significant insights that emerged. It therefore makes little sense either to divorce the two or to prioritise one over the other. As it happens, the interplay between inner relationship and outer relationship continued throughout the period Jung was writing in his Black Books and then *The Red Book*.

Having highlighted the crucially important role in Jung's psychological development of his personal, outer relationship with Sigmund Freud, I now intend to turn my attention to a series of other outer relationships between Jung and various significant female figures. This history has suffered from a peculiarly Jungian fate, in that, both in Jung's writings and subsequently in the writings of his followers, it has tended to become subsumed into an account of the constellation and fashioning of the anima archetype. Such an account runs the risk of circularity because it assumes the priority of inner, intrapsychic dynamics over outer relationships. However, it also risks distorting our understanding of the development and character of Jung's ideas in that it blinds us to the contributions of those flesh-and-blood women who, in their own right, made a vital contribution to his psychology. If to reduce these women to shadowy prototypes of the anima offers one kind of distortion, a different, though equally reductive, kind of distortion can be found in the salacious or gossipy treatment of Jung's intimate relationships. The latter approach, which assumes that outer relationships can provide "nothing but" romantic/sexual banalities, is, in a sense, the shadow of the former. The effect of both approaches is to erase the real women involved.

A psychology that gives due weight to the event of human relationship needs to discern psychological value *in outer relationships* as well as intrapsychic relationships so that we can begin to discern the complex interweavings that make up the field in which both are held together. Moreover, if we want to gain a more rounded understanding of the experiences that informed Jung's development of the anima concept, we need to pay close attention to the nature of those highly relational experiences.

## Mother – Wife

A figure who was undoubtedly crucial to Jung's development, though neglected in most accounts of that development, was Jung's wife. Emma Jung figures as little more than a shadowy figure in *MDR*, though, according to Shamdasani, the *MDR* protocols contain more extensive "significant" comments by Jung on his wife (Shamdasani, 2005, p. 82). In the light of this paucity of evidence, and until we have access to private diaries and/or letters, it is impossible to speak authoritatively about specific ways in which the relationship influenced and affected the evolution of Jung's psychology.

One of the only two remarks Jung makes in *MDR* about Emma concerns the period of the "confrontation with the unconscious." There, he emphasises how important it was at a time of huge inner disturbance that he was able to maintain the outer normality of his life: "[M]y family and my profession always remained a joyful reality and a guarantee that I also had a normal existence." (Jung, 1989, p. 189) The important implication lying behind this statement is that in this period, Jung found it necessary to maintain psychological balance by sealing his inner disturbance away from the "safe" zone of normality. As we have seen, in *MDR* Jung proudly describes his childhood ability to secrete from public view those dreams, experiences, and feelings that he experienced as most personally significant. In his childhood and youth, this process seems to have maintained a prophylactic barrier between personality No. 1 and personality No. 2. During the confrontation with the unconscious, a period of extreme disorientation, it is perhaps not surprising that Jung reverted to this defensive strategy of segregating the two parts of his life. In Chapter 6, I shall look more closely at this tendency toward compartmentalisation in Jung's life and its consequences for his psychology.

The fact remains that Jung rarely comments directly on his relationship with Emma except to make it clear how important her dependable presence was to his psychological health at this point. According to C.A. Meier (who knew both Emma Jung and Toni Wolff as friends and analysands), Emma Jung was not suited to the job of accompanying Jung on his 1913 journey into the unknown: "Going into the depths, no, that wasn't her kind of fish." (Quoted in Clay, 2016, p. 230) However, because of what begins to look like a persistent tendency toward compartmentalisation in Jung—keeping Emma Jung in the No. 1 realm of "wife and mother" and Toni Wolff in the No. 2 compartment of "anima figure" —it is hard to know how much Meier's judgment represents merely a post hoc acknowledgment of what had become concretised in an arrangement that all concerned seemed to have colluded in maintaining.

What seems likely is that this tendency of Jung's to separate the women in his life into two mutually exclusive categories relates to his childhood relationship with his mother. As we have seen, as a child, Jung saw Emilie Jung in two radically different guises. In her No. 1 daytime mode, she was the loving, reliable mother whom the infant Jung required, but in her nighttime, No. 2 mode, she was frightening, unpredictable, uncanny, and exciting. Jung's difficulty in bridging the radical gulf between these two modes (a problem that presumably reflected Emilie's experience of her own psychological difficulties) seems to have encouraged Jung to categorise his relationships accordingly. As mentally healthy wife and mother, Emma was required by Jung to stay within the realm of No. 1. His No. 2 personality, on the other hand, seems to have been attracted to women who evoked something of the instability and excitement of his mother's No. 2. However, as we will see, this persistent tendency to divide up the feminine in this way was to prove highly problematic, both for himself and for his psychology.

## Anima – Soul

In the period of The Red Book, Jung portrays himself as engaged in an attempt to refind his "soul." (Jung, 2009, pp.231ff) There are at least three ways to interpret this notion, which, although identifiably different are not mutually exclusive. According to the first, the refinding of soul equates to a psychological shift in the direction of personality No. 2. A second interpretation would regard it as bound up with the discovery of the notion of *anima* (contrasexual archetype). The third evokes Jung's erotic connection with several women, culminating in his relationship with Antonia (Toni) Wolff. The first and second of these factors are evidently intrapsychic events, while the third is an inter-psychic and interpersonal event, taking place in the outer world.

There is a Black Book entry where Jung writes to his "soul": "I found you again only through the soul of the woman." (quoted in Shamdasani, 2009, p. 233 n.49) This sentence plays upon a significant ambiguity. The phrase "the soul of the woman" here may mean anima (soul as *inner* woman), or it may refer to a connection with a real woman, an *outer* event that has resulted in a reconnection with his inner soul. Jung's failure to clarify the ambiguity would imply that, for his purposes, the two are indistinguishable.

Jung's first and most extensive account of the *Auseinandersetzung* is, of course, to be found in *The Red Book*. When, 10 years later, he gave an account of these events in the 1925 seminar (Jung, 1990), he put particular emphasis upon the importance, within that process, of his discovery of the anima archetype. According to Jung, the earliest example of what he describes as "communications with split-off portions of the unconscious" (Jung 1990, 44) (later given the official title, "active imagination"), was his encounter with a female voice. Jung, beginning to write down in sequence the "uncanny" events he had been experiencing, was informed by this voice that what he was engaged in was not science but art. In the account given in *MDR*, Jung tells us, "I knew for a certainty that the voice had come from a woman. I recognized it as the voice of a patient, a talented psychopath who had a strong transference to me. She had become a living figure within my mind." (Jung 1989, p.185)

Despite an enormous amount of speculation with regard to this "talented psychopath," (see e.g. Kerr, 2011; Shamdasani, 1999) it seems to me that what is most significant about this detail is not so much her specific identity as the fact that Jung's anima showed up in the shape of a real-life woman with whom Jung had been involved in an intense erotic transference relationship. Despite Jung's subsequent emphasis upon the intrapsychic nature of his relationship with this imaginal figure, the way in which she made her inaugural appearance tied the whole event inextricably to an outer flesh-and-blood relationship between Jung and an actual woman.

There is a defensive tone both to Jung's description of the woman in question ("a talented psychopath") and to his focus on the transferential element of the relationship ("who had a strong transference to me"). Jung evidently seeks to simultaneously bolster his status as scientist/doctor and undermine the status of the woman in question. What ensures the failure of this strategy is that, by providing too much information and yet also not enough, Jung provokes the curiosity of the reader. Jung's skimpy description of this proto-anima woman fits (at least) three women—Sabina Spielrein, Maria Moltzer, and Toni Wolff—and his defensiveness almost certainly stems from the fact that none of these relationships was either objectively transparent or professionally boundaried in the way Jung seems to be trying to convince us was the case.

Given what we know about the depth and complexity of these important relationships, Jung's brief statement that the woman in question had "had a strong transference" to him looks suspiciously like an apotropaic gesture and a half-truth. Perhaps we should take note of Jung's own suggestion that when a man identifies with his persona, "the anima is inevitably projected upon a real object, with which he gets into a relation of almost total dependence." (Jung 1921, para. 807) In fact, Jung repeatedly emphasises that the anima archetype is encountered first and most commonly *in projection*. This would all seem to imply that, when it came to this, the first appearance of the anima in Jung's psychological life, the crucial transference projection is far more likely to have been that of Jung onto the woman rather than the other way round, though, as we shall see, any hard and fast distinction between the two only serves to obscure the all-important interactive and relational field within which both operate.

When Jung remarks in the 1925 seminar, "I was in analysis with a ghost and a woman," (Jung, 1990, p. 46) he seems to be implying that at this moment of extreme psychological dislocation it was this anima figure who took on the role of analyst so that Jung became anima's patient. I shall argue that what prepared the ground for this fascinating inversion was the quasi-analytic roles that Spielrein, Maria Moltzer and Wolff had taken on within their relationships with Jung. In this context, the question of whether or not these relationships took an actively sexual form (however important it may be with regard to questions of professional ethics) is secondary to the significance of the mutuality and reciprocity they exhibited, since each of these three analysands, at crucial moments, played the role of Jung's analyst.

## Ghostly Analysis

Jung's characterisation of the anima figure as a "ghost" inevitably reminds us of his long-standing interest in spiritualism, an interest that he had inherited from his mother and her family. This interest, with which Jung's "mother's No. 2 sympathized wholeheartedly" (Jung, 1989, p.100), had made a significant contribution to Jung's fascination with psychological matters (Jung, 1989, pp.98ff). In a spiritualistic séance, the medium both summons up and speaks to the spirits. This (predominantly female) figure who gives voice to the "other" had loomed large in the work of those psychological investigators (William James, Frederic Myers and Theodor Flournoy) who, as we have seen, had strongly influenced Jung before his encounter with Freud, and had made an important contribution to the development of his model of the psyche. James and Flournoy in particular are known for the close working relationships they developed with gifted mediums—Mrs. Leonora Piper for James (Richardson, 2007, p. 257ff) and Hélène Smith for Flournoy (see Shamdasani, 1994). The medium who played a parallel role for Jung was his cousin Helene Preiswerk. James, Myers, and Flournoy (and indeed Jung) agreed that, from a psychological perspective, the spiritual, ghostly figures who spoke through the medium represented split-off aspects of the medium's psyche, or in Jung's later terminology, splinter-psyches or complexes. However, when it came to the actual relationship between psychological investigator and medium, and to the dynamics that were inevitably constellated between them, what seems to have remained invisible to contemporaries were precisely those transferential dimensions that were to later preoccupy Freud and Jung in their analytic work.

In his account of Flournoy's relationship with Hélène Smith, Tony James suggests: "[Flournoy] is ... in many ways an accomplice of his chosen medium ... and bypasses ... issues of transference and countertransference." (James, 1995, 266) To "bypass" such issues is, of course, to remain unconscious of them. The contributions of many of those who worked in this field before Freud are characterised by an obliviousness with regard to the complex reality of transference. All kinds of knotty transferential complexities were woven, unanalysed, into the relationships between investigator and medium—complexities which were by no means new but had long shown up in the shape of disturbances within the unexamined though highly active field within which magnetisers and hypnotists encountered their patients. These disturbances had the capacity, therefore, to powerfully distort their "scientific" results.

Such issues, not surprisingly, also continued to bedevil the relationships between psychoanalysts and their analysands, but one of Freud's major contributions was to bring these transferential distortions in the relationship into the light of conscious attention. As Ellenberger points out, there was nothing really new in these problems: "[Transference] was a reincarnation of what had been known for a century as rapport and which Janet had recently brought back into focus as somnambulic influence." (Ellenberger, 1970, p. 490) However, even Janet's acknowledgment of "somnambulic influence" fell far short of providing the kind of transformative insight that Freud retrospectively applies to the abrupt and problematic termination of Breuer's analysis of "Anna O" in 1882.

It was at this point that a thoroughly awkward fact became too obvious to ignore: Patients, and particularly female patients, had a tendency to form close, often erotic, bonds with their magnetisers, investigators, and psychoanalysts. As Ellenberger puts it, "Freud's innovation lay not in introducing the notions of resistance and transference, but in the idea of analyzing them as a basic tool of therapy." (Ellenberger, 1970, p. 490) Freud's breakthrough was to recognise that what at first seemed both embarrassing and inconvenient had the potential, if understood in the right way, to not only provide the analyst with vital information about the patient's psyche but also to *transform the nature of analysis itself*, transmuting it from what had hitherto been a primarily archaeological exercise—digging up original traumata and exposing them to the light—into a real-time healing process enacted (or reenacted) *within and through the analytic relationship itself.*

For all the theoretical differences I have identified between Jung and Freud, neither man disputed the crucial importance of the transference, describing it, as early as 1907, as "The Alpha and Omega of the analytical method." (Jung, 1946 para. 358) Shamdasani has done a great deal to undermine the influence of what he calls a "Freudocentric" reading of Jung's psychological development, but however compelling this revisionist approach may be, it gets into difficulties when it comes up against the crucial fact that transference as the central event of psychoanalysis was almost completely unrecognised by those influential precursors whose importance Shamdasani has done so much to reclaim: Myers, James, Flournoy, and Janet. When it comes to the actual dynamics of psycho-analytic work, Freud was important to Jung because only he could offer Jung the key he needed to achieve what would, as we will see in Chapter 6, eventually lead to Jung's mature understanding of the mutual and reciprocal dynamics that operate in transference/countertransference.

## Four Women

The crucial next step in the development of depth psychology was to be the recognition and appreciation of these interpersonal dynamics. This process of recognition was, as it happens, closely bound up with the unfolding of Jung's personal and professional relationships. It is important to remember that the context not only of Freud's famous 1906 comment that "essentially, one might say, the cure [Heilung] is effected by love ... and transference," (Freud and Jung, 1977, pp. 12–13) but also of the first conceptualisation of countertransference in 1909 (Freud and Jung, 1977, p.145) was that of Jung's relationship with Sabina Spielrein with all its erotic/therapeutic complexities.

However, before we review the implications of that much-discussed affair, we need to place it in a wider context. In his 1961 paper, *Psychiatry and its Unknown History*, Ellenberger identifies a pattern of relationship, whereby,

[A] psychiatrist … has made one of his patients—most often a *female* patient and generally a *hysterical* one—a special object of psychological investigation. The psychiatrist develops unconsciously with this patient a long complex, and quite ambiguous relationship the result of which will be very fruitful for medical science. (Ellenberger, 1993b, pp. 239-40 italics in the original)

This pattern, or something like it, may be discerned in Jung's relationships with Helene Preiswerk, Sabina Spielrein, Maria Moltzer, and Antonia Wolff. Despite the important differences between these women and despite the differences between the relationships they had with Jung, there are nonetheless identifiable factors that recur in all four cases. These factors are of interest because, as we will see, not only do they contribute to our understanding of the development of Jung's anima concept, but they also provide us with the means to interrogate that concept and, therefore, Jung's psychology as a whole.

## Helene Preiswerk

Never less than astute, Sabina Spielrein couldn't help noticing that, when it came to the relationship with Jung, she was, as it were, not altogether alone with him. In a 1906-07 diary entry, Spielrein attributes these words to Jung: "Yes … a few years ago, I knew a similar woman; she too seemed to me like a goddess, but in the end she turned out to be just a flighty girl." (Spielrein, 2001, 169) As Spielrein was aware, this woman, who Spielrein was to go on to describe as her "prototype," was Jung's cousin, Helene Preiswerk, the teenage medium who had provided him with the material for his doctoral dissertation (Jung, 1902). As we have seen, Jung's comments in *MDR* on the source of the anima show him attempting to disguise the complex reciprocities contained in his relationships with Spielrein (or Moltzer), by squeezing them into the familiar doctor/madwoman binary. However, this pattern was first enacted in Jung's narration of the Preiswerk affair in his doctoral dissertation; there, too, he chose to erase his own countertransferential involvement by depicting himself as objective scientist and Preiswerk as a pathological "case."

We know frustratingly little about the truth of the relationship between Jung and Preiswerk. However, we know enough to be very wary when reading Jung's account of it, an account that was later disputed both in detail and in general by Preiswerk's family (Zumstein-Preiswerk, 1975). What we do know is that Preiswerk showed early promise as a medium and that from as early as 1895, Jung set up seances with her and other family members. Shamdasani, who has gone back to Jung's original reports of the seances (Jung, 1895), points out that, although in his 1902 account Jung presents himself "as not [taking] any of this remotely seriously," (Shamdasani 2015, p. 293) back in 1898, he was an enthusiastic and active participant in the seances. In fact, he was sufficiently enthusiastic about them to fantasise about writing "a work on Helene Preiswerk akin to Kerner's *The Seeress of Prevost*," (Shamdasani 2015, p.293) a book he himself had given to his cousin for her 15th birthday in 1896.

We can surmise from contemporary documents that both Jung and his cousin were caught up in a kind of folie-à-deux that not only inflated Jung's ambition to create a partnership along the lines of Kerner and Friederike Hauffe, but that pushed Preiswerk into increasingly desperate attempts to provide the kind of mediumistic results that she believed Jung was looking for.

In a controversial 1984 paper (Goodheart, 1984), William Goodheart suggests that throughout the period of the seances not only was Jung unconsciously fighting the erotic bond between Preiswerk and himself, but that the theoretical developments that emerged in his doctoral dissertation were formulated in order to further this defensive position. I will return to this question in chapter 6 when I look at certain difficulties that Jung encountered in his clinical practice.

At any rate, as Ellenberger implies, these events were sublimating an erotic charge between Jung and his cousin, whether or not either partner was conscious of it at the time (Ellenberger 1993a, p. 304). Eventually, this bubble of mutual self-deception was burst by the mocking laughter of some student friends whom Jung had invited to a seance. At this painful moment, one assumes, Jung, too, saw all too clearly the absurdity of what he and Helly had co-constructed. If, in Ellenberger's words, Jung's portrait of Preiswerk in his 1902 doctoral dissertation is "governed by contempt," (Ellenberger 1993a, p. 304) then Jung's contempt is, I would suggest, intended to distance him from his own embarrassment at this youthful folly.

As Shamdasani points out, by the time Jung came to write up these events for his dissertation, he had discarded the model of a partnership à la Kerner and Hauffe and replaced it with one closer to that of Flournoy and Smith (Shamdasani, 2015, p. 295). No longer rewriting *The Seeress of Prevost*, Jung now sought to replicate *From India to the Planet Mars*. Discarding the role of faithful and supportive amanuensis of a medium's visions and dreams, he now saw himself as a scientist who understood that the "spirits" to which his accomplice gave voice were really expressions of her own divided psyche. Preiswerk was thus demoted from "gifted medium" to "pathological case," and Jung was simultaneously elevated to the position of doctor, with all the scientific objectivity that role brings with it. As a result of this shift, Jung undoubtedly achieved a significant gain in psychological insight, since, as we have seen, he was introduced to a complex psychological model of inner multiplicity that would well serve his future work. Nonetheless, there was a commensurate loss, and one that in some ways distorted the "scientific" narrative presented. In the doctoral dissertation, what was completely erased was the dimension of complex reciprocity that showed up as the "rapport" between medium and seance-goer—in this case a rapport with distinctly erotic overtones.

Significantly, when Jung decided in 1925 to offer "a brief sketch of the development of my own conceptions from the time I first became interested in problems of the unconscious," he began it with an account of the Preiswerk episode, which he described as "an impetus for my future life." (Jung, 1990, p. 3) By 1925, Jung had apparently gained some insight into the factor that had, at least partly rendered the episode so important for him: While it was actually happening, he tells us, "I overlooked the most important feature of the situation, namely my connection with it. The girl had of course fallen deeply in love with me, and of this I was fairly ignorant and quite ignorant of the part it played in her psychology." (Jung, 1990, p. 5) Unfortunately, Jung's acknowledgement of the erotic complexities of the relationship remained compromised, since it ignored the fact that what Jung describes as his "connection with" the situation actually consisted of his own relationship with Preiswerk, i.e., not only her feelings for him, but his feelings for her. We can retrospectively discern the intensity of Jung's bond with Preiswerk in some of Spielrein's writings, such as the diary entry in which she says (to Jung), "You held the young woman [Preiswerk] in greater esteem than anybody else, and [you said] that you thought she was destined for you." (Spielrein, 2001, p. 169) Spielrein is making the point not that Jung had loved Preiswerk in an ordinary romantic sense but that his love entailed the attribution to her of enormous, fateful, importance. This tone can also be detected in Spielrein's letter to Freud of June 20, 1909, where, having referred to a dream of Jung's in which Preiswerk appeared in a white robe, she goes on, "[Preiswerk] was supposed to be very pretty and intelligent. This girl was deeply rooted in him, and she was my prototype. … [H]e would sometimes turn reflective when I said something to him; such and such a woman had spoken in just this way, etc. And it was always this girl!" (Carotenuto, 1984, pp. 105–6)

As we have seen, in many ways the Jung/Preiswerk collaboration fits the pattern of relationship between psychiatrist and female patient identified by Ellenberger (Ellenberger 1993b). In such relationships, according to Ellenberger, the analyst allows "himself to be misled for a long time by his patient—or, rather, by the mythopoetical operations of the patient's unconscious—as well as by his own illusions and expectations." (Ellenberger, 1993b, p. 253) This pattern discerned by Ellenberger inevitably begs a question about the nature of the psychological factor underlying this dynamic, which presumably consisted in some kind of reciprocal interaction between the "illusions and expectations" of the analyst and the workings of the patient's unconscious as traced through transference and countertransference phenomena. Ellenberger's examples include Anton Mesmer and Maria Theresia Paradis, Kerner and Hauffe, Jean-Martin Charcot and Blanche Wittmann, Janet and Leonie, Breuer and Anna O, and finally Jung and Preiswerk.

Not surprisingly, at the time of the séances Jung was unaware of such dynamics, and even at the time of his reworking of the material in his doctoral dissertation he revealed no real understanding of the unconscious dynamics within the relationship. However, the "case" clearly possessed a more than ordinary significance for Jung. His nagging desire to make sense of what had happened and what had not happened seems to have led directly to what Shamdasani has represented as an almost obsessive revisiting of the Preiswerk case in later texts.[3]

## Sabina Spielrein

For all their differences, Jung's later relationships with Spielrein, Moltzer and Wolff possessed important common factors with the Preiswerk relationship. We have seen something of this in the Spielrein comments I have already quoted, such as her description of Preiswerk as her "prototype," clearly indicating an intuition that Jung was engaging in some kind of unconscious repetition.

Jung's unconsciousness of the mutually active erotic component that underpinned his relationship with Preiswerk led directly to his defensive representation of Preiswerk as a pathological case. However, a few years later, it proved less easy to dismiss Sabina Spielrein as merely a "case," although Jung was not above attempting it, especially when writing in collegial mode to Freud. Nonetheless, the overtly erotic complexities of the relationship between them were plain to all. Indeed, recent accounts of the Spielrein narrative have tended to highlight this erotic dimension, sometimes sensationalising it (as in the David Cronenberg film *A Dangerous Method*) and sometimes utilising it in order to initiate long-overdue and inevitably heated discussions of boundary violations (as in Gabbard and Lester, 2016). These contrasting focuses have made it more difficult to achieve a comprehensive understanding of the relationship's contribution to Jung's psychology (or indeed of its contribution to Spielrein's psychology, a subject that exceeds the bounds of this study).

I am going to concentrate here not upon the intellectual/theoretical aspect of the relationship but rather its performative, mutual, and reciprocal dimensions, through which both partners blindly, painfully, and messily worked through dynamics and experiences that would eventually bear theoretical fruit in the profoundly intersubjective (or perhaps trans-subjective) model of psychotherapy that Jung developed in his pioneering 1946 study, *Psychology of the Transference* (Jung, 1946).

Jung and Spielrein met in the Burgholzli in 1904; she a very challenging "hysterical" case of 19 years, he an ambitious psychiatrist of 29, four years out of medical school. She became his first "psychoanalytic" case, though at the time he had done little more than read Freud's *Interpretation of Dreams*. Nonetheless, the talking cure was apparently a success, and after five months, Spielrein seemed mostly cured, though the talking was to continue within the context of a close friendship that had developed between doctor and patient. By now, Spielrein was deeply in love with Jung, and within a year, Jung was returning that love. In the meantime, Spielrein had entered medical school, intending to emulate Jung by becoming both psychiatrist and psychoanalyst. By 1909, rumours of scandal led Jung to temporarily break with her, but they remained close until at least 1911, when Spielrein went to Vienna where, under Freud's aegis, she became a full-fledged psychoanalyst. Jung and Spielrein remained in friendly correspondence until 1919.

We possess vivid, albeit fragmentary, evidence about the relationship, pieced together from Jung's letters to Spielrein and Freud, Spielrein's letters to Jung and Freud, and entries from Spielrein's diary at the time. Although the Jung/Spielrein connection was to begin in a thoroughly asymmetrical (though conventional) dynamic of "mad" patient and "sane" doctor, it was to develop, in the period 1905-11, into something far more complex: a relationship possessing elements of both reciprocity and mutuality. Not only did Jung come to return Spielrein's erotic feelings, but the erotic connection between them seems to have been inextricably bound up with an intellectual bond, whereby Jung's ideas were channeled through Spielrein's critical intelligence and returned transformed, and Spielrein's ideas underwent a parallel process. What also appears to have occurred at times was an inversion of the original analytic dynamic such that Jung became patient and Spielrein analyst. It is clear from the surviving letters of both parties and from Spielrein's journal entries that Jung felt able to expose his vulnerabilities to Spielrein in a context of intimacy and mutuality, and that she, in turn, was capable of reflecting them back to him through a psychoanalytic lens. See for example Spielrein's insight in this passage from a 1908 letter to her mother:

> He is for me a father and I am a mother for him, or, more precisely, the woman who has acted as the first substitute for the mother … and now he has fallen in love with me, a hysteric; and I fell in love with a psychopath, and is it necessary to explain why? (Quoted in Lothane, 2015, p. 130)

At times then, during the Spielrein relationship Jung played the role of patient, in receipt not only of her penetrating analytical interpretations but also of her love and support. For example, in his letter to Spielrein of December 4, 1908 he writes:

> Give me at this moment something back of the love and patience and unselfishness that I was able to give to you during the time of your illness. Now I am the sick one … (Quoted in Carotenuto, 1984, pp. 195–6)

It is interesting to see in Spielrein's writings at the time what appear to be pre-echoes of ideas that Jung was later to develop. For example, Spielrein's diary entries contain passages that indicate an awareness of the tendency to project onto the partner contrasexual aspects of the psyche (Spielrein, 2001, p. 162 and p. 168). She also observes Jung's doubleness, identifying "two speakers" within him (Spielrein, 2001, p. 156). Here, she writes in terms similar to Jung's own when describing the contrast between Eros and Logos, a familiar motif in the mature Jung, but also evoking *MDR*'s passages on his two personalities. Spielrein's reflections on the transformative power of unrequited love (Spielrein, 2001, p. 163) find parallels, 40 years later, in Jung's *Psychology of the Transference*, where he reflects upon the contributions of instinct to psychic transformation (Jung, 1946, para. 471). I am not suggesting that Jung took his ideas from

Spielrein, or vice versa, but merely that the relationship was fertile and creative and that its reciprocity enabled both partners to deepen, in tandem, the personal and theoretical dimensions of their understanding.

In 1919, after the liaison had finished, Jung wrote a letter in which he overtly and very clearly attributed to his relationship with Spielrein a key psychological insight:

> The love of S [Spielrein] for J [Jung] made the latter aware of something he had previously only vaguely suspected, namely of a power in the unconscious which shapes our destiny, a power which later led him to things of the greatest importance. (Covington and Wharton, 2015, p. 57)

With this apparently generous comment, Jung acknowledges that Spielrein's love for him was an important factor in the development of his psychological ideas. At first glance, Jung appears to give due weight to the relational aspect of the encounter, indicating that the insight in question was gained thanks to an event of Eros. However, by stressing that the love in question was Spielrein's (active) love for Jung (passive), Jung is really recycling the old psychotherapeutic pattern whereby the (male) doctor achieves clinical insight as a result of the (female) patient's erotic projection upon him. The female patient provided the (irrational) Eros, and the male doctor provided the (rational) Logos—and the result was an insight (of Jung's) "which later led him to things of the greatest importance."

Setting aside the important matter of Spielrein's own *intellectual* contribution and the insights gained by her, what this account erases is Jung's (irrational) *erotic* contribution. This factor remains invisible because it doesn't fit the male/logos, female/eros binary, or the assumption that this is a narrative about male scientists making important discoveries. There are clear parallels between the Jung-Spielrein relationship and the Jung-Preiswerk relationship. There, it was Preiswerk who provided the (irrational) mediumism and Jung who provided the (rational) analysis, resulting in an insight (of Jung's) that was "an impetus for [his] future life."

If the relationship with Spielrein really did introduce Jung to "a power in the unconscious" that led him "to things of the greatest importance," we might wonder why the source of such an important insight (i.e., the relationship with Spielrein) was subsequently written out of his account. This is not a question about priority or even about individuals receiving their due, though both these points are important. By suppressing the actual circumstances of the insight gained, i.e., the experiential and relational dimension, Jung failed to provide his readers with crucial information about the nature of that insight. If, as Jung seems to be implying, his understandings of the workings of the objective psyche grew directly out of the mutual erotic complexities of his relationship with Spielrein, it was surely his scientific obligation to find a way to convey something of these formative dynamics to his readers.

Assuming that Jung is being sincere in this passage, another question that arises is what is Jung referring to when he claims that as a result of the relationship, he became aware of "a power in the unconscious"? The period of the Spielrein relationship coincided with much of the work Jung did on the feeling-toned complex, but although the complex is "a power in the unconscious," it seems unlikely that Jung is referring to the complex here. What seems to me more likely is that he is suggesting that the erotic complexities of their entanglement enabled him to take an important step in his awareness and articulation of what was eventually to be called the anima.

In the 1925 seminar, and later in *MDR*, Jung gives a highly dramatic version of the revelation of the anima. He represents the anima's first appearance as a spontaneous intrapsychic event, which was only tangentially related to an actual woman who happened to have an erotic transference onto him. It seems to me more likely that this moment of insight was in fact the product of a process of gradual realisation over years, and moreover that the conceptualisation of the anima was directly related to the complex twists and turns of his *outer* relationships. As we have seen, Spielrein herself touched on something resembling a rudimentary version of Jung's contrasexual archetype and its projection within their erotic connection:

What really is this abominable thing that is love? … What do we love in the other? Our own ideal. … Still you must be aware that my 'unconscious' does not want to have anything to do with what your 'unconscious' rejects. … The complexity of the situation makes me adopt the unnatural role of the man and you the feminine role. (Spielrein, 2001, p.157, p.162, p.168)

It seems far from unlikely that it was in and through his relationship with Spielrein that Jung first achieved insight into the anima, which he later described as "[functioning] as a bridge, or a door, leading to the images of the collective unconscious," (Jung, 1989, p. 392) and which was eventually to be identified with the "soul" refound at the time of *The Red Book*.

The creation narrative whereby the anima springs fully formed and Athena-like from Jung's head provides us with an anima that, already fully interiorized and appropriated, can seamlessly contribute to Jung's *inner* process. It follows that, when it comes to *outer* relationships, such an anima can only show up in projected form. As he puts it in the 1925 seminar, "If a man cannot project his anima, then he is cut off from women. It is true he may make a thoroughly respectable marriage, but the spark of fire is not there, he does not get complete reality into his life." (Jung, 1990, p.140) This prioritisation of the inner, intrapsychic relationship with the anima has the effect of reducing the outer relational world to a mere arena for projections (see Brooke, 2015, p. 77). So it is that a Jungian like Aldo Carotenuto can describe a mature relationship with a woman as representing "the rapport with the inner reality of the anima, which has only a projective link with persons in real life." (Carotenuto, 1985, pp. 51–52)

What I am suggesting here, however, is that the anima was, in fact, the product of a process of co-creation. She emerged from intricate and reciprocal *outer* relationships: not only the bond with Spielrein, but also those with Preiswerk, Moltzer and Wolff. If this is so, then psychological life—and indeed the dynamic unconscious itself—needs to be sought not only *inside* the individual, but within and through the living relations shared between persons. The emphasis thus moves from individual to individuation, a process that occurs not only through outer and inner relations but within the relations between those relations.

In the last chapter, we saw how in the period 1902-12 Jung sought and found in his outer relationship with Sigmund Freud the opportunity to achieve a living engagement between his No. 1 personality (i.e., his ego) and the energies, ideas and dynamics that he associated with his No. 2 personality. We also noticed that this meeting provided both men with a fruitful opportunity for intellectual cross-fertilisation. As a living engagement, it not only informed Jung's own psychological and theoretical development (especially in the realm of transference/countertransference) but also brought a reciprocal enrichment to that of Freud.

We have now also become aware of the ways in which the relationships with Preiswerk and Spielrein add another dimension to this picture by bringing into focus a further facet of the ongoing interaction between personality No. 1 and personality No. 2. If, as I have suggested, Jung's development of the anima archetype was constellated as much by the interactive nature of his relationships as it was by his own private inner psychic dynamics—or rather, that the two are inextricably intertwined— then the notion of individuation needs to be revisioned to allow for the new dimension of complexity that the reciprocal interplay between inner (No. 2) and outer (No. 1) processes must involve.

## Maria Moltzer

Our skimpy knowledge of Sabina Spielrein and her relationship with Jung seems abundant when we compare it with what we know of Maria Moltzer (1874-1944). She was a Dutch woman, an heiress of the Bols fortune, who, having turned her back on family money on the grounds that it derived from the selling of alcohol, worked as a nurse at the teetotal Burghölzli. Subsequently, with Jung's help, Moltzer became a trusted colleague and an analyst in her own right (see Shamdasani, 1998). Alongside Emma Jung and Toni Wolff, Moltzer accompanied Jung to the Weimar psychoanalytic congress of September 1911. We know that she occasionally attended to Jung's correspondence while he was away (Moltzer, 1912) and that she was joint translator of his 1912 Fordham lectures (subsequently published under the title *The Theory of Psycho-analysis* [Jung, 1912b]). We are also told that Moltzer subsequently "worked closely with Jung as his assistant." (Shamdasani, 2003, p. 57) In fact, as Jung told American psychiatrist Smith Ely Jeliffe in 1915, he "trusted ... cases entirely to her with the only condition, that in cases of difficulties she would consult me. ... Later on Miss M. worked quite independently." (Quoted in Shamdasani, 2003, p. 57)

Moltzer enjoyed what Lance Owens describes as an "intricate relationship" with Jung, which, Owens speculates, may have included a reciprocal mutual analysis: "something not entirely unlike what had informally happened with Spielrein over the prior years." (Owens, 2015, pp. 36–37) In support of this idea, he quotes Freud's letter to Ferenczi of December 1912. Provoked by a belligerent letter from Jung where he claims that he—unlike Freud—had at least experienced analysis (Freud and Jung, 1977, p. 535), Freud responded, "The master who analyzed him could only have been Fraulein Molzer [sic] and he is so foolish as to be proud of this work of a woman with whom he is having an affair." (Freud and Ferenczi, 1993, p. 446)[4]

Although, as Jung acknowledged in print, Moltzer made a major contribution to his theory of types by "[discovering] the existence of [the intuitive type]," (Jung, 1921, para. 773 n. 68) she was by no means an orthodox Jungian and went on to develop what Shamdasani describes as an "individual interpretation of Jung's concepts." (Shamdasani, 1998, 104) What I am here interested in is the way in which Moltzer's ideas and Jung's ideas from this period seem to have emerged from the kind of reciprocal relationship that Jung had previously enjoyed with Spielrein.

In the summer of 1916, for example, Moltzer delivered papers to the Zurich Analytical Psychology Club on two topics: the relation of the individual to the collective, and the process of individuation. As Shamdasani points out, Jung's paper "Adaptation, Individuation, Collectivity" (Jung 1916a), dated October 1916, "can in part be read in terms of a response to or dialogue with Moltzer's positions." (Shamdasani 1998, 104) Indeed, even Moltzer's ideas on intuition, which Jung acknowledged as a major influence, were by no means identical to those of Jung. As Shamdasani puts it, "it appears that Jung developed his concept of this type through extensively reworking Moltzer's concept."

It seems eminently possible that this kind of creatively dialogical way of working might have emerged through the experience of a quasi-analytical relationship between Jung and Moltzer (if we assume that Freud's sneering comment has some basis in fact) and that such a relationship was similar to what Jung had also experienced with Spielrein, whereby a mutual psychological understanding of some depth enabled a fruitful though challenging engagement of ideas and emotions, leading to new insights, on both sides.

Another relevant reference to Moltzer from a slightly earlier period occurs in Jung's 1915-16 correspondence (on the subject of psychological types) with his erstwhile analysand Hans Schmid-Guisan. In the last letter of the correspondence, dated January 16, 1916, Schmid-Guisan writes to Jung: "Once you told me that it repeatedly struck you how your secretary Moltzer rendered thoughts that you had told her in a more acceptable and lively form." He goes on:

So perhaps the extravert has the capability of clearly formulating thoughts, and the introvert provides the matter in the form of his thoughts. Vice versa, the extravert provides matter in the form of his feelings, while they are given form by the introvert. The extravert finds the form only through the intersection with other circles. The extravert projects his incapability of finding a form for his feelings into the introvert, and that is why he always wants to correct the introvert's feelings. Perhaps the introvert, too, inasmuch as he wants to correct at all, has the analogous tendency to correct the form of the thoughts of the extravert. (Jung and Schmid-Guisan, 2013, pp. 155-156)

Putting aside the particular *typological* point Schmid-Guisan is making here, he is clearly pointing to a mutual and reciprocal interaction between Jung and Moltzer whereby a relational give and take between different individuals can achieve highly creative results. This is precisely what seems to have also occurred within Jung's relationship with Spielrein, and, as we will see, it was also to occur in the case of Toni Wolff.

As it happens, the Schmid-Guisan correspondence followed the same pattern, in that Jung deliberately set out to create a dialogue within which extravert feeling type met and engaged with introvert thinking type. Since Schmid was an erstwhile patient of Jung's, this encounter provides us with yet another example of Jung engaging in a quasi-analytical relationship with a client and, within that relationship, achieving important insights that feed back into his developing psychology. And yet again, the *outer* relationship proved to be crucial to insights that, when they achieved their final textual form, were represented as primarily the products of an *inner* process.[5] I shall look more closely at the correspondence with Schmid in the next chapter.

## Toni Wolff

Until very recently, standard accounts tended to delineate Toni Wolff's role in Jung's life by using terms like *femme inspiratrice, Soror Mystica,* or, in Jungian terms, anima figure (e.g. Hannah, 1976). This way of characterising Wolff had the advantage of maintaining Jung's status as sole heroic discoverer of the underworld/unconscious. Wolff's existence as an actual woman who mattered in Jung's life was, of course, acknowledged, but her significance within the mythic development of Analytical Psychology remained firmly attached to her famed ability to mirror an *inner* aspect of Jung by embodying his projected anima. From the point of view of the Jung family, this portrayal also retained the virtue of endowing Jung's wife, Emma, with a far more substantial existence than that of Wolff.

Unfortunately, in reality this arrangement failed to honour either woman's existence as a whole person, since it succeeded only in furthering the problematic compartmentalisation we have already identified. In Emma's case, it insists upon locating her sphere of influence in a realm quite separate from that of Jung's real "soul" work, which, we are reminded, did only and could only occur on the *inner* level. In Wolff's case, on the other hand, the kudos gained from her proximity to Jung's "soul" work only serves to emphasise her erasure as an actual woman.

To a certain extent, this particular Jungian narrative has in recent years undergone a change in the light of various attempts to allow Wolff a more three-dimensional presence in the history of Analytical Psychology. For example, in her 2017 book-length study of Wolff, Nan Savage Healy insists upon using the term "collaborator" to describe her role in the work that Jung was undertaking during the *Red Book* years (Healy, 2017). This usage marks a significant shift in perspective, because although for two partners to work as collaborators does not necessarily imply a symmetrical or equal relationship, it does nonetheless imply a relationship that contains elements of reciprocity and dialogue.

As we have seen, Shamdasani tends to follow Jung's narrative for the creation of *The Red Book* by representing it as the product of a state of inner solitude. In Shamdasani's introduction to *Liber Novus*, Wolff's contribution is barely mentioned. Perhaps understandably, the Jung family has attempted to divert attention from Wolff's role in Jung's life. Moreover, the "auntification" of *MDR* apparently led to a chapter derived from the Jaffe protocols and devoted to Wolff's role in Jung's life being excised from the final text (Elms, 1997). Nonetheless, it seems clear from the testimony of those who were close to both Jung and Wolff that Toni Wolff was a far more active participant in Jung's "confrontation with the unconscious" than has been generally acknowledged.

According to Barbara Hannah, Wolff "had not the slightest wish … to experience the unconscious at first hand," though "[s]he had no doubt whatever of its objective existence." (Hannah, 1976, p. 119) It was Wolff's "calm attitude" that enabled her to offer "the firmest support" to those (including Jung) who did encounter it through active imagination. Tina Keller, who worked analytically with both Wolff and Jung, offers support to this claim when, in direct contrast with Jung's statement that Wolff "was disorientated and in the same mess" as himself (Shamdasani, 2009, p.204), suggested that "[Wolff] helped Dr. Jung in his confrontation with the unconscious." (Swan, 2009, p. 27) Keller tells us that, although Wolff understood "how close he … felt to insanity," she was "able to accompany him into those dangers and thus to anchor him to reality." (Swan, 2009, p.

28) Liliane Frey-Rohn, who was a close friend of Wolff's, agrees with this estimation:

> Without Toni Wolff he couldn't have made it because she had brakes in a way and she was stopping him always when he had a temperament where he was losing himself completely without boundaries and Toni Wolff stopped him and always brought him back to reality and that was tremendously important for Jung (Frey-Rohn, 1986).

Irene Champernowne, describing the way in which Wolff, as her analyst, translated her "inner material and ... helped [her] to coordinate" then adds: "I think she also did this for Jung." (Champernowne, 1968) Indeed, Jung himself is quoted as remarking to Isabelle Hamilton Rey that Wolff had "a peculiar ability to stabilize an individual doing the work." (Mullen, 1975, p. 75) What seems clear is that, during the period of the so-called "confrontation with the unconscious," Wolff and Jung collaborated very closely. Although Jung was alone when undergoing the intrapsychic events (active imaginations, dreams, and visions) that are recounted in *The Red Book*, Wolff was a regular and active participant in the reception, analysis, and processing of the images they contained.

In light of the fact that both Spielrein and Moltzer seem to have acted at various times in the role of Jung's analyst, it is evidently significant that various Jungian authors have also suggested that Toni Wolff served Jung in the same way during this period. For example, John Ryan Haule states that during Jung's "own brush with psychosis ... Toni Wolff became his analyst." (Haule, 1996, 105)[6] Certainly, as Haule also points out, it is striking how many echoes there are of Jung's previous relationship with Spielrein, in which, as we noted, the doctor/patient relationship was, at times, inverted. It is surely also significant that Wolff, Spielrein, and Moltzer all later went on to become analysts in their own right.

It is nonetheless worth asking what it might mean to suggest that at this point Wolff became Jung's analyst? Evidently, Wolff (25 years old in 1913) was not in a position to perform anything like the full range of analytical work that we would expect from any psychotherapist. However, it does seem as though, at a time when Jung himself clearly felt in danger of being overwhelmed, Wolff was not only able to engage with Jung in a way that stabilised him and enabled him to continue to return, again and again, to encounter the highly challenging and disturbing images that flowed from his unconscious psyche, but that her intelligence and sensitivity contributed to a dialogical process that eventually fed into Jung's ability to comprehend the symbolic meaning of what was occurring. What is beyond doubt is that Wolff provided important support to Jung throughout this difficult period.

However, the fact remains that Jung's descriptions of his encounter with the unconscious in *MDR* make no mention of Wolff. For example, Jung's account of his miniature building activities by the side of Lake Zurich (Jung, 1989, p. 172), lead the reader to assume that Jung was alone at the time, yet several sources tell us that he was invariably accompanied by Wolff and sometimes by his son Franz (Healy, 2017, p. 117; Bair, 2004, p. 730 n. 37) Elsewhere, when he says that, overwhelmed by unconscious material, he "took great care to try to understand every single image, every item of my psychic inventory, and to classify them scientifically," (Jung, 1989, p. 192) there is no indication that this work of amplification was being conducted with the active and energetic collaboration of another person—Toni Wolff.

In the context of *MDR*, this apparent airbrushing of Wolff from the account can probably be explained as an attempt to avoid embarrassment for Jung's family, and particularly Jung's wife, since Wolff was Jung's mistress at the time. However, this does not explain why in the 1925 seminar that constitutes the first detailed description of his confrontation with the unconscious, Jung also failed to mention Wolff's involvement. Although Wolff did not personally attend the seminar, the participants would have known her and would have been fully aware of Jung's intimate relationship with her. However, her absence from the actual seminar is matched by her absence from its textual content. To read the seminar now, knowing the level of collaboration with Wolff that had actually taken place, certain passages are particularly striking: For example, when Jung discusses the first appearance of the anima and its inaugural statement, "That is art," Jung reflects:

A living woman could very well have come into the room and said that very thing to me, because she would not have cared anything about the discriminations she was trampling underfoot. Obviously it wasn't science; what then could it be but art, as though those were the only two alternatives in the world. That is the way a woman's mind works. (Jung, 1990, p. 42)

Jung's casual misogyny is disappointing but sadly not surprising. However, what is startling is the fact that a "living woman" in the form of Toni Wolff was indeed coming into Jung's room on a regular basis at the time he describes. This leads one to suspect that Jung considered Wolff, whose "discriminations" he seems to have highly valued, as something other than a "living woman" at this time. When later Jung says that the experience of the anima was "like the feeling of an invisible presence in the room one enters," (Jung, 1990, p. 46) it is hard not to read this as an implicit commentary on his erasure/interiorisation of Wolff's visible presence as living woman.

It is certainly true that in the 1925 seminar, and later in *MDR*, Jung was primarily interested in making available to his audience the *content* of his dreams, fantasies, and visions, i.e., the intrapsychic meeting between Jung's conscious ego and the products of his unconscious; his prime aim was to convey the existence of an autonomous objective psyche with which the conscious ego could communicate. The relationship Jung wanted to focus upon was that between conscious and unconscious *within a single psyche*. No doubt he believed that these inner waters would have been muddied were he to have drawn attention to another factor—his outer relationship with Wolff.

However, this argument founders against the fact that throughout his writings, Jung made a point of repeatedly offering detailed descriptions of the experiential process that had enabled him to engage with the unconscious, revealing precisely how he had (and by extension how anyone might) use this technique (active imagination) in order to facilitate a psychological event of this kind. As Shamdasani puts it, "He took his own experiences as paradigmatic." (Shamdasani, 2009, p. 205) In the light of these points, the question remains why Jung chose to exclude from all of these accounts the role of his collaborator—Toni Wolff.

In fact, Jung's decision to narrate the story of his encounter with the unconscious as a journey undertaken entirely alone fits the pattern we have already ascertained when examining his relationships with Moltzer, Spielrein, and before that with Preiswerk. Despite the clear importance of these outer relationships, not only on a personal level, but crucially in terms of that intertwined field in which Jung's own self-knowledge was all but indistinguishable from the development of his psychological ideas, Jung consistently chose to portray his experience as an inner process, undertaken alone.

Hitherto I have concentrated upon the similarities between Jung's relationships with Spielrein, Moltzer, and Wolff. However, it is important to also pay attention to the differences between them. Over the period between Jung's first encounter with Spielrein (1904) and the writing of *The Red Book* (begun in 1913), there seems to have been a distinct shift in the balance within Jung's relationships with these women, which is best illustrated when we look at contrasts between the protagonists on the theoretical/intellectual level.

For all Spielrein's youth and inexperience, her writings on psychology (e.g., the dissertation written toward the end of her liaison with Jung and the paper 'Destruction as the Cause of Coming into Being' [Spielrein, 1994]), all remain relatively independent of Jung's theoretical influence. They are clearly not "Jungian," as we can see from her immediate acceptance by Freud into the psychoanalytic fold in Vienna in 1912. In fact, her ideas, which are in some ways independent also of Freud's influence, show distinct originality. The relationship with Jung, and the tension and friction that it generated, was a spur for both partners, as we have seen, to develop their ideas, but those ideas remained quite separate.

When it comes to Moltzer, Jung's willingness to, as he put it, "[trust] cases entirely to her," implies that he was confident in her ability to purvey an authentically Jungian style of analysis. However, her theoretical ideas, as contained in the papers she delivered in 1916 to the Zurich Psychology Club (Shamdasani, 1998), were, as we have seen, far from being slavishly Jungian and contained a certain originality of perspective. For all Moltzer's broadly Jungian sensibility, there is enough of a theoretical divergence to allow Jung to engage in what Shamdasani calls a "dialogue with Moltzer's positions." (Shamdasani, 1998, p. 104) If Shamdasani is correct in his identification of Moltzer as the original of the anima, we can perhaps detect a critical perspective in Jung's disparaging and scornful rejection of the anima's suggestion that what he is doing is art.

In Wolff's writings, however, one never senses any threat of theoretical divergence from the Jungian line. Although Wolff did make original contributions to the theory of Analytical Psychology, such as "Structural Forms of the Feminine Psyche," (Wolff, 1956) these nonetheless took the form of amplifications of Jung's ideas and occupy a position squarely within the classical Jungian tradition.

It is also, I think, highly significant that Wolff, unlike Spielrein or Moltzer, was assigned a quasi-official position in Jung's life. In this way the compartmentalisation we have noted segregating the world of Emma and the children from that of Toni Wolff became institutionalised. It was an arrangement that seems to have been accepted by all. However painful and difficult this situation undoubtedly was for both Emma and Toni, it became, in time, the status quo. Jung later described such an arrangement to Henry Murray as "difficult but possible and for some men psychologically advantageous." (Douglas, 1997b, p. 132) However "advantageous" this arrangement seemed to Jung, it is hard not to regard it as regressive, since as a concretisation of the split between the two sides of Jung's life, it marks a significant retreat from the model of play and interplay between "the opposites" that Jung generally represented as essential to psychological life. By segregating his relationship with his wife and family from his relationship with Wolff, Jung was in a sense creating a firewall between his No. 1 personality and his No. 2 personality. Jung retained the capacity to move from one to the other at will, but Emma and Toni were, as it were, confined to the realms assigned to them: to Emma the No. 1 dimension of ordinary life, the "responsibilities [and] entanglements" of family; and to Toni the No. 2 dimension of "soul." We can see the same solution played out architecturally in his decision to alternate between two homes: Küsnacht and Bollingen.

## Anima Figures

As we have seen, within the official narrative of Jungian psychology, the story of Jung's relationships with Preiswerk, Spielrein, Moltzer, and Wolff tends to be subsumed into the myth of Jung's discovery of his inner figures, and in particular of the anima archetype, which he describes as gatekeeper of the deep unconscious and which becomes more or less identified with psychological interiority:

> The inner personality is the way one behaves in relation to one's inner psychic processes; it is the inner attitude, the characteristic face, that is turned towards the unconscious ... the inner attitude, the inward face, I call the anima. (Jung, 1921, para. 803)

However, when we look more closely at this narrative, as it applies to Jung's relationship with Wolff, various problems emerge. I shall utilise an egregiously "classical" Jungian source here, that of Barbara Hannah's 1974 book, *Jung: His Life and Work* (Hannah, 1976), a text that Shamdasani describes as "the only indispensable biography of Jung." (Shamdasani, 2005, 71) Hannah was an intimate associate of Jung, Emma Jung, and Toni Wolff from 1929 onward, and having outlived the protagonists, she clearly felt authorised to write openly about the relationship between Jung and Wolff, a relationship that during Jung's life was a well-kept, albeit open, secret.

Hannah describes Jung's confrontation with the unconscious, and his relationship with Wolff as "two facets of the same problem." (Hannah, 1976, p. 118) In 1913, she explains, Jung was not so much engaged in a relationship with Wolff as caught in the spell cast by his unconscious anima. Unfortunately, Hannah claims, "Jung ... did not yet know that the anima frequently projects herself into a real woman and that this projection endows that woman with the whole numinous quality of the unconscious." Wolff herself, according to Hannah, contributed to this situation by being a particularly gifted "anima figure," one that was "most fitted to carry the projection of [Jung's] anima." (Hannah, 1976, p. 118) Hannah shifts here from a statement about Jung's inner dynamics and his projection of an inner figure (the anima) onto a real woman (Wolff), to a supposedly objective statement about Wolff's own nature as an "anima figure." She is echoing ideas and usages to be found in Jung's writings, in which the term "anima figure" is used in two different ways: first, to describe a female figure appearing within a man's psyche, for example in *MDR*, "Salome is an anima figure" (Jung, 1989, p. 181); and second, to describe a real woman in the outer world on whom a man projects his anima:

> When an inner process cannot be integrated it is often projected outside. It is, indeed, the rule that a man's consciousness projects all perceptions coming from the feminine personification of the unconscious onto an anima figure, i.e., a real woman, to whom he is as much bound as he is in reality to the contents of the unconscious. (Jung, 1958, para. 714)

Although both these descriptions are concerned with psychological processes within the man's psyche, the latter idea leads Jung sometimes to talk in an apparently objective way about a certain kind of woman for whom, he claims, it comes naturally to attract such projections: "There are certain types of women who seem to be made by nature to attract anima projections; indeed one could almost speak of a definite 'anima type.'" (Jung, 1925b, para. 339) When Hannah refers to Wolff as an "anima figure," she is using the term in this latter sense. However, we should note that in Jung this usage is invariably negative in tone, for example, "But as long as a woman is content to be a femme à homme, she has no feminine individuality. She is empty and merely glitters—a welcome vessel for masculine projections." (Jung, 1941, para. 355) By contrast, Hannah appears to want to depict Wolff's role as an "anima figure" in a much more positive way: "[Wolff] had an extraordinary genius for accompanying men—and

122

some women too, in a different way—whose destiny it was to enter the unconscious." (Hannah, 1976, pp. 118–119)

There are, however, some important questions that arise from Hannah's characterisation of Wolff and her situation. First, was it really a "gift" for Wolff to have been called to the role of vehicle for the projections of others? In this role, Wolff, we are told, accompanied Jung (and others) "into the unconscious" although as Hannah also tells us, Wolff herself "did not ever enter the unconscious on her own account." Hannah's hyperbolic description of Wolff as a "genius" cannot entirely deflect our attention from the fact that to be an "anima figure" means neither more nor less than to be a magnet for projection. The stone that Jung carved in memory of Wolff after her death described her as "Lotus, Nun, Mysterious." Christian nuns are described as brides of Christ because they voluntarily surrender romantic, sexual, or family relationships with others in order to devote themselves selflessly to Christ. Presumably, as Jungian nun, Wolff was doing much the same in order to devote herself selflessly to Jung and the Jungian cause. For Jung to describe Wolff as "mysterious" says very little about her and a great deal about Jung, in the same way that the descriptor "anima figure" says nothing about the woman and everything about the man who perceives her in this way.

Second, and more important, Hannah tells us that at the start of the relationship, Jung was "largely" projecting "the positive aspect of the anima" (Hannah, 1976, p. 125) onto Wolff, but that after he became aware that the anima was in fact an *inner* figure, he "became less dependent on the mediation of the outer woman in the unconscious and was able to face it entirely alone." (Hannah, 1976, p. 125) Hannah is keen to reassure us that "taking back projections and becoming less dependent does not mean becoming less related." (Hannah, 1976, p. 125) In fact, she goes on to tell us that "as Jung saw the inner anima and made the tremendous effort to come to terms with her, so he was set free more and more for real individual relationships." (Hannah, 1976, p. 125.)

If we apply this narrative framework to Jung's relationship with Wolff, we would expect the first period of their connection to consist of a kind of delusional bond—lacking in genuine relatedness, but then in the later period, as Jung achieved increasing awareness of his inner figures, that the relationship would become more real and gain depth and weight. However, according to Healy in her recent book on Wolff and Jung, this is the opposite of what occurred. Jung and Wolff were never again as close as they had been during the *Red Book* years, and by the 1930s, Jung was all but ignoring her, to her intense sadness and regret (See Healy, 2017, pp.203ff.). When the allure that accompanied Wolff's role as "anima figure" faded, Jung seems to have simply lost interest. Contrary to the happy picture that Hannah paints of a settled ménage à trois, in which a just and equitable distribution of psychic labour provided both Emma and Toni with the opportunity to develop into their best selves, the reality was that over the years Toni became increasingly estranged from Jung and increasingly bitter about her fate (Healy, 2017, pp. 287ff).

It may be that Wolff's estrangement from Jung was accompanied by a deeper connection between Jung and Emma, such that the compart-mentalisation we have identified as particularly active during the *Red Book* years broke down and Jung became increasingly able to experience both No. 1 and No. 2 within his relationship with his wife. In the wake of Emma's death, Jung had a significant and moving dream:

> [Emma] stood at some distance from me, looking at me squarely. She was in her prime, perhaps about thirty, and wearing the dress which had been made for her many years before by my cousin the medium. It was perhaps the most beautiful thing she had ever worn. Her expression was neither joyful nor sad, but, rather, objectively wise and understanding, without the slightest emotional reaction, as though she were beyond the mist of affects. I knew that it was not she, but a portrait she had made or commissioned for me. It contained the beginning of our relationship, the events of fifty-three years of marriage, and the end of her life also. Face to face with such wholeness one remains speechless, for it can scarcely be comprehended. (Jung, 1989, p.296)

Here Emma is wearing a dress made by Helly Preiswerk, an image that would suggest that the No. 2 anima pattern we have identified in Preiswerk, Spielrein, Moltzer, and Wolff has been finally brought together in a coniunctio with the No. 1 dimension hitherto evoked by Emma as wife and mother, both aspects, as Jung describes it, "interwoven into an indescribable whole." (Jung, 1989, p.296)

## Inner and Outer

What seems to have occurred during the *Red Book* period is a shift in Jung's focus from complex and challenging outer relationships to complex and challenging inner relationships. As we have seen, Jung's withdrawal from the relationship with Freud coincided with the development of increasingly idiosyncratic ideas, ideas that he at first declined to expose to Freud's challenging gaze. I have argued that Jung's tendency to secretiveness was closely bound up with his experience of this transition as a resurgence of an aspect of his personality that had for some years, he felt, been in abeyance: Personality No. 2. In its new form, this private interior aspect of Personality No. 2 became transmuted into an emphasis within Jung's psychology upon the priority of the internal world.

Jung acknowledged that individuation is a highly relational process, but he now understood that the relations that matter psychologically occur on the intrapsychic level. It is as though the intense and turbulent dialogical dynamics that characterised Jung's intimate relationships during the period 1902-13 were transferred tout court from the outer sphere to the inner sphere. It was no longer a question of Jung in dialogue with Freud, but of Ego in dialogue with Wise Old Man, and instead of the erotic complications that characterised Jung's relationship with Spielrein, we find the *inner* romance of Ego and Anima. The inner other has, in effect, replaced the outer other, who becomes redundant. As Hannah put it, Jung, "less dependent on the mediation of the outer woman in the unconscious ... was able to face it entirely alone." (Hannah, 1976, p. 125)

## Analysis—Inner or Outer?

Of course, when it comes to relationships that occur within the vessel of psychoanalytic work, it is far from easy to make a clear distinction between inner and outer dimensions. The complexities of transference and countertransference dynamics make differentiation extremely difficult. Under these circumstances, it might be objected that Jung's relationships with Spielrein, Moltzer, and Wolff were never truly—or at least never solely—outer relationships since, in all three cases, Jung first and foremost took the role of psychoanalyst and doctor, and all three women first met Jung as a patient. However much these relationships seem to have been characterised by elements of both mutuality and reciprocity, the fact remains (a fact now supported by a considerable literature to which, of course, Jung had no access) that no relationship that is first formed within the crucible of psychoanalytic work can ever fully escape the shadows of its origins. The initial projections that each of these women will necessarily have made onto Jung as healer or even saviour, could never completely be overcome, nor could Jung's projections onto his patients qua patients.

If the inevitable transference/countertransference dynamics that will arise within any analysis are indeed "the alpha and omega of the psychoanalytic method," then these relationships, initiated as analytic bonds, will have constellated significant inner dynamics in both partners, traces of which would inevitably persist, however successful the course of the analysis. For example, Spielrein's outer relationship with Jung would always be shadowed by powerful residues of her inner relationship with her inner healer/saviour, and Jung's relationship to her would always be shadowed by indelible traces of his own inner relationship with what would eventually become articulated as his anima (a projection discerned by Spielrein in the form of Jung's attachment to her "prototype" Helene Preiswerk).

In fact, it seems to have been the active presence of this *inner* dimension that rendered these relationships particularly prone to what was to what we might call appropriative interiorisation by Jung. Perhaps it would be preferable to describe the process as *reinteriorisation* since

Jung was, in effect, placing back into his inner world what had, at least partly, emerged there in the first place.

However, to focus too much on this aspect of the picture would be to distort it. Although these relationships were all inevitably imbued with and coloured by projections of inner dynamics (on both sides), it is also the case that truly outer elements also came into play as the relationships developed, since each participant also appeared as outer "other" to his or her partner in the dance of relationship, and indeed it was the psychological heat generated by the ongoing interplay of inner and outer within the crucible of the relationship that itself created something new for both partners.

## Jung's Interiorisations

We can see this particularly clearly in Jung's relationships with the three women I have focused on in this chapter. The dimension of the feminine had over the years presented itself repeatedly to Jung as an outer "other." Over the period of his relationships with Preiswerk, Spielrein, Moltzer, and Wolff, the feminine (which had originally presented itself to Jung in the powerfully alien form of his mother's No. 2 personality) became gradually less and less "other" such that eventually (in the case of Wolff) it seems to have become almost entirely domesticated.

This process of interiorisation was arguably Jung's great achievement during this period. It consisted of a creative appropriation of those outer elements (elements that were "other" to Jung) through an operation that blended them together with those inner elements that he had first intuited as a child in the form of his No. 2 personality. Jung's account in *MDR* of personality No. 2 contains no overtly "feminine" characteristics (other than the parallel drawn with his mother's No. 2). The introduction of the inner feminine as gatekeeper and guide to the collective unconscious was a new development that emerged out of Jung's experiences in relationship with these women. This process of amalgamation shaped a new inner landscape that would eventually bear fruit in the form of the ideas, images, and concepts of Analytical Psychology.

This discussion of Jung's significant relationships has opened up the question of the relative importance of the inner realm and the outer realm in the psychology that Jung was developing during this crucial period. In the next chapter, I want to look more closely at the way in which Jung, during the years 1913-17, pursued the concept of individuation as a purely interior process and at the potential difficulties this was to create for Analytical Psychology.

1 If we follow Bair in dating the "confrontation with the unconscious" as lasting from autumn 1913 to the end of 1917 (Bair, 2004, p. 242), then this period includes Jung's July 1914 lectures in London and Aberdeen. According to Bair, he also lectured in Bern and attended meetings in Munich (Bair, 2004, p. 248). During this period, Jung was working hard to disentangle his psychology from Freud's and find new ways to conceptualise and express his psychological ideas. Several of the works from this period were crucially important as first attempts to articulate what was to become the mature psychology, e.g., his essay on the Transcendent Function (Jung 1916d), which remained unpublished at the time. Other significant works from this period include 1916's The Structure of the Unconscious (Jung 1916c), and 1917's rewriting of New Paths in Psychology (Jung 1917a): together these, in the words of the editors of the Collected Works, "marked a turning point in the history of analytical psychology, for they revealed the foundations upon which the greater part of Professor Jung's later work was built … [they] contain the first tentative formulations of Jung's concept of archetypes and the collective unconscious, as well as his germinating theory of types." (Read, Adler, & Fordham, 1953, p. v) The years 1913-17 are, of course, constitute precisely the period in which these ideas were being generated. We also know that between 1915 and 1916 Jung was developing his ideas on typology by engaging in a dialogue-via-correspondence with Schmid-Guisan (Jung & Schmid-Guisan, 2013). The idea that Jung could have written and lectured on these crucial and groundbreaking topics without reading a book is obviously absurd.

2 Shamdasani draws attention to this point, "[MDR] furthers the myth of Jung's heroic descent and self-generation, after he has freed himself from

the shackles of Freudian psychology, founding a foundling psychology, without antecedents, with no prior model to follow, only the counter exemplar of Freud." (Shamdasani, 2005, 31) Shamdasani's point here is directed against those who would ignore significant influences upon Jung other than Freud.

3 Shamdasani (Shamdasani, 2015) has suggested that Jung reworked the Preiswerk material in numerous ways according to whatever research interest was current at the time. For example, in 1902, it was framed as abnormal psychology (Jung, 1902, passim); in 1903, in terms of the psychology of the unconscious (Jung, 1903); in 1907 as an exemplum of hysteria (Jung, 1907, para. 10); in 1912, he found in it the emergence of primordial images from the phylogenetic unconscious (later the collective unconscious) (Jung, 1912/1955, para. 95); in 1921, in the context of "Psychological Types"—as the prospective tendency of the unconscious (Jung, 1921, para. 701n); in 1925, as the initial impetus for his whole interest in psychology (Jung, 1990, p. 3); in 1935, he tells us that the idea of the independence of the unconscious came to him through studying S.W. (Jung, 1935a, p.123); in 1939's "Concerning Rebirth," it was an example of enlargement of the personality (Jung, 1939 para. 219n.); in 1943, he discussed the case's significance in the development of Analytical Psychology in "On the Psychology of the Unconscious" (Jung 1943, para. 199) and described it as a "decisive experience." It should be said that Shamdasani's point has been hotly contested by Andrea Graf-Nold (Graf-Nold 2016).

4 This idea is perhaps backed up by Jolande Jacobi's recollection: "I heard from others, about the time before he [Jung] met Toni Wolff, that he had a love affair there in the Burgholzli with a girl—what was her name? Moltzer." (quoted in Shamdasani, 2003, p.57 n. 3)

5 It is, I think, of note that Jung was willing to acknowledge publicly the importance of the correspondence with Schmid-Guisan when it came to the writing of *Psychological Types* (Jung, 1921, pp. xi–xii) and that this was also the context in which he acknowledged Maria Moltzer's contribution with regard to the intuitive type. It seems to me that Jung's willingness to give due weight to the contribution of others, and to his relationships

with others in this context, is due to the fact that, unlike most of Jung's psychological works, his book on the types necessarily and evidently required input from sources external to Jung's own inner psyche. This is why, as he puts it to Schmid, he makes the specific point that

> What originally led me to [the problem of types] were not intellectual presuppositions, but actual difficulties in my daily analytical work with my patients, as well as experiences I have had in my personal relations with other people." (Jung & Schmid-Guisan, 2013, p. 39).

Later, he described *Psychological Types* as "taking shape from the countless impressions and experiences of a psychiatrist in the treatment of nervous illnesses, from intercourse with men and women of all social levels, from my personal dealings with friend and foe alike, and, finally, from a critique of my own psychological peculiarity." (Jung, 1921, p. xi) When it came to ideas to do with the intrapsychic dynamics of the process of individuation, he seems to have been far more reluctant to acknowledge the fact that his ideas often derived from experiences of outer relationship with real people.

[6] See also Anthony, 1999, p. 30, Bair, 2004, p. 249, and the interview with Frieda Fordham in which she states, "Jung was the patient, and Toni Wolff was the analyst." (Fordham, 1968)

# CHAPTER 5
# Inner and Outer

I have argued that the problematic dynamic that Jung experienced with regard to his two personalities, and his eventual understanding of the significance of that dynamic within his own psychological development played a crucial role in the gradual formation of Analytical Psychology as a coherent psychotherapeutic approach. In this chapter, I intend to focus on the period 1913-17, during which important shifts occurred within Jung's life and work as that brought him new understandings of that dynamic and its significance. I shall go on to argue, however, that it also introduced elements that continue to shadow and problematize the development of Analytical Psychology.

As we have already seen, Jung's own highly mythicised account of his "Confrontation with the Unconscious" (as found in the 1925 seminar [Jung, 1990] and in *MDR* [Jung, 1989]) should not be confused with an objective account of what was occurring at the time. In what follows, I therefore intend to keep Jung's own account in tension with those aspects of the period in question that Jung seems to have chosen to ignore or downplay.

The topic I intend to focus upon in this chapter is Jung's persistent articulation of an opposition between the inner world and the outer world. First, I want to look into how this opposition relates to Jung's two personalities and, second, how Jung integrated it into his mature psychology.

## Jung and Interiority

The theme that runs through Jung's early life and his early psychological work is that of engagement with the other (Papadopoulos, 1991). With Jung's split from Freud, there was a significant shift toward a prioritising of *intrapsychic* relationships with *inner* others rather than outer relationships with outer persons. Of course, throughout this period Jung continued to maintain these latter relationships in both work and family arenas, but it was the inner encounters that he was later to describe as his "confrontation with the unconscious" that mattered *psychologically*.

Since Jung's tendency to prioritise the inner over the outer will be the prime focus of the final chapters of this book, it is worthwhile at this point to attempt to contextualise Jung's particular employment of these concepts within the wider history of Western thought.

The concept of an "inner realm," which can be unproblematically differentiated from an "outer world," has become inextricably bound up with the modern understanding and experience of subjectivity. However, it is important to remember that this way of understanding our experience stems from a culturally conditioned metaphorical usage. The experience of choosing not to communicate a feeling or thought outwardly to others leads easily to the idea that in some way one is holding the feeling "inside" oneself, in a private or secret space known only to oneself. However, even this common experience has its conceptual history. Jean Starobinski discusses the way in which, in archaic European thought, the body's interior became metaphorised into a space of interiority. In Homer, "the act of hiding a thought, a design, a speech, even in constituting the dimension of the unsaid, constitutes an 'interiority,' an abstract mental region superadded to the image of the carnal inside: thus, phrenes comes to acquire the further meaning of mind..." (Starobinski, 1975 p. 337) In this way the boundaries of the interior become identified with the skin.

However, this highly metaphorical inner/outer binary was to take on a quasi-ontological form in the wake of the 17th-century Cartesian distinction between *res cogitans* and *res extensa*. Henceforth, the encapsulated "inner" thinking space—the mind—was to be seen as radically separate from all that existed outside of it. Despite various challenges to this radically dualistic approach, the assumption that this, or something very like it, accurately describes our experience of the world, remains deeply embedded in modern thought. Within psychoanalytic thinking, this shows up in, for example, the notion that psychological life is a realm in which "[o]thers and cultural history are 'internalized' into mental representations … and one's 'inner' needs, feelings, fantasies and conflict are 'projected' outwards onto others." (Brooke, 2013, p. 5)

Brooke goes on to summarise the situation in this way:

> The problem is that psychological life is ultimately located theoretically in a place within us, separate from the world in which psychological life actually takes place. We are left with a theory still rooted in an anthropology that locates all meaning in an interior place called mind and thinks of the world as pure material realm, accessible only to the assumptions and methods of natural science—ultimately physics and mathematics. (Brooke, 2013, p. 5)

Brooke is keen to point out that although in many respects Jung's psychology implicitly undermines these categories and assumptions, it remains the case that Jung's constant differentiation of the inner world and inner experience from the outer world and outer experience and his prioritisation of the former over the latter, repeatedly reminds us that he remains inextricably entangled in a post-Cartesian vision (Brooke, 2013, p.116).

When it comes to the two personalities, as we have seen, Jung's *inner* world tends to be strongly identified with personality No. 2. In Jung's imaginal landscape, this realm is persistently imaged in the form of a cavelike interior location, which combines the qualities of inwardness, hiddenness and depth. It is, in effect, an encrypted space beneath and behind the surface, and thus co-signifies Jung's notion of "the secret." In *MDR*, this shows up as the chamber in which Jung meets the underground phallus (Jung, 1989, pp. 11-12), the cave in which Jung lit fires (Jung, 1989, p.19), the dream of digging a hole in a burial mound (Jung, 1989, p.85), and, of course the cave beneath the basement that is featured in the house dream which inspired the idea of the collective unconscious (Jung, 1989, pp. 158-9). Finally, we see it in the dark cave that Jung entered when inaugurating the series of active imaginations that constitutes Jung's confrontation with the unconscious (Jung, 1989, p.179).

Personality No. 1, on the other hand, is described as that aspect of Jung which engages with the *outer* world, and indeed with outer persons. The images associated with it are closely bound up with the notion of exteriority: As Jung says, it points "irrevocably outward," on a path "into the limitations and darkness of three-dimensionality." (Jung, 1989, p.88) This surface-bound exteriority contrasts starkly with the deep, inner journey that Jung is eventually required to undergo at the time of his confrontation with the unconscious.

The implications of this phenomenology of interiority are wide-ranging. Most importantly, the subjectivity of the psychological individual becomes identified with interiority, secrecy, and depth. This means that the realm of exteriority (outer world, outer relationships, the social, the collective) is banished to a secondary dimension, regarded as psychologically barren, unless and until it can be elevated to the psychological via processes of introjection and thereby achieve an interiority of its own.

Jung's confrontation with the unconscious was experienced as an enantiodromic swing in the direction of the concerns, themes, and motifs of personality No. 2, and away therefore from personality No. 1. This inevitably took the form of a turning away from the outward-facing dimension of his life through which he experienced relationship with individual other people, or with the outer collective.

It might be argued that Jung's 1913-17 swing in the direction of personality No. 2 concerns—the inner, solitude, the intrapsychic, dreams, visions—functioned as a *temporary though necessary* stage in his development, because it prepared the ground for him to subsequently return to a balanced position from which he could engage with both inner concerns *and* the outer world, thus enabling him to pursue his career as creator of Analytical Psychology and writer of the *Collected Works*. In the next chapter, I shall attempt to address this question and will go on to ask whether Jung and his psychology, as we now know it, remained shadowed by a long-term one-sidedly introverted bias.

However, what complicates this question is Jung's tendency to represent himself, in his own accounts, as having been more one-sided than he in fact was. For example, in *The Red Book,* as we have seen, he tends to paint himself as focused entirely upon his inner world, while in reality Jung's "outer" relationships during the period (not only those that he overtly acknowledges, with, for example, Emma Jung and the family, but also those with, e.g., Toni Wolff and Hans Schmid-Guisan) continued to register as far more psychologically significant than we might expect to be the case from Jung's own accounts. This said, Jung's deliberate decision to characterise his myth of this period in this way itself tells us a great deal about his perspective—or at least the perspective he wishes his readers to identify as his. I shall argue that this choice itself, in fact, provides further evidence for an ongoing persistent one-sidedness in Jung's approach—and that this one-sidedness long outlives the *Red Book* period.

Wolfgang Giegerich, in a penetrating review of *The Red Book*, points out that although Jung represents his active imaginations as immediate experiences of the unconscious (Jung compares them, for example, to volcanic eruptions [Jung, 1989, p.199]), a close reading of *The Red Book's* text leads one to question these claims. First, as Giegerich says, "Much of the content of the *Red Book* is directly derived from Jung's reading (200b). It is the work of a scholar and in fact largely took place in his library (203a)" (Giegerich, 2010, p. 373; references are to pages and columns in Jung, 2009). Second, his confrontation with the unconscious, far from being a spontaneous eruption of the unconscious, was, in fact, a carefully constructed scientific experiment, or as Giegerich puts it, a "deliberate technical undertaking."

Third, despite Jung's claims that it "happened in a way that I neither expected nor wished for," (Jung, 2009, p. 338) Jung's writing is informed by a "powerful will or craving underlying it all." (Giegerich, 2010, p. 373) As Giegerich puts it, "[I]n general the text is soaked in the rhetoric of wanting, longing, expectation," (Giegerich, 2010, p.373) and this points to an unconscious agenda, albeit one that is hidden from Jung's conscious ego.

Fourth, the figures who appear in the text are often given names that evoke Gnostic antecedents (Abraxas, Phanes, etc). This archaizing style has the effect of invoking an aura of ancient depth, but, as Giegerich suggests, the content it masks "needs to be inferred and reconstructed exclusively from the modern text and its modern context." (Giegerich, 2010, p. 375) Giegerich argues that *The Red Book* is a product of the intellectual, cultural, and political world of 1913 and only makes sense when understood as a response to that world. It represents, "Jung's wrestling with the spiritual situation of contemporary Christianity and at the same time, as it were, his 'Answer to Nietzsche.'" (Giegerich, 2010, p.376) In short, *The Red Book* performs an—albeit unconscious—engagement with the intellectual context of Jung's time, though it is dramatized in a mythic (archetypal) form. Jung's determination to prioritise the inner (archaic) over the outer (contemporary) apparently renders him blind to the numerous ways in which his own "inner" experiences are, in fact, embedded in an "outer" personal and cultural context.

## 1913 to 1917: Four Texts

This blindness of Jung's is also consistent with his determination to downplay the extent and importance of the outer activities he engaged in at the time he was writing it—such as lecturing, teaching, and writing (Jung, 1989, p. 193). In fact, these latter activities are particularly significant because they offer us evidence of the ways in which Jung, even at this early stage, was already beginning to formulate responses—on a theoretical/psychological level—to his dreams, visions, and inner dialogues. These responses differed in style and approach from the responses to be found in *The Red Book*, where Jung utilised what he later called an "esthetic" approach to the same questions (Jung, 1989, p. 188).

Because these texts deliberately address the relation of outer world to the inner world and of the individual to the collective, they are particularly valuable for this enquiry. I intend to focus here upon the typological experiment that Jung initiated in 1915 in the form of an outer dialogue with his friend and ex-analysand Hans Schmid-Guisan (Jung and Schmid-Guisan, 2013). I shall then go on to examine a text from 1916, "The Transcendent Function," (Jung, 1916d) which also bears on this question. Finally, I shall look at Jung's statements on the relation of individual and collective in his paper "Adaptation, Individuation, Collectivity." (Jung, 1916a) The first place we need to look, however, is of course *The Red Book* itself.

## *The Red Book.*

When approaching this topic, it is extremely important to remember that Jung's text *Liber Novus*, or *The Red Book* (Jung, 2009), is far more than an account of the various experiences that made up Jung's "confrontation with the unconscious." Shamdasani, *The Red Book's* editor, has described it as the:

> most carefully composed work when set beside all of Jung's published and unpublished writings. There is no other work that I have come across in his published writings—I've studied the manuscripts of the published corpus as well as the unpublished corpus—which went through such a high degree of elaboration and correction in editing. (Casement, 2010, p. 44)

In Shamdasani's view, *The Red Book* is "a work of psychology ... in a literary and prophetic form." (Casement, 2010, p. 39) It is clear then that, far from being a verbatim record of Jung's engagement with his inner figures, *The Red Book*, in fact, represents a serious attempt to reconfigure these experiences into psychology. It should also be borne in mind that, although throughout his life Jung emphasised the seminal importance of his experiences at this time, the particular elaboration of those experiences that we find in *The Red Book* he eventually dismissed as "esthetic" and abandoned "in favour of a rigorous process of understanding," (Jung, 1989, p. 188) i.e., a process of understanding that would take a form that was less "literary and prophetic."

## The Two Spirits and Enantiodromia

One of the recurrent motifs of *The Red Book* (and henceforth of Jung's psychology as a whole) is the importance of psychic balance, a state that Jung equates with the avoidance of one-sidedness. As I have argued, this motif can be traced back to the insight that Jung gained in the wake of *MDR*'s storm lantern dream. Jung realised that he needed to maintain contact not only with personality No. 1, in the form of what we might summarise as the everyday, outward-facing, conscious ego, but also with all that comes with personality No. 2, which henceforth took the form of the numinous inner other. What Jung learned from the storm lantern dream was that to reject *either* of the psychological dimensions the two personalities occupy is to risk becoming unhealthily one-sided.

In the period of *The Red Book*, this theme of psychic balance took on a strongly enantiodromic tone.[1] According to this narrative Jung had, during the years 1902-13, become one-sidedly dominated by personality No. 1 and had thus neglected or even forgotten personality No. 2. In 1916's The Transcendent Function, Jung used abstract psychological terms to describe the resulting shift:

> Life today demands concentrated, directed functioning and with it the risk of considerable dissociation from the unconscious. The further we are able to detach ourselves from the unconscious through directed functioning, the more readily can a powerful counter-position be built up in the unconscious, and when this breaks loose it may have devastating consequences. (Jung, 1916, pp. 148-149)

However, in the more personal language of *The Red Book,* this shift was depicted in terms of a pressing need for Jung to refind his "long disavowed soul." (Jung, 2009, p. 232) In his introduction to *Liber Novus*, Shamdasani describes this situation succinctly:

> Jung realized that until then, he had served the spirit of the time, characterized by use and value. In addition to this, there existed

a spirit of the depths, which led to the things of the soul. In terms of Jung's later biographical memoir, the spirit of this time corresponds to personality No.1, and the spirit of the depths corresponds to personality No.2. Thus this period could be seen as a return to the values of personality No.2. (Shamdasani, 2009, p. 208)

The implication is that Jung's long subjection to "the spirit of this time" constellated a compensatory need for a renewed allegiance to the "spirit of the depths," and this seems to have led to a major shift of his conscious orientation in favour of those values, themes, and motifs that were characteristic of his No 2 personality. What accompanied this shift was a concomitant rejection of the values and themes of the spirit of this time and personality No. 1.

## Midlife?

In the early sections of *The Red Book,* Jung seems to be diagnosing himself with some kind of ego-inflation: "Filled with human pride and blinded by the presumptuous spirit of this time, I long sought to hold that other spirit away from me." (Jung, 2009, p. 229) However, when he recognises the reality of what he was later to label the "objective psyche," Jung undergoes a compensatory adjustment. This realisation leads him (his ego) to take up a less elevated position within the psychic economy.

An adjustment of this kind is often a feature of a successfully encountered midlife crisis, and indeed *The Red Book* has been understood by many to describe a crisis of this kind (see, for example, Stein, 2012). One of the earliest readers of *The Red Book,* Cary Baynes, seems to have seen it in this way. She commented to Jung:

[*The Red Book*] is no cry of the young man awakening into life but that of the mature man who has lived fully and richly in ways of the world and yet knows almost abruptly one night, say, that he has missed the essence. The vision came at the height of your power when you could have gone on just as you were with perfect worldly success" (Quoted in Jung, 2009, p. 232 n. 44).

Baynes' comments are ambiguous in a way that becomes significant when we look more closely at Jung's notion of psychic balance: Does she mean to suggest that to "live fully and richly in ways of the world" always entails missing "the essence" because the two forms of success—outer and inner—are by definition mutually exclusive? Such an interpretation points to a binary choice between the outward path and the inward path, and strongly implies that only the latter is psychologically correct. Or does she mean that the dimension that has been excluded can and should be recognised precisely because it needs to be integrated into life in a way that will enable one to achieve balance and live even more "fully and richly"? This is a question that we shall return to.

## Psyche and History

In the early sections of *The Red Book*, Jung seems keen to establish a link between the inner world of the subjective psyche and the outer world of historical events. For example, Jung sets out to show us that his dreams and visions are intimately related to the outbreak of world war.[2]

What Jung implies here is that there is an intimate and meaningful relation between deep inner phenomena (within Jung) and those forces, energies and tendencies that operate behind objective outer events (outside Jung). The explanation Jung offers in the account contained in *The Red Book* (though not in the later accounts) is that the prime mover within both dimensions is the spirit of the depths: "the depths in me was at the same time the ruler of the depths of world affairs." (Jung, 2009, pp. 230-231) It is only when we embrace the spirit of the depths, Jung argues, that we begin to understand this crucial hidden relation between psyche and history. Most people miss this connection, Jung suggests, because they are operating solely from the perspective of the spirit of this time, which, as Jung puts it, "would want to make you believe that the depths are no world and no reality." (Jung, 2009, p.242, n.112) This is why, according to Jung, psychological analyses that derive solely from the realm of the spirit of this time (and we should note that this would emphatically include *psychoanalytic* explanations) can never be as comprehensive as analyses that derive from an understanding of the spirit of the depths. Jung clearly also believes that we are missing something essential when we utilise factors that are solely social or political or historical to explain world events such as the outbreak of world war: The required insight can derive only from the spirit of the depths.

However, even if Jung is right about the tendency for contemporary understandings to be one-sided in the direction of the spirit of this time, it would not necessarily follow that the solution to the problem is to become one-sided in the other direction—that of the spirit of the depths. The latter may be, in a sense, more comprehensive than the former, in that it allows for unconscious factors, but this would not eradicate the potential value of, for example, historical, political, or economic factors. According to the logic of the storm lantern dream, Jung should at this point seek to harness the hermeneutic strengths of *both* spirits, (both personalities, if Shamdasani is right) by bringing each into contact with the other. For example, historical (spirit of this time) factors might be brought into play with what Jung will go on to describe as archetypal (spirit of the depths) factors, in a potentially creative meeting between the social/political and the soul-oriented.

Instead, however, Jung sets up a binary choice between spirit of this time and spirit of the depths: These are, he insists, mutually exclusive options between which the individual must choose. In effect, he must dwell entirely in one personality or entirely in the other.

There are several different factors that complicate this issue. The first is that, although within *The Red Book,* Jung one-sidedly favours the spirit of the depths over the spirit of this time, he also persistently emphasises the psychological need to bring together the opposites. He tells us, for example, that the spirit of the depths combines both God and God's shadow, contains both sense and nonsense, and is "the beginning and the end." It also "turns into meaning and then into absurdity, and out of the fire and blood of their collision the supreme meaning rises up rejuvenated anew." (Jung, 2009, p. 230)

However, there are two ways in which the dialectic Jung describes here differs from that of the storm lantern dream. First, in *The Red Book*, the tension of opposites appears to take place within only one dimension, that of the spirit of the depths. As we have seen, the spirit of this time, perceived as irredeemably secular, contemporary, rational, and superficial, is excluded from this crucible of creative conflict. As an active and dynamic factor within psychological development, therefore, personality No. 1 seems, at this point, to have been left out of the picture.

Second, as Wolfgang Giegerich has pointed out, the opposites that Jung brings together in *The Red Book* tend to be logical contraries, whereby "one and the same term is at one and the same time affirmed and denied." (Giegerich, 2010, p. 388) These opposites are different in kind from the opposites that we tend to find in Jung's psychological works, e.g., thinking and feeling, extraversion and introversion, which parallel the oppositional qualities of the two personalities. When confined to the spirit of the depths (personality No. 2), the opposites take on an absolute—even cosmic— character that needs to be distinguished from the role of the opposites in individuation.

It might be argued that *The Red Book*'s apparent one-sidedness (in favour of the spirit of the depths) should be seen rather as the product of a movement that is short-term and compensatory to Jung's previous one-sidedness (in favour of the spirit of this time). In *The Red Book*, Jung himself emphasises the enantiodromic aspect of what was occurring: "Because I was caught up in the spirit of this time, precisely what happened to me on this night had to happen to me, namely that the spirit of the depths erupted with force, and swept away the spirit of this time with a powerful wave." (Jung, 2009, p. 238) Even if this is the case, what remains unclear is whether, once this violent compensatory swing has occurred and personality No. 2 has become reinstated as an important psychic element, we should expect Jung, at some later point, to find a way to bring the two personalities (or two spirits) back into a creative dialogue.[2] This is an important question that I will return in the next chapter when I look more closely at Jung's differing approaches to psychic balance and his tendency to compartmentalise inner world and outer world.

## The Killing of the Hero.

As we have seen, the early sections of *The Red Book* are dominated by the conflict within Jung between the spirit of the depths and the spirit of this time, a conflict that clearly results in the victory of the former over the latter. This struggle seems to culminate in the two striking and important interventions from Jung's unconscious that occur in December 1913. The first is his initial "active imagination" of the red crystal, the dead blond hero, and the black scarab, and the second is the dream of the killing of Siegfried that follows shortly after.

The images found in both vision and dream occupy a pivotal position in Jung's narrative of his confrontation with the unconscious and therefore within the development of Jung's psychology as a whole. They have, not surprisingly, elicited a great deal of commentary and interpretation, some of which I will review in what follows. I want to focus here upon the motif of the killing of the hero, which occurs in both the vision and the dream. As Jung himself indicates in *The Red Book*, this particular image has something to tell us about the way he imagined and conceptualised the conflict between the spirit of the depths and the spirit of this time, and therefore between personality No. 2 and personality No. 1 (Jung, 2009, p. 240).

On December 12, 1913, Jung had a vision in which, having "plunged down into dark depths," he witnessed the body of a murdered hero "with blond hair and a wound in the head." (Jung 1989, p. 179) Very disturbed by his inability to work out the meaning of this striking image, six days later (on December 18), Jung dreamed that he himself, aided by a brown-skinned savage, murdered the hero Siegfried.[3]

Before the posthumous publication of *MDR* in 1961, only a small circle of Jungians (those entitled to study the 1925 seminar on Analytical Psychology—not published until 1990) was acquainted with either vision or dream. The publication of *The Red Book* has enabled us to study much earlier versions of these important products of Jung's unconscious.[4]

According to Jung, the imagery of both dream and vision provided variant forms of the same unconscious material. After the vision, Jung tells us in the 1925 seminar, he "could not … grasp the significance of the hero killed." (Jung, 1990, p. 48) It was only the subsequent dream that enabled him to achieve some understanding of it: "In this dream something was fulfilled that had been suggested in the cave. The slain hero was there and here the murder is accomplished, so we can say of the dream that it is an elaboration of the vision in the cave." (Jung, 1990, p. 61)

## A Typological Interpretation.

What makes it particularly hard to gain a comprehensive understanding of the psychological importance of the image of the killing of the hero is what Marco Heleno Barreto (in a paper on the Siegfried dream) has described as the "complex (or overdetermined, in the psychoanalytic sense) meaning" of this image (Barreto, 2016, p. 92). To approach the image today is to be confronted by several different and perhaps conflicting reflections from Jung himself, as well as numerous wildly divergent interpretations from subsequent commentators.

In the 1925 seminar, Jung gave an interpretation of the killing of the hero that utilised the typological tools he had developed in his recently published *Psychological Types* (Jung, 1921). In his book, Jung suggested that we all have access to four different conscious attitudes—thinking, feeling, sensation and intuition—but that each of us tends to identify with a "superior" function by means of which we navigate the world. The functions are, for Jung, arranged in oppositional pairs: Thinking is the opposite of feeling, and sensation is the opposite of intuition. This means that the "superior" function is inevitably mirrored by an opposite "inferior" function—a function that remains mostly in the unconscious and is, by definition, extremely difficult for the conscious ego to access. In the 1925 seminar, Jung suggests that in his Siegfried dream, the image of his killing of the hero pointed to an unconscious need to cease identifying with his "superior" function, i.e., thinking. Jung's unstated implication was that there was a psychological requirement for him to live much more in his inferior function, the function of feeling. Looking back to his 1913 dream, he tells us, "I deposed my superior function … as soon as the main function is deposed, there is a chance for other sides of the personality to be born into life." (Jung, 1990, pp. 56–57) He then goes on to amplify this idea by suggesting that the killing of the hero is connected with the sacrifice of the superior function in order to get at the libido necessary to activate the inferior functions. If a man has a good brain, thinking becomes his hero and, instead of Christ, Kant, or Bergson, becomes his ideal. If you give up this thinking, this hero ideal, you commit a secret murder— that is, you give up your superior function. (Jung, 1990, pp. 48-49)[5]

This notion of the sacrifice of the superior function is explored more comprehensively in the first chapter of *Psychological Types*. There, Jung points to the examples of early church fathers Tertullian and Origen, each of whom, he suggests, exhibited extreme one-sidedness, though in diametrically opposite ways. Jung suggests that both dealt with this situation by sacrificing their respective superior functions (in Tertullian's case, it was a "sacrificium intellectus," and in Origen's, it took the form of a "sacrificium phalli"). As a result, Jung tells us, "The original type has actually become reversed: Tertullian, the acute thinker, becomes the man of feeling, while Origen becomes the scholar and loses himself in intellectuality." (Jung, 1921, para. 27)

In the 1925 seminar, Jung appears to be suggesting that we can identify a similarly enantiodromic swing from one extreme to the other in the dream of the killing of the hero. However, since neither Tertullian nor Origen is a model of psychic balance, either before or after his sacrifice, it seems unlikely that Jung wants us to regard him as requiring an equally radical solution to his situation. This perhaps implies that for Jung the sacrifice of the superior function was a short-term necessity—a response to his extreme one-sidedness at the time—and that this enantiodromic shift would constitute merely a temporary moment within an overall process, eventually resulting in a more balanced stance whereby the opposites would be able to creatively engage.

## Introversion and Extraversion.

However, when we look more closely at the ideas about introversion and extraversion that Jung was developing at the time, it becomes more difficult to interpret the killing of the hero as merely a temporary moment in the onward march toward psychic balance. It is worth paying particular attention to the introversion/extraversion binary at this point because it brings together all the topics most relevant to the theme of this chapter: the question of the two personalities, the question of inner versus outer, and the question of how Jung's personal "inner" experiences influenced the later development of his psychological theory. I shall address the issue by looking first at Jung's 1913 formulation of the two attitude types and then by taking a closer look at Jung's 1915 correspondence with Hans Schmid-Guisan.

According to Jung's ideas on typology, each of the four "types" could take either an extraverted form or an introverted form. At the time of the December 1913 Siegfried dream, Jung's typological system was not yet perfected; as we have seen, it reached its full and final form only in 1921. Three months before the dream, in September 1913, Jung had made an important start on that work by presenting his initial articulation of the two attitude types—introversion and extraversion—at the Munich psychoanalytic congress. On this occasion, which also happened to be Jung's final encounter with Freud, he delivered a lecture delineating the essential features of extraversion and introversion and went on to compare Freud's (extraverted) psychoanalysis with Adler's (introverted) "individual psychology." (Jung, 1913)

Jung made it clear in Munich that although the two "modes of psychic reaction" (extraversion and introversion) are considered to be "opposite movements of libido," it remains the case that they "may operate alternately in the same individual." (Jung, 1913, para. 861) The libido, "depending on the individual, is directed sometimes to our inner life, sometimes to the objective world." (Jung, 1913, para. 869) In order to remain healthy, therefore, the psyche needs to "maintain the balance between the two psychological opposites of extraversion and introversion." (Jung, 1913, para. 872) A balanced person will be able to direct libido in the direction of either inner life or outer world, depending upon the person's psychological needs at the time. A one-sided libido—whether inner-directed or outer-directed—might suggest a diagnosis of either schizophrenia or hysteria, the two pathological forms that introversion and extraversion can respectively take (Jung, 1913, para. 859). Jung's argument is that that in order to attain psychic balance, the individual needs to gain enough self-knowledge to understand which attitude is dominant in his/her psyche and then attempt to achieve a more balanced state in which libido can be invested in either inner or outer dimensions, whichever is appropriate at the time.

However, Jung went on to inform his audience that even among "normal" persons, one rarely finds a perfect balance between the two attitude directions; most, Jung says, "are distinguished by the pre-dominance of one or other of the two mechanisms." (Jung, 1913, para. 862)

At this point, Jung's paper shifts its focus from the action of intro-version and extraversion within a single psyche to the actions of two different kinds of people: the extraverted and the introverted. Jung likens these two types of person to William James' "tough minded" and "tender minded" but makes a subtle though significant shift in his classification by renaming them the "materially-minded" and the "spiritually-minded." (Jung, 1913, para. 864)

By altering the focus of his analysis in this way, Jung is preparing the ground for the polemical final section of his paper, in which he positions Freud's psychology—diagnosed as extraverted—against that of the introverted Adler. It is the extraversion of Freud's psychoanalysis, he suggests, that makes it "reductive, pluralistic, causal, and sensualistic. ... [T]he dominant note in Freudian psychology," he goes on, "is a centrifugal tendency, a striving for pleasure in the object." (Jung, 1913, para. 881)[6]

Jung ends with this: "The difficult task of creating a psychology which will be equally fair to both types must be reserved for the future." (Jung, 1913, para. 882) Jung clearly wants us to see him as just the person who can create just such a psychology, and this means presumably that he believes himself capable of holding the theoretical high-ground here, achieving with Olympian even-handedness a balance between the one-sided extraversion of Freud and the respective one-sided introversion of Adler.

We should note that Jung's paper fails on both a personal and a theoretical level to maintain anything resembling an Olympian detach-ment from this particular fray, since it represents (and would certainly have been received as representing) an out-and-out *rejection* of the ideological position—now labelled as one-sidedly extraverted—that he had spent the previous 10 years closely identified with: that of psychoanalysis. Jung implies that a crucial psychological dimension (that of Adlerian introversion) is *completely absent* from Freud's psychology. Jung's unspoken message is that, having spent years aligned with Freud's fatally one-sided position, he will be able to achieve a properly balanced psychology only by making a direct move away from extraversion and toward the hitherto relatively unexplored dimension of introversion.

For Jung, it is Freud's stress upon the psychic mechanism of transference (*Übertragung*) that highlights the close alignment between psychoanalysis and extraversion. In the same way that the hysteric transfers his inner preoccupations onto the outer analyst, so it is that the extravert, so Jung informs us in the 1913 paper, "projects upon the object his own illusions and subjective valuations," (Jung, 1913, para. 860) in this way hoping to "forget these painful contents and leave them behind him." (Jung, 1913, para. 861) We can trace back this linkage between the dynamics of transference and the dynamics of extraversion to a point made by Jung in *Transformations and Symbols of the Libido* (1911-12):

> It is generally to be expected that the two basic mechanisms in psychoses, transference and introversion, are to a great extent also very expedient normal modes of reaction to complexes: transference as a means to flee from the complex into reality, introversion as a means to detach oneself, with the complex, from reality. (Jung, 1912b, p. 182)

At this stage in the development of Jung's thinking, transference and extraversion are regarded as interchangeable terms; this is made clear in the 1952 update of *Transformations*, published as *Symbols of Transformation*, where Jung simply replaced the word *transference* with the word *extraversion* in the relevant passage (Jung, 1912/1952, para. 259).

It is also notable that at this point Jung saw introversion and extraversion primarily through a pathological lens. The extravert is someone who tends to manage difficult inner phenomena by projecting them onto the outer objective world. The introvert, on the other hand, is someone who makes problematic outer phenomena more manageable by transforming them into inner processes.

Jung's earliest use of the word "introversion" occurs in one of his talks at Clark University in 1909, in which he discusses the case of his daughter. Introversion, described as a process whereby part of the love hitherto directed toward an outer object becomes turned inward, is there linked by Jung to an increase of fantasy activity. (Jung, 1909, para. 13) The same process was to be fulfilled in Jung's own life when, in 1913, his investment in outer relationships was replaced by a shift toward introversion, and he experienced the huge explosion of fantasy activity that was to be recounted in *The Red Book*.

By late 1913, Jung no longer regarded introversion as a predominantly pathological retreat from outer difficulties. By then, it had become the royal road to individuation, and as we shall see, for Jung it was to become all but identified with the notion of psychology itself. We are left, however, with a problematic mismatch between, on the one hand, the notion of psychology as essentially introverted and, on the other, Jung's doctrine of psychic balance, whereby as Jung puts it, the healthy psyche needs to "maintain the balance between the two psychological opposites of extraversion and introversion." (Jung, 1913, para. 872) This tension (which parallels the tension we have identified in *The Red Book*, between the spirit of this time and the spirit of the depths) remained unexamined and unresolved.

## An Extraverted Hero

Jung's vision and dream of the killing of the hero occurred three months after the delivery of his paper on typology. In the 1925 seminar, Jung tells us that he was bewildered that the hero figure in the dream was named Siegfried, since he was consciously repelled by the "exaggeratedly extraverted" character of the Wagnerian hero (Jung, 1990, p.56). It seems plausible that the image of the hero and of his assassination pointed to Jung's previous personal, theoretical, and professional identification with Freud's psychology and Jung's need to eliminate that aspect of his identity that had been hitherto bound up with psychoanalysis. If so, it marked a powerful reaction against what Jung now saw as Freud's one-sidedness and particularly the "exaggerated" extraversion of the psychoanalytic approach. In the 1913 paper, Jung had combined his own words with the words of William James in order to pointedly describe the extravert as

> "materialistic and pessimistic," for he knows only too well the uncertainty and hopeless chaos of the course of things. He is "irreligious," being incapable of asserting the realities of his inner world against the pressure of external facts; a fatalist, because resigned; a pluralist, incapable of all synthesis; and finally a sceptic, as a last and inevitable consequence of all the rest. (Jung, 1913, para. 868)

Jung focused here upon the gulf between his own psychological approach and that of Freud. At this stage, Jung saw his psychology as everything Freud's was not: religious, synthetic, optimistic, and spiritual. If Freud's was extraverted, then Jung's was necessarily introverted.

In 1913, however, Jung was experiencing not only an outer rebellion but also an inner revolution. The enantiodromic swing that seems to have occurred in that year involved a massive reaction not only against Freud and psychoanalysis but also against the extraverted personality that Jung himself had inhabited during his psychoanalytic years, a personality now characterised in *The Red Book* as the "spirit of this time."

Various biographers and commentators have chosen to identify the figure of Siegfried in Jung's dream with the person of Sigmund Freud. Frank McLynn, for example, tells us in his biography of Jung that the psychologist's own interpretation of the dream "shied away from the obvious meaning. It is a commonplace of Jungian hermeneutics that Siegfried stands for Freud and that the murder and guilt represent Jung's 'parricide.'" (McLynn, 1998, p. 237)[7]

By naïvely mapping an outer person (Freud) onto an inner dream-figure (Siegfried), MacLynn transforms the dream into an easily read narrative about Jung's personal need to dispatch his erstwhile intellectual hero. In Ronald Hayman's biography of Jung, a different, though similarly reductive, linkage is made. This time the figure of Siegfried gets mapped onto Sabina Spielrein's longed-for but imaginary love child (also called

Siegfried, for which see Carotenuto, 1984). It was Jung's "need to keep silent" about Sabina Spielrein, Hayman informs us, that stopped him from "writing honestly about this dream." (Hayman, 2002, p. 176)

Despite their interpretive shallowness, both these approaches have value if they are repositioned into a more complex and comprehensive context whereby Jung's *inner* conflicts are brought into tension with the *outer* developments we have been discussing. One lens of this binocular perspective pictures Freud as Siegfried, the extraverted hero who needs to be deposed (and by extension the extraverted psychoanalysis that Jung needed to reject [murder] in favour of an introverted approach). The other lens gives us Siegfried as Jung's own libido during the pre-*Red Book* period—an extravertedly intellectual and emotional energy that animated not only Jung's bond with Freud but also Jung's relationship with Spielrein, (and by extension with the fantasy fruit of that relationship—Siegfried). Only a three-dimensional hermeneutic—one that brings both lenses together—can begin to capture the complexity of the 1913 psychological revolution that Jung was undergoing at this time.

In the short term at least, Jung failed to take up a binocular approach of this kind. Instead, what seems to have happened is that Jung experienced a profound enantiodromic change in *how he understood and experienced his own engagement with the world*. Jung now realised that for years he had been behaving in what he understood with hindsight to be an extraverted way, in the sense that he had been projecting outward (for example, onto his outer relationships with Freud and with Spielrein) processes that should properly be understood as *inner* phenomena. It was now apparent to him that he had been guilty of committing a kind of psychological category error.

In 1913, Jung was in no doubt that the image of the killing of the hero pointed to a need to terminate this "exaggeratedly extraverted" approach. From now, Jung would ensure that the psychology he developed would prioritise an *introverted* approach. When, later in *The Red Book*, Jung met and dialogued with figures such as Philemon and Salome, he understood himself to be entering a level of reality within which it was finally possible for him make a *direct* encounter with those autonomous forces and energies that, in an outer (and, he now believed, indirect) form, he had been meeting and wrestling with for years. The absolute reality of this inner dimension of existence was reflected in Jung's term for it: the "objective psyche." As we will see, the problem that arrived with this development was a tendency to segregate this objective psyche from the subjective, personal psyche and to prioritise the former.

## The Introversion of Jung's Psychology

It is an evangelically introverted Jung who tells us in *The Red Book*, "Within us is the way, the truth, and the life." (Jung, 2009, p. 231) It might be argued that this prioritisation of inner engagement over outer engagement is a defensive move by Jung signalling a schizoid retreat and that it points to a strain of solipsism in Jung's psychology. We can only do justice to this question by looking more closely at Jung's approach, on both a personal and a theoretical level, to the inner and outer worlds, and the interaction between the two as it reveals itself within the development of Analytical Psychology. Certainly, at the time of *The Red Book* it seemed to Jung that the shift toward introversion was the only way he could make contact with that dimension of human experience that is fundamentally deeper and more primordial than any that can be reached through the horizontal (superficial) level of ordinary human engagement. This is the same dimension, of course, that he had experienced in childhood in the form of personality No. 2 and which he describes in *MDR* as "God's world." By making vertical contact with his "soul" he is, he believes, simultaneously making contact with a universal dimension that remains invisible so long as one operates solely on the horizontal level of the spirit of this time. Hence, Jung's need to make a strict differentiation between these two dimensions, the spirit of this time and the spirit of the depths, and to reject the former and embrace the latter.

While he had been under the (extraverted) sway of the spirit of this time, Jung had regarded outer events and outer relationships as primary. His inner response to these outer phenomena had been therefore a secondary event, constellated by the former. However, with the newborn perspective of *The Red Book*, Jung is enabled to see that only introversion leads into that dimension of verticality that can be described as truly psychological. To be under the sway of the spirit of the depths therefore means to prioritise introversion—to see inner events and relationships as primary because they are primordial, and outer events or relationships as secondary because they are changeable and time-bound.

It was this highly introverted approach that dominated the subsequent period of Jung's life and work. It is especially apparent in *The Red Book*, but it is not limited to this work or this time. We can recognise exactly the same approach in the words with which Jung introduces his memoir:

> Outward circumstances are no substitute for inner experience. Therefore my life has been singularly poor in outward happenings. I cannot tell much about them, for it would strike me as hollow and insubstantial. I can understand myself only in the light of inner happenings. (Jung, 1989, p. 5)

Elsewhere he remarks, "perhaps [my] 'Outer' experiences were never so very essential anyhow, or were so only in that they coincided with phases of my inner development." (Jung, 1989, p. ix) This is the authentic voice of the introverted Jung, fully in the sway of personality No. 2.

## Two Kinds of Balance

In those parts of *The Red Book* that we have hitherto examined, Jung unequivocally champions the inner and rejects the outer. However, it should also be acknowledged that *The Red Book* also contains passages that seem far more equivocal, as we can see in this excerpt from the draft:

> For you must know that your inner life does not become richer at the expense of your outer one, but poorer. If you do not live on the outside, you will not become richer within, but merely more burdened. This is not to your advantage and it is the beginning of evil. Likewise, your outer life will not become richer and more beautiful at the expense of your inner one, but only poorer and poorer. Balance finds the way. (Jung, 2009, p.188)

Here, Jung seems to suggest not only that the inner life enriches the outer, but that an engagement with the outer world also enriches the inner, an idea that flies in the face of the emphasis we have identified elsewhere on the absolute priority of the inner. We can gain a better understanding of this apparent contradiction if we look more closely at what in this context Jung means by "balance" and how it is that such balance "finds the way"?

Jung suggests elsewhere in *The Red Book* that psychic balance consists of a bringing together of opposites, however painful and difficult that may be: "You achieve balance ... only if you nurture your opposite. But that is hateful to you in your innermost core, because it is not heroic." (Jung, 2009, p.263) This approach becomes characteristic of Jung's later psychology. However, we need to note that the psychic balance Jung recommends is an *inner* balance, to be achieved within the vertical dimension of soul. For example, Jung expounds upon the need for men to be in touch with their *inner* feminine (Jung, 2009, p. 263) and upon the therapeutic value of engaging (consciously) with the *inner* figures of the unconscious. In these examples, psychic balance is achieved through the painful and difficult process of bringing consciousness into dialogical relation with its opposite—located in the unconscious. It is an interaction that occurs on the intrapsychic level.

However, when what needs to be achieved is a balance between the inner world and the outer world (a balance that "finds the way"), Jung seems to take a quite different approach. To understand why in this case Jung utilises this divergent approach, we need to look at the only place in *The Red Book* where Jung directly addresses the question of what a living balance between the inner and outer dimensions of life might look like. Reviewing the first 25 days and nights of his confrontation with the unconscious, during which he has been won over by the spirit of the depths, Jung tells us:

> But the spirit of the depths had gained this power, because I had
> spoken to my soul during 25 nights in the desert and I had given
> her all my love and submission. But during the 25 days, I gave all

my love and submission to things, to men, and to the thoughts of this time. I went into the desert only at night.

Thus can you differentiate sick and divine delusion. Whoever does the one and does without the other you may call sick since he is out of balance. (Jung, 2009, p.238)

Jung's implication is that the balance between inner and outer requires a strict compartmentalisation of the two dimensions. While one is living in the *outer* world (engaging presumably with wife, career, clients, children, etc.), one should devote oneself entirely to that world. But then when one turns to the *inner* world, one needs to commit oneself equally to that realm. The two will thus alternate like day and night. Significantly, what Jung does *not* recommend is a direct engagement *between* these opposites.

In "Psychology of the Unconscious Processes" (Jung, 1917b) (one of the papers that emerged toward the end of his confrontation with the unconscious), Jung tells us that

[i]n order to differentiate the psychological ego from the psychological non-ego, man must necessarily stand upon firm feet in his ego-function; that is, he must fulfil his duty towards life completely, so that he may in every respect be a vitally living member of human society." (Jung, 1917b, pp. 416-417)

Here, Jung emphasises the need to maintain two quite separate psychological domains by stressing the importance of differentiating ego from nonego. This idea is also consistent with Jung's remarks in *MDR* about the period of the *Auseinandersetzung*:

Particularly at this time, when I was working on the fantasies, I needed a point of support in "this world," and I may say that my family and my professional work were that to me. It was most essential for me to have a normal life in the real world as a counterpoise to that strange inner world. My family and my profession remained the base to which I could always return, assuring me that I was an actually existing, ordinary person. (Jung, 1989, p.189)

It is precisely the fear that his inner wanderings may lead him, like Nietzsche, to feel like "a blank page whirling about in the winds of the spirit" that leads Jung to require a "counterpoise" that will remind him that he is, after all, a three-dimensional solid Zurich burger, firmly tethered to the daylight world of normality.

What we need to note here is that Jung is operating with two quite different conceptions of balance. In *intrapsychic* balance, the conscious ego "nurtures the opposite," which means breaking down any compartmentalised separation between conscious and unconscious, and entering into a difficult interaction with the inner other, whether it takes the form of the shadow, or the inner feminine or any of the other figures Jung encounters in *The Red Book*. In his contemporary paper *The Transcendent Function*, Jung showed how such an interaction might enable one to emerge into a newly transformed psychological position. However, when it comes to the opposites of inner and outer, Jung appears to recommend a completely different approach by which each pole is required to remain radically separate from the other. Jung values the inner precisely to the extent that it has nothing to do with the outer, and vice versa. This approach depends then upon the kind of compartmentalisation that Jung argues directly *against* when it comes to achieving intrapsychic balance.

Jung's mention of Nietzsche in this context is highly significant. In *MDR*, Jung tells us that "Nietzsche had lost the ground under his feet because he possessed nothing more than the inner world of his thoughts." (Jung, 1989, p.189) During his student years, Jung's powerful personal identification with Nietzsche had brought up an intense fear that his own No. 2 personality was as morbid as that of Nietzsche's Zarathustra and that he was therefore in real danger of becoming lost in the madness that Nietzsche experienced in his last years. This old terror that he would suffer Nietzsche's fate had been revived by his confrontation with the unconscious, and it now underpinned his urgent need for a separate but solid outer counterpole of normality.

The aspects of Nietzsche's fate that Jung found particularly terrifying are worth paying attention to:

> [H]e fearlessly and unsuspectingly let his No. 2 loose upon a world that knew and understood nothing about such things… he fell head first into the unutterable mystery and wanted to sing its praises to the dull, godforsaken masses. That was the reason for the bombastic language, the piling up of metaphors, the hymnlike raptures—all a vain attempt to catch the ear of a world which had sold its soul for a mass of disconnected facts. (Jung 1989, p.103)

This is ostensibly a description of Nietzsche's *Also Sprach Zarathustra.*, However, it might be more accurately seen as referring to Jung's own *Red Book*, a work that, as he acknowledges, is full of "bombastic language" (Jung, 1989, p.178) that seeks to express the "unutterable mystery" (of the spirit of the depths) and "sing its praises," and is intended to "catch the ear of a world which had sold its soul for a mass of disconnected facts," (i.e., has given itself over to the spirit of this time). It is perhaps not surprising then that, under these highly threatening circumstances, Jung's old fear of emulating Nietzsche's fate was revived. As a result, he felt the need to insure himself against madness by retaining a solid foothold in external normality by insisting upon the kind of *cordon sanitaire* that would keep his outer, No. 1, life safely compartmentalised and separated from his inner No. 2.[8]

We should also note that by choosing a notion of balance that meant in effect taking up alternating, mutually excluding counterpositions, Jung was reverting to that stage he describes in *MDR*, when, aware of the existence of both personalities, he could occupy only one personality at a time. As we have seen, Jung transcended this stage only after his storm lantern dream, which enabled him to recognise the need for a simultaneous engagement with both opposites. However, when it came to inner and outer, Jung was, it seems, deliberately (and defensively) holding on to a regressive position.

We need now to examine some of the writings of the period of *The Red Book*, in which we find Jung wrestling with precisely the same issues: inner and outer, and how to find a creative balance between the two.[9]

## The Schmid-Guisan Dialogue.

Jung's approach to the inner/outer opposites was closely related to his attitude to introversion and extraversion. We can unpack this relation further by looking more closely at the way Jung himself developed his ideas on typology during the *Red Book* years. As we saw, Jung's first detailed writing on typology from 1913 indicated a clear intention to take on the "difficult task of creating a psychology which will be equally fair to both types." (Jung, 1913, para. 882) Here, Jung highlighted the importance of developing a psychological approach that could recognise the differences between introversion and extraversion, while integrating them into a single psychology that could allow for both.

Two years later, in June 1915, Jung contacted his respected friend and ex-analysand Hans Schmid-Guisan, with a view to starting a correspondence specifically designed to encourage research into this question (Jung and Schmid-Guisan, 2013). As John Beebe puts it, Jung seems to have designed this correspondence as "a kind of Platonic dialogue, a dialectical discourse." (Beebe and Falzeder, 2013, p.18) It deliberately employed a dialogical form in order to enable an investigation and exploration of the differences (but also the possibilities of relationship) between an introvert (Jung) and an extravert (Schmid-Guisan).

If the correspondence began life as a rather abstract dialectical exercise, it rapidly, and perhaps not surprisingly, acquired a more personal character. The letters between the two men are of particular interest and value, not only because of what they tell us about the evolution of Jung's ideas about typology, but also because they give us a rare insight into how a close friend and colleague regarded Jung and his psychology during that crucial period when *The Red Book* was in the process of being written and important new ideas were coalescing.

In his final four letters, Schmid-Guisan takes up a position that is respectfully critical of certain aspects of Jung's approach (Jung and Schmid-Guisan, 2013, pp.142-156). His criticisms can be dismissed (and probably were dismissed by Jung at the time) as fatally distorted by Schmid-Guisan's's one-sidedly extraverted position. However, I would argue that Schmid-Guisan's thesis deserves serious attention. He suggests that Jung's introverted bias renders him blind to his own one-sidedness (Jung and Schmid-Guisan, 2013, pp.152-153). This critique is particularly forceful because Schmid-Guisan's argument emerges from a perspective that is broadly sympathetic to Jung's psychology. Schmid-Guisan is not suggesting that Jung's psychology is intrinsically one-sided. On the contrary, he remains committed to the fundamental principles of Analytical Psychology and especially its recognition of the need for balance between the opposites. His argument is that Jung's introverted bias distorts his approach to certain aspects of that psychology.

As Beebe notes in his introduction to the letters, the two men soon found themselves engaging in an important dispute about the process itself. The question was whether or not this dialogical process itself possessed the capacity to engender mutual understanding between the two types, as represented by Schmid-Guisan (Extraversion/feeling) and Jung (Introversion/thinking) (Beebe and Falzeder, 2013, pp.18-19).

In 1913, Jung had argued that Adler's introverted perspective was irreconcilable with that of Freud since each type was in possession of a radically different kind of truth. Since they "speak a different language," no real communication was possible (Jung, 1917b, para. 80). Schmid-Guisan, on the other hand, argued that, when it came to mutual understanding, what mattered most was the relationship between the two men (as enacted within the correspondence) and that this was the case whether or not they disagreed. As Schmid-Guisan explained, psychic transformation required precisely this tension between opposites: "I have never viewed the problem of the types as the existence of two truths, however, but I rather envisaged, from the genetic point of view, the existence of two poles between which psychic development occurs." (Jung and Schmid-Guisan, 2013, p.48)

Jung responded by arguing that miscommunication between the two types would inevitably bring about what he called "disastrous violation of the other" (Jung and Schmid-Guisan, 2013, p.62) (a suggestion that perhaps hints at Jung's old terror of being misunderstood). Schmid-Guisan suggested in response that the relationship between the two types will inevitably involve a clash of perspectives, but that this struggle is precisely what holds the potential for the emergence of meaning and further mutual understanding:

> I have never felt this opposite nature of the two types as anything tragic but only saw a meaningful interaction of nature in it. What you felt as a violation, I felt as a meaningful force. I felt this force as unpleasant, or as a violation, only so long as I believed I had to submit completely to your thinking. (Jung and Schmid-Guisan, 2013, p.70)

Schmid-Guisan's point is that such an interaction will be experienced as crushing or wounding only if one partner insists upon totally eclipsing the other by imposing his own perspective. As the correspondence unfolds, this is precisely how Schmid-Guisan begins to experience Jung—as attempting to erase his perspective.

For the moment, Schmid-Guisan's conviction that outer relationship can enable psychological understanding gets strongly countered by Jung's insistence that such insights can only emerge from an *inner, intrapsychic* engagement. Jung's tactic of responding to Schmid-Guisan by, as Beebe puts it, "repeatedly asserting first principles derived from an internal standard of truth," (Beebe and Falzeder, 2013, p.19) begs the very question that is at issue.

In Jung's fifth letter, he articulates his disagreement with Schmid-Guisan by reframing the idea of the two irreconcilable "truths"—describing one as rational and the other as irrational. He goes on, "The two truths have indeed something to do with the two 'realities,' which we might call the 'psychological' and the 'real' one." (Jung and Schmid-Guisan, 2013, p.76) Later, he develops this idea in an important passage: Both types (introverted and extraverted), he suggests, "can find their own irrational (i.e., psychological) truth only in themselves, and with it the true source of energy, because life flows from ourselves and not from the objects." (Jung and Schmid-Guisan, 2013, p.77) Jung's implication is that for both extravert and introvert psychological work (i.e., the process later to be titled individuation) is of necessity *inner* work, and therefore that *psychology itself* should be seen as residing in the inner (irrational) realm. By differentiating the two realms in this way—outer, rational, real vs inner, irrational, psychological—Jung implicitly excludes the possibility that psychological development might emerge from interaction or relation between the two—which is precisely Schmid-Guisan's position.

In response to these arguments, Schmid-Guisan warns that Jung's emphasis upon the overriding value of inner union with the unconscious introduces the dangerous possibility

> that by and by an analyst might easily come to believe he could replace experience via the object by analysis—the weapon that enables him to withstand the ensnaring powers of the unconscious—or, at the most, that he will accept experience only as a "necessary evil". One might easily get to that point if one took your phrase, "life flows from ourselves, and not from the objects," too literally. (Jung and Schmid-Guisan, 2013, p.97)

Here, Schmid-Guisan deliberately imagines an extreme perspective according to which outer experiences and outer relationships are evaluated as, at best, an opportunity for inner development and inner relationship. Unbeknown to Schmid-Guisan, this hypothetical position was very close to the perspective that, as we have seen, Jung was articulating in *The Red Book*. Schmid-Guisan goes on to advise anyone holding such a perspective that he "must learn for his part that there is life not only in himself but also in the object, and that he cannot bear children without being fertilized by the object." (Jung and Schmid-Guisan, 2013, p.97) Taking this lesson rather personally, Jung shot back a highly defensive response. Schmid-Guisan, astonished that Jung was responding so personally to his analysis of the "dark sides" of inferior introversion, replied: "I would never have believed that you felt that this concerned you." (Jung and Schmid-Guisan, 2013, p.116)

After five months and four exchanges of letters, Jung terminated the correspondence with this rebuff: "Your letter strengthens my conviction that reaching an agreement on the fundamental principles is impossible, because the point seems to be precisely that we do not agree." (Jung and Schmid-Guisan, 2013, p.131) Jung thus arrived decisively at the destination one suspects he was aiming for from the start. He had convinced himself that the experiment had somehow proved the impossibility of communication between the introvert and the extravert. Reading through the whole correspondence, it is hard not to see Jung's conclusion as at best premature. If two people disagree, this says nothing about their ability to communicate, nor would such a disagreement necessarily obviate the emergence of psychological understanding (conscious or unconscious). Nonetheless, what was more than clear was that Jung had had enough.

Upset at Jung's attempt to close down the conversation, Schmid-Guisan took the opportunity to express some serious doubts about the way in which Jung had managed the whole experiment. In his last two letters, written in a noticeably more personal tone, he outlined, as Beebe puts it, "some of the ways he felt his extraverted commitment to relationship (Eros) had been slighted, and even short-changed, by Jung's introverted stance as an analyst." (Beebe and Falzeder, 2013, p.26) However, it is important to note that Schmid-Guisan was not merely making a personal point. He was stepping outside Jung's 'dialectical experiment' in order to critique its very premises. Schmid-Guisan's central argument was that if, like Jung, one approaches psychology solely from an introverted perspective, one will necessarily, on a feeling level, remain blind to the principle of relationship with the other, or as Schmid puts it, "the power of Eros." (Jung and Schmid-Guisan, 2013, p.149) This kind of blindness will inevitably handicap the resulting psychology.

Schmid-Guisan concluded by telling Jung that he had initially engaged in the correspondence because of "the feeling that it is not yet possible for you to acknowledge an important, divine as well as devilish, power of the inner life of all humans, and because I was worried about the effects of your one-sidedness on our work." (Jung and Schmid-Guisan, 2013, p.152) Presumably, nothing in Jung's subsequent actions had allayed Schmid-Guisan's fears with regard to this latter problem. He closed with jokey prophecy about the future of the Jungian world which was perhaps more serious and more prophetic than he knew. He pictures the wise old Jung sitting in a tower on the Obersee, having become Nietzsche's heir, father to none, friend to none, and sufficient unto yourself. Vis-à-vis, here and there, a few other male and female introverts are living, each in their tower, loving humankind in those "farthest away," thus protecting themselves against the devilish love of their closest "neighbors." And, from time to time, they meet in the middle of the lake, each in their motorboat, and prove to each other the dignity of man. (Jung and Schmid-Guisan, 2013, p.154)

Jung, of course, had the last word. In the obituary that Jung wrote when Schmid-Guisan died in 1932, he stated that it was the correspondence with Schmid-Guisan that had enabled Jung "to clear up a number of fundamental questions. The results are set forth in my book on types".[10]

## The Transcendent Function

A year after he terminated the Schmid-Guisan correspondence, Jung wrote a paper titled, *The Transcendent Function* (Jung, 1916d). Here, Jung highlighted and amplified the dynamic he had touched on in his letters to Schmid-Guisan whereby the conscious ego engages with the "irrational" realm of the unconscious. The technique he describes (later to be called active imagination) was, of course, also the means Jung himself had chanced upon when encountering the figures of Philemon, Salome, and all the other characters that populate *The Red Book*. In *The Transcendent Function*, Jung underlined the specifically dialogical nature of the relation between ego and unconscious, directly comparing the interaction between ego and unconscious to

a dialogue … between two human beings with equal rights, each of whom gives the other credit for a valid argument and considers it worth while to modify the conflicting standpoints by means of thorough discussion, and in this way to strike a balance or at least make a compromise. (Jung, 1916d, p.175)

In the year since the correspondence, Jung seems to have incorporated Schmid-Guisan's argument that dialogue can enable psychological understanding, but he has made it his own by ensuring that the dialogue in question unfolds, not in the outer world, but between two inner figures.

Jung goes on to offer a reflection on the world war, still raging as he wrote: "The present day shows with appalling clarity how little able people are to let the other man's argument count. This capacity however is an essential, basic condition of any human community." (Jung, 1916d, p.175) The best way any individual could learn to develop such a capacity, Jung suggests, would be "by having it out with the unconscious, which contains the other standpoint with all possible distinctness, since consciousness is largely one-sided." (Jung, 1916d, p.175) Jung seeks to solve the problems of outer conflict by prioritising an *inner* dialogue; he suggests that we address our difficulties with the outer other best by "having it out" with our inner other.

In 1957, Jung undertook an extensive revision of this 1916 paper (Jung, 1957b). By comparing the two we can discern differences in approach and emphasis between early Jung and late Jung. Sometimes Jung merely elaborates the original's prioritisation of the inner with a new amplification. For example, in 1957, the "long conflict" between ego and unconscious, "demanding sacrifices from both sides," gets compares to the analytic relationship: "Such a rapprochement could just as well take place between patient and analyst, the role of devil's advocate easily falling to the latter." (Jung, 1957b, para. 186) At first glance, this reference to the analytical relationship seems to be a recognition that outer relationships can contribute to individuation. On reflection, however, we can see that Jung is merely emphasising that the patient's projection onto the analyst gives the helpful *illusion* of outer engagement. The analyst merely plays the part of "devil's advocate" on behalf of the patient's inner other.

Elsewhere, however, it is possible to detect a subtle but important shift in emphasis in the later reworking. In 1957, Jung adds a supplementary thought to the sentence quoted above:

Everyone who proposes to come to terms with himself must reckon with this basic problem. For, to the degree that he does not admit the validity of the other person, he denies the "other" within himself the right to exist—and vice versa. The capacity for inner dialogue is a touchstone for outer objectivity. (Jung, 1957b, para.187)

Jung's emphasis upon the importance of the other's "validity" implies that inner and outer possess equal status. There also seems to be an element of mutuality in the suggested relation of "inner dialogue" and "outer objectivity." In fact, Jung subtly stresses outer over inner: Anyone who fails to "admit the validity of the other [outer] person" will inevitably deny "the "other" within himself the right to exist." (Jung, 1957b, para.187) The writer of this sentence is recognisably the author of 1946's *Psychology of the Transference*, where he writes "the human connection ... is at the core of the whole transference phenomena, and it is impossible to argue it away, because relationship to the self is at once relationship to our fellow man." (Jung, 1946 para. 445)

## Inner and Outer in 1916.

Although in the original 1916 paper Jung pays very little attention to the significance of the outer other, he does place a strong emphasis upon the crucial nature of "the opposites" and the therapeutic necessity to avoid one-sidedness by bringing the opposites into relation with each other. This emphasis pervades all of Jung's later writings, and, as we have seen, it is a motif that runs through *The Red Book* (Jung 2009), the correspondence with Schmid (Jung and Schmid-Guisan, 2013), *The Transcendent Function* (Jung, 1916d), and the more theoretical works Jung wrote in 1916-17 such as "The structure of the unconscious," (Jung, 1916c, §442ff) "Adaptation, Individuation, Collectivity," (Jung, 1916a), and "The Psychology of the Unconscious Processes." (Jung, 1917b)

As I have argued, by articulating the notion of the creative nature of the tension of opposites, Jung revives in a newly conceptualised form the struggle he had endured in childhood and early adulthood between personalities No. 1 and No. 2, a struggle that taught him early about the potential perils of psychological one-sidedness.

It may be that Jung made the theoretical decision to identify the realm of psychology with the inner, irrational realm (and with introversion itself), in part, in order to restore some validity to the experience of interiority under threat from a hostile outer world that had excluded it as a reference point. However, the effect of that decision was to banish the outer-facing dimension from psychological work. Henceforth, the outer world (what Jung describes as "the real" as opposed to "the psychological") became a suitable object for psychology *only* to the extent that it may be, has been, or is rendered psychological through a process of interiorisation or introjection. As I have argued, a truly binocular approach (i.e., one consistent with the logic of the two personalities) would have allowed for both inner and outer dimensions to be brought into creative tension and thereby transcend both.

## Adaptation and Collectivity

I want to end the chapter by looking at a paper that Jung wrote and delivered in Zurich in October 1916, titled *Adaptation, Individuation, Collectivity*. (Jung, 1916a). Unfortunately, this lecture is written in such an abbreviated form that it verges on incoherence. However, since it deals with precisely the questions we are addressing here—that of the relation between individuation and collectivity—it is worth making an attempt to reconstruct Jung's argument.

According to Jung, the individuating person meets two challenges with regard to adaptation: "Adaptation to outer conditions" and "Adaptation to inner conditions." (Jung, 1916a, para.1084) By "outer conditions" Jung apparently means "conscious judgments ... formed of objective things." (Jung, 1916a, para.1085) "Inner conditions" seem to be more or less equivalent to the unconscious. Problems of adaptation arise, Jung suggests, for two quite different reasons. One derives from exaggerated extraversion whereby the subject "neglect[s] the inside," and the other derives from exaggerated introversion, which entails "neglect of the outside in favour of adaptation to the inside." (Jung, 1916a, para.1088)

As it happens, this paper includes one of Jung's earliest uses of the term "individuation" in the technical sense we find in his later psychology.[11] Here, Jung tells us that individuation is "against all adaptation to others," (Jung, 1916a, para.1094) and it has the effect of cutting "one off from personal conformity and hence from collectivity." (Jung, 1916a, para.1095) This segregation from collective norms leads, according to Jung, to an experience of "tragic guilt" (Jung, 1916a, para.1094).[12] In order to assuage this guilt, the individuating person must "offer a ransom in place of himself, that is, he must bring forth values which are an equivalent substitute for his absence in the collective personal sphere. ... Only to the extent that a man creates objective values can he and may he individuate." (Jung, 1916a, para.1095)

Jung clarifies the nature of the process of individuation by telling us, "Individuation is exclusive adaptation to inner reality." (Jung, 1916a, para.1095) It is, he explains, a process of adaptation to "those facts or data which force themselves upon my inner perception from the unconscious, independently of my conscious judgment and sometimes even in opposition to it." (Jung, 1916a, para.1086) Interestingly, this sentence is a close paraphrase of Jung's description in *MDR* of what he learned from the inner figure Philemon: "I understood that there is something in me which can say things that I do not know and do not intend, things which may even be directed against me." (Jung, 1989, p.183) It clearly indicates that Jung, as so often, is creating psychological theory out of his own personal experience of individuation, in this case that of his confrontation with the unconscious, whereby he himself attempted to adapt to "inner reality" (i.e., the unconscious). It would therefore be fair to assume that Jung too was left with "tragic guilt" as a result of the "destruction of [his] aesthetic and moral ideal." (Jung, 1916a, para.1094) If this is the case then, Jung is saying that the ransom for his introversion—his retreat from the outer collective world—will consist of his ability to bring back from the underworld certain "objective values," such as, we may assume, an entirely new psychology of individuation.

The compressed nature of the following section makes it very hard to follow Jung's argument. However, it would seem that, at this point, Jung is offering us two differing versions of individuation. For both, the necessary first step appears to be that the individuant breaks his connection with both society and with God—and consequently experiences the guilt Jung mentioned earlier. One possibility is that he offers "his good" to the soul, which in turn brings it to God (apparently identical to "the polarized unconscious") and eventually receives from God (the unconscious) a "gift" that the individual can pass on to mankind—presumably in the form of the new values mentioned earlier (Jung, 1916a, para.1103).

However, interestingly, Jung mentions another possibility. Rather than offering his "good" (his love) directly to the soul, the individuant may also offer it to a human being "who stands for his soul." This person then passes it on (in a way not specified) to God, and then the gift returns, via the lover, to the individuant, who is now able to directly offer the gift to his soul and thus begin to "receive it again from God." (Jung, 1916a, para.1103) Speaking now in the first person, Jung concludes with this restatement of the two possibilities: I can either "discharge my collective function" by giving my love directly to the soul and thus receiving the objective values that alone can redeem me, or, "as a lover, by loving the human being through whom I receive the gift of God." (Jung, 1916a, para.1104)

Jung reminds us that although this second means of individuation seems to involve a genuinely outer relationship, in fact the "discord between collectivity and individuation" (Jung, 1916a, para.1105) remains absolute; it is always the case that "if a man's libido goes to the unconscious, the less it goes to a human being; if it goes to a human being, the less it goes to the unconscious." (Jung, 1916a, para.1105) How then, we ask ourselves, could an individuation via a real outer human lover possibly work? Jung spells out the answer, an answer which by now we should have been able to predict, by telling us that it only works if the lover is the object of "true love," a concept he helpfully explains by telling us that it means that the lover needs to be a "representative of the unconscious" —only then does the libido "go direct to the unconscious." (Jung, 1916a, para.1105)

## Soul

We can witness this notion, or something very like it, articulated in a different form in the section of *The Red Book* titled "Refinding the Soul." The narrative follows Jung's return to, and recognition of, his (feminine) Soul. The way that Jung writes about the soul and his joyous return to her leaves the reader wondering whether what is occurring should be seen as a purely intrapsychic phenomenon or whether Jung is simultaneously referring to a literal romantic reunion with an actual lover. What gives weight to the former interpretation is Jung's implication that a close relationship with his soul in no way conflicts with a state of solitude: "My soul, my journey should continue with you. I will wander with you and ascend to my solitude." (Jung, 2009, 232) As we have seen, Jung's relationship with Toni Wolff, (described by Barbara Hannah as his "anima," or soul-figure [Hannah, 1976, 118]), commenced and flourished during the period during which these texts were written. But what should we make of the fact that throughout this period of "solitude" Jung was closely accompanied by Wolff?

What this conundrum seems to point to is that, although Wolff was physically present during much of Jung's confrontation with the unconscious, he engaged with her as if she functioned solely as an inner figure. Such an approach would be consistent with Jung's frequent implication that outer persons and situations are to be seen as valuable only to the extent that they facilitate Jung's inner connection to the autonomous powers of the unconscious. This idea seems to lie behind this passage, for example:

> I shall learn that my soul finally lies behind everything, and if I cross the world, I am ultimately doing this to find my soul. Even the dearest are themselves not the goal and end of the love that goes on seeking, they are symbols of their own souls. (Jung, 2009, p. 233)

Jung's liaison with that "dearest" of *outer* persons, Toni Wolff, may have contributed to the constellation of Jung's reunion with his Soul. However, this is the case not because she is herself "the goal and end of [Jung's] love," but rather because she is uniquely capable of symbolizing Jung's Soul on an *inner* level. On this psychological level, it is Jung's love for his Soul that matters, not his love for Wolff. In the terms of his *Adaptation, Individuation,*

*Collectivity* paper (Jung, 1916a), Wolff was the "true love" who, as a "representative of the unconscious" enabled Jung to pursue individuation by going "direct to the unconscious." (Jung, 1916a, para.1105)

In *The Red Book*, Jung amplifies this idea: "He whose desire turns away from outer things, reaches the place of the soul." (Jung, 2009, p. 232) He goes on:

> [The fool] forgets the way of his soul, never to find her again. He will run after all things, and will seize hold of them, but he will not find his soul, since he would find her only in himself. Truly his soul lies in things and men, but the blind one seizes things and men, yet not his soul in things and men. He has no knowledge of his soul. How could he tell her apart from things and men? He could find his soul in desire itself but not in the objects of desire. (Jung, 2009, p. 232)

From the point of view of individuation, what matters is not Wolff herself as a separate person but the psychological event of Jung's *desire* for Wolff. This is a crucially important point because it implies that, for Jung and for his psychology, the outer world is significant only to the extent that it aids or hinders our connection to the inner world. It should be remembered that, in a quite different compartment of Jung's life, there existed another "dearest," his wife, Emma. However, as we saw in the last chapter, by virtue of her position in the No. 1 compartment, she was, at this stage at least, disqualified from functioning as a Soul symbol, since her role was to supply sufficient psychic ballast to enable Jung to safely pursue his inner journey from a stable base.

Having reviewed several of Jung's works from this period, it has become increasingly clear that when it comes to psychic balance, Jung holds to a consistent, albeit arguably contradictory, approach. To summarise: Jung persistently informs us that individuation consists in the bringing together of the opposites; however, he also strictly limits this process to the *inner* dimension, which he identifies with the realm of the unconscious. This fact privileges introversion as the only way to enter such a realm, and it means that psychology itself becomes defined as inner-facing and introverted. It also means that I, qua individuating person, must necessarily cut myself off from the collective, from "the human being," unless, as we have seen, that person can be a "representative of the unconscious"— a placeholder for my "soul." Therefore, only solitude can provide the conditions for individuation to occur. The encounter with the unconscious that then follows may, it is true, take the form of a dialogical confrontation with the "other," but it must necessarily be an *inner* other. It is only after the lonely process of individuation has concluded that I can return to the outer world of society, clutching the hard-won, newly created objective values that alone can bring redemption.

Jung hereby ring-fences individuation in such a way that excludes the possibility that psychological growth might occur through an encounter with the outer other, whether in the form of the outer collective or in the form of the outer person. By defining individuation in this way, Jung explicitly rules out the notion of individuation-through-extraversion that Schmid developed during his correspondence with Jung, whereby a challenging and authentic relation with another person (or, one assumes, with the outer collective) has the capacity to enable an individual to become who he is.

However, despite Jung's determination to define individuation (and psychology itself) in this narrow way, there are hints throughout the works of this period that such limitations are in fact misplaced and perhaps even incoherent given the overall thrust of his psychology. For example, in *Adaptation, Individuation, Collectivity*, Jung makes the interesting suggestion that "[t]he unconscious is, as the collective psyche, the psychological representative of society." (Jung, 1916a, para.1102) Here, he hints at the possibility that the relationship between outer and inner collective is one of complex mutuality. Although Jung expressly differentiates the outer function ("The collective function in relation to society") from the inner function ("The collective function in relation to the unconscious"), he acknowledges that "from the 'mystical' or metapsychological point of view," (Jung, 1916a, para.1101) these two apparently different functions are in fact identical. In another text from the same year, Jung emphasises the close relationship between the individual and the collective when he points out that

[t]he human psyche is both individual and collective, and . . . its well-being depends on the natural co-operation of these two apparently contradictory sides. Their union is essentially an irrational life process that can, at most, be described in individual cases, but can neither be brought about, nor understood, nor explained rationally. (Jung, 1916c, para. 486)

This vision of the relationship between individual (inner) and collective (outer) opens up the possibility that the process of individuation might necessarily consist in a process of confrontation and dialogue not only with the *inner* unknown other (collective unconscious as interiority) but with the *outer* unknown other (collective in the form of outer person or group). Under these circumstances, individuation might be expected to require either outer or inner confrontations depending upon which attitude type was, at the time, dominant. However, there is a clear contradiction between such an idea and Jung's notion that introversion is uniquely the road to psychological transformation.

In *MDR*, Jung remarks that during this period he "felt the gulf between the external world and the interior world of images in its most painful form." (Jung, 1989, p.194) All he could see at the time was "an irreconcilable contradiction between 'inner' and 'outer.'" However, Jung then adds this important point: "I could not yet see that interaction of both worlds which I now understand."

This sentence implies that Jung's understanding of the relation of outer and inner underwent a transformative shift in the period subsequent to that of *The Red Book*. In the next chapter, I intend to explore the nature of that shift and what it means for Analytical Psychology as a contemporary psychological and psychotherapeutic discipline.

1 Described in the *Critical Dictionary of Jungian Analysis* as "a psychological 'law' first outlined by Heraclitus and meaning that sooner or later everything turns into its opposite." (Samuels, Shorter, and Plaut, 1986, p.53) It operates in this way: "If an extreme, one-sided tendency dominates conscious life, in time an equally powerful counter-position is built up in the psyche. This first inhibits conscious performance and then, subsequently, breaks through ego inhibitions and conscious control." (Samuels, Shorter, and Plaut, 1986, p.53)

2 This is a theme that will, of course, become developed and amplified in various different ways within Jung's mature psychology. As we will see in chapter 6, it provides Jung with the theoretical background to support his claims that Hitler's rise was primarily a mythic/archetypal event, rather than a political/social/historical event.

3 In *The Red Book,* the vision is recounted on pages 237-38 and the dream on pages 241-42. In the 1925 seminar, both vision and dream are described on pages 47-48. In *MDR*, the description of both vision and dream occurs on pages 179-80.

4 That Jung left so many versions of both dream and vision is a testament to their vital importance to him, both at the time and later. Their contemporary significance to Jung cannot be exaggerated; in *The Red Book* he says, "I felt certain that I must kill myself if I could not solve the riddle of the murder of the hero." (Jung, 2009, p.242)

5 Jung then adds this interesting comment:

> With all of this I give you the impure thoughts that lay back of the Types, where I have carried over into abstract terms the contest between the superior and inferior functions, first seen by me in the symbolic form of the slaying of the hero. (Jung, 1990, pp.48-49)

Here, Jung draws attention to the specific kind of transmutation whereby, depending upon one's perspective, either the base metal of his personal experiences—Jung's "impure thoughts"—become transmuted into the gold of abstract theory, or the gold of Jung's personal experiences become reduced to the base metal of abstract theory. The process here is one whereby the unconscious conflict between Jung's own superior and inferior functions (presumably, in the language of *The Red Book*, between spirit of this time and spirit of the depths) is revealed to Jung in symbolic terms in the dream/vision (blond hero versus brown savage), the conscious understanding of which enables Jung to subsequently reframe the conflict in abstract and universal terms in the form of Jung's text, *Psychological Types*.

6 The emphasis upon the dominant type as in some way defining the individual achieves its apotheosis in Jung's 1921 book on typology. However, its effect is not only that of positing a taxonomy of individuals whereby mutual incomprehension becomes the norm, and of thereby setting the stage for a reductive typological system such as Myers-Briggs, but more importantly, it takes attention away from the crucial fact that individuals are more similar than they are different, in that all individuals operate in the world via all four functions. This approach makes it difficult, for example, to look into the way in which feeling operates relationally among and within individuals.

7 A survey of interpretations of the Siegfried dream can be found in Shamdasani's *Jung Stripped Bare by His Biographers, Even* (Shamdasani, 2005).

8 We can see another aspect of this compartmentalisation in Jung's determination to keep *The Red Book* private—the inner narrative was to be kept away from outer eyes.

9 When we look at Jung's differing attitudes to psychic balance, it might be argued that we should differentiate between two contrasting versions of the Inner/Outer split: 1) The outer qua personal relationships with other people; and 2) the outer qua social and historical culture in general (materialism, psychology without a "soul," etc.). Balance would be considerably easier to achieve with regard to the former version of

the inner/outer split than the latter. In a world in which the social and cultural dimension defines itself so as to exclude and marginalise the inner, how could any individual hope to achieve balance? We can answer this question if we remember that Jung's notion of balance is not about the achievement of a finished state of equilibrium; it is concerned with the ongoing emergent experience of engagement between inner and outer. Understood in this way, to bring one's soulful inner realm into tension with a soulless and materialist outer culture would involve allowing the feeling of being hopelessly marginalised and excluded to inform the experience. The result might not feel like balance, but the process would be true to the logic of the two personalities and of Jung's transcendent function. If, on the other hand, one cuts off and compartmentalises one realm from the other, one simply obliterates the possibility of any interaction.

[10] The introverted bias that distorts Jung's typological writings was apparent to at least one of his close followers. C. A. Meier writes, "With his typology book, Jung, in keeping with his own introversion, is attempting a sort of apologia for this attitude." (Meier, 1989, p.92) Meier goes on to suggest that this lack of balance is justified on the grounds that is intended to compensate for the one-sided extraversion of the dominant culture.

[11] The word "individuation" occurs in Jung's 1912 *Transformations and Symbols of the Libido* (Jung, 1912/1952, para 180), but there it seems to have a philosophical meaning (as found in Schopenhauer and von Hartmann) (Shamdasani, 2003a, p.306 n.41). Although, according to Shamdasani, "[*The Red Book*] presents the prototype of Jung's conception of the individuation process, which he held to be the universal form of individual psychological development," (Shamdasani, 2009, p.207) the word individuation does not occur in the text. By the time Jung wrote the 1916 paper *Adaptation Individuation Collectivity* (Jung, 1916a), the concept seems to have become fully formulated. It first occurred in a published form in 1921's *Psychological Types* (Jung, 1921).

<sup>12</sup> This theme echoes Jung's comment in *The Red Book*, "I know, I have stridden across the depths. Through guilt I have become a newborn." (Jung, 2009, p.242)

# CHAPTER 6

# From Wotan to Christiana Morgan and Back Again: The Limits of the Archetypal/Personal Split

> The serious problems in life… are never fully solved. If ever they should appear to be so it is a sure sign that something has been lost. The meaning and purpose of a problem seem to lie not in its solution but in our working at it incessantly. This alone preserves us from stultification and petrifaction. (Jung, 1931b, para. 771)

I have suggested that during the period in which Jung began to formulate the concepts that would structure his mature psychology, his psychological writings were haunted by an unacknowledged one-sidedness, especially when it comes to the question of the relationship between the inner world and the outer world. This one-sidedness is carried through into the mature psychology in ways that distort its capacity to engage meaningfully with the outer dimension, whether collective, (i.e., the dimensions of the social and the political) or individual (the other person).

I ended the last chapter with a passage from *MDR* in which Jung suggested that at the time of writing *The Red Book,* he could see only "an irreconcilable contradiction between 'inner' and 'outer.'" And yet, Jung added, "I could not yet see that interaction of both worlds which I now understand." It is not immediately apparent from the context what Jung means by this last sentence, although he is clearly implying that in his later psychology, the inner dimension and the outer dimension no longer occupy the radically separate compartments we have noted in Jung's writings at the time of the confrontation with the unconscious. Now, (at the time of writing *MDR*) Jung understands these dimensions to be engaged in a relationship that is far more interactional than he previously thought possible. In this chapter, I want to begin by focusing on two arenas of his mature psychology in which this interactional connection can be identified. The first is that of psychotherapy itself.

## Jung's Two Models of Psychotherapy

When it comes to Jung's approach to the dynamics of psychotherapy, it is possible to identify two quite different analytic models embedded in Jung's writings—a one-person model and a two-person model (Giannoni, 2003). According to the first model, the process of individuation is primarily intrapsychic and moreover requires no intervention from outer influences. It follows that the role of the therapist is to act as a kind of companion and mentor facilitating the analysand's inner journey, which will take place (as in Jung's case during his confrontation with the unconscious) through intrapsychic encounters with *inner* others. We can see an excellent example of this approach in Jung's therapeutic relationship with Peter (Godwin) Baynes (1882-1943), Jung's translator and friend, who was to become Jung's assistant on his journey to Africa in 1925-26 (Burleson, 2005). During his first analysis with Jung, in Zurich in 1921, Baynes was encouraged by Jung to follow his own example—conducting active imaginations and engaging with the figures he encountered. In a contemporary notebook, Baynes described the relationship with Jung in this way:

> He is always in the background, felt rather than seen. He ... seems to be hardly concerned with the actual nexus and incident of one's life. He is essentially a guide. He shows one the way but the actual business of analysis and self-evaluation he has left almost entirely to my own efforts. Actually, he knows very little about me and seems to care very little ... yet I am as deeply under his directing influence as ever. (Jansen, 2003, p.129)

## From Wotan to Christiana Morgan and Back Again:
## The Limits of the Archetypal/Personal Split

When Jung left Zurich on vacation, Baynes remarked, "My analysis has certainly improved while he has been gone and it is done as it were under Jung's eye." (Jansen, 2003, p.129) Clearly, such a style of analysis neither develops within nor depends upon a close relational connection between analyst and analysand.

Within this model of analysis, Jung by no means excludes the possibility that transference will occur during therapy, but he suggests that if it does so, it will take the form of the analysand projecting inner figures onto the analyst. These figures may be parental—derived from the patient's personal history—or, under some circumstances, archetypal (e.g., anima, animus, wise old man, etc.). These projections will, at a later stage, need to be withdrawn as the individuant becomes better acquainted with his or her cast of inner figures. As an example of an archetypal transference (and echoing Baynes' own idealising projection onto Jung), Jung mentions a patient who dreamed of Jung as a Godlike father figure. He interprets the dream as "the unconscious … trying to create a god out of the person of the doctor, as it were to free a vision of God from the veils of the personal." (Jung, 1928b, para 214)

The patient's (pseudo-)encounter with the analyst resembles then Jung's encounter with those women who carried Jung's anima projections. In both cases, an outer person acts as a kind of stand-in, required to carry the projection until such time as the individuant can take it back. At that point, individuation can resume its proper *intrapsychic* form. The point is that even when it *seems* to be occurring in or through an *outer* dimension, the transformational process is in fact taking place on the *inner* level. It is this model of analysis that Jung has in mind when, as we have seen, he characterises the individuation process as essentially a solitary exercise. According to this model, it is only when the process is completed and the newly individuated person is ready to finally return to the outer world that a more relational approach can be taken up toward the outer world and wider society.

However, in those of Jung's writings that directly address questions of practical psychotherapy, it is possible to discern a very different model of analysis. In contrast with the one-person model's emphasis upon intrapsychic development, this model highlights those dimensions of psychotherapy that, because they are relational, mutual, and inter-subjective, require a genuine meeting between two persons. For example, in 1929's "Problems of Modern Psychotherapy," Jung tells us:

> For two personalities to meet is like mixing two different chemical substances: if there is any combination at all, both are transformed. In any effective psychological treatment the doctor is bound to influence the patient; but this influence can only take place if the patient has a reciprocal influence on the doctor. You can exert no influence if you are not susceptible to influence. (Jung, 1929, para.163)

Such comments are difficult to reconcile with, for example, Baynes's description of his analysis with Jung. Here, Jung takes us far beyond the one-person model whereby the individuant utilises the analyst as a relatively neutral figure, a target for projections that are later to be taken back. According to the two-person model, the psychotherapeutic event is a genuine meeting—both reciprocal and mutual—and therefore an authentically relational encounter. Such a notion is founded upon Jung's stated assumption that "We cannot fully understand the psychology of the child or that of the adult if we regard it as the subjective concern of the individual alone, for almost more important than this is his relation to others." (Jung, 1931a, para. 80)

From this perspective, the transformational aspect of the individuation process is closely entwined with—if not identical to—actual engagement with another person: "No longer is [the analyst] the superior wise man, judge, and counselor; he is a fellow participant who finds himself involved in the dialectical process just as deeply as the so-called patient." (Jung, 1935b, para. 8)

Jung's ideas on the theory and practice of psychotherapy are articulated in their most complete form in his *Psychology of the Transference* (Jung, 1946). Here, Jung conveys a strong conviction that the individuation process, as pursued within analysis, is intrinsically relational: "The unrelated human being lacks wholeness, for he can achieve wholeness only through the soul, and the soul cannot exist without its other side, which is always found in a 'You.'" (Jung, 1946, para. 454) This is a process that necessarily entails not only the patient's total involvement but also a mutual and reciprocal counterinvolvement by the therapist as what Jung describes as the "whole man" (Jung, 1946, para. 367): "The doctor is inclined to demand … total effort from his patient, yet he must realize that this same demand only works if he is aware that it applies also to himself." (Jung, 1946, para. 367) In *MDR*, Jung clearly states that in psychotherapy, transformation requires a two-person encounter:

> For psychotherapy to be effective, a close rapport is needed. …
> The rapport consists … in the dialectical confrontation of two opposing psychic realities. If for some reason these mutual impressions do not impinge on each other, the psycho-therapeutic process remains ineffective, and no change is produced. Unless both doctor and patient become a problem to each other, no solution is found. (Jung, 1989, p.143)

Though he rarely uses the term *countertransference*, Jung's persistent stress upon the importance of mutuality within therapy, and its value for therapeutic understanding, ensures his position as a pioneer in the field. Indeed, in his *History of Countertransference*, psychoanalyst Alberto Stefana acknowledges Jung's role as "the person who probably preceded everyone on the issue of countertransference." (Stefana, 2017, p.35)[1]

Jung's writings on psychotherapy indicate that awareness and analysis of the countertransference offer the analyst insights that he/she might otherwise miss. As he puts it, "It is futile for the doctor to shield himself from the influence of the patient and to surround himself with a smoke-screen of fatherly and professional authority. By so doing he only deprives himself of a highly important organ of information." (Jung, 1929, para.163)

The issue of countertransference is important to the argument of this book because it points to the fact that the psychological transformation emerges not solely from the inner work of the patient, important though that is, or solely from the mentoring, suggestions, or interpretations of the therapist, but rather from the relationship dynamics that develop *between* the analyst and analysand. Jung's *Psychology of the Transference* uses alchemical imagery to depict the complexity of conscious and unconscious relations between the analytic partners. Jung illustrates this dynamic with a useful diagram.

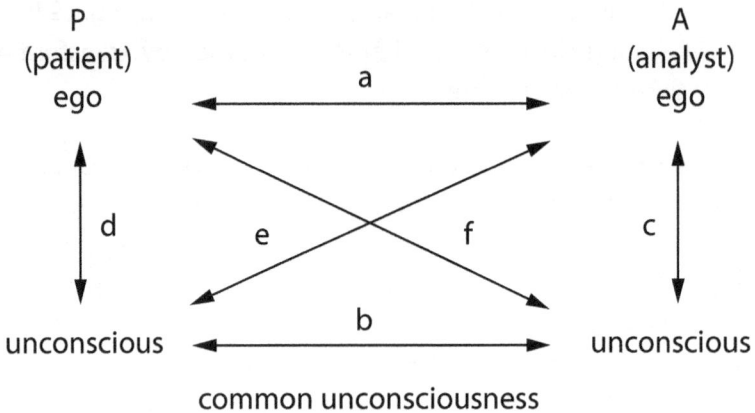

*Figure 4.* Jung's Transference/Countertransference diagram
from *Psychology of the Transference*

The arrows in the diagram help us differentiate various relational connections. These include the ordinary ego-to-ego conscious connection (a), and the projective connections we have encountered in the one-person model (e and f). However, the level of relational connection that Jung is referring to when he characterises the therapeutic encounter as a mutually transformative chemical combination also involves the relation depicted by arrow (b). This is the connection he refers to when he suggests, "Even the most experienced psychotherapist will discover again and again that he is caught up in a bond, a combination resting on mutual unconsciousness." (Jung, 1946, para.367) Elsewhere he takes this idea further: "The patient, by bringing an activated unconscious content to bear upon the doctor, constellates the corresponding unconscious material in him." (Jung, 1946, para.364)

Jung uses the term "the third" to articulate that dimension of the therapeutic event (and the vessel that contains it) which reveals itself in the form of the dynamic field within which the analytic relationship itself operates: "Psychological induction inevitably causes the two parties to get involved in the transformation *of the third* and to be themselves transformed in the process." (Jung, 1946, para.399) Joe Cambray suggests that, in terms of Jung's diagram, "[t]he "third" could be understood as emerging from [its] combined pathways ... especially those in the central region (paths a, b, e, and f)." This relational process therefore offers analyst and analysand the chance to coconstruct transformative meaning "from our mutual experiences, conscious and unconscious, atop an archetypal base." (Cambray, 2012, p.85)

## Therapy and Synchronicity

It is significant that Cambray's useful comment, which highlights the interaction of both personal *and* archetypal aspects within the analytic encounter, is to be found in a book on the subject of synchronicity, a topic that took a great deal of Jung's attention and time in his later years. Synchronicity, like the transference, arguably exemplifies the interaction of both inner and outer dimensions. On occasion, Jung himself linked the two topics: "The relationship between doctor and patient ... especially when a transference on the part of the patient occurs, or a more or less unconscious identification of doctor and patient, can lead to para-psychological [i.e. synchronistic] phenomena." (Jung, 1989, p.159)

Nonetheless, on the whole, Jung's writings on synchronicity focus more upon the wider theoretical implications of his idea rather than the emergence of synchronicities within clinical settings and their meanings within that interactional context. This has not prevented several of his followers from expanding upon parallels between the clinical and the synchronistic, and especially Jung's suggestion that analysis occurs in a "third" field, which operates outside (on top of, or beneath) those intrapsychic processes that occur *within* the analytic partners *as individuals* (Main, 2007). For example, Hans Dieckmann reported that a research project investigating the unconscious interaction between analyst and patient showed "an astonishing increase in the phenomena of synchronicity" when the researchers "started to keep more accurate records of the subliminal perceptions of the analyst." (Dieckmann, 1976, p.27)

This link between the clinical and the synchronistic is of interest to this inquiry because it throws light upon the problem of the relation of inner to outer. Jung's ideas on transference/countertransference do so by drawing attention to the relation between the inner world of the individuant and the outer encounter with the analyst (via "the third"). Jung's ideas on synchronicity come at the same problem but from a different perspective. Jung defines synchronicity as "the simultaneous occurrence of a certain psychic state [inner] with one or more external events [outer] which appear as meaningful parallels to the momentary subjective state." (Jung, 1952, para.850) Although this definition mentions merely "parallels" between outer and inner, what drew Jung's attention to what he emphatically described as a *connecting* principle was the potential of synchronistic events to bring about psychological transformation.

Let us take a closer look at the ur-example of synchronicity, the episode that Jung most often refers to when explaining the idea. It occurred during the analysis of a young woman patient Jung describes as "psychologically inaccessible." He tells us that he was unable to make headway in analysing her and therefore confined himself to "the hope that something unexpected would turn up, something that would burst the intellectual retort into which she had sealed herself." (Jung, 1952, para. 982) Jung describes what happened next:

> Well, I was sitting opposite her one day, with my back to the window, listening to her flow of rhetoric. She had had an impressive dream the night before, in which someone had given her a golden scarab—a costly piece of jewellery. While she was still telling me this dream, I heard something behind me gently tapping on the window. I turned round and saw that it was a fairly large flying insect that was knocking against the window-pane in the obvious effort to get into the dark room. This seemed

to me very strange. I opened the window immediately and caught the insect in the air as it flew in. It was a scarabaeid beetle, or common rose-chafer (Cetonia aurata), whose gold-green colour most nearly resembles that of a golden scarab. I handed the beetle to my patient with the words, 'Here is your scarab'. This experience punctured the desired hole in her rationalism and broke the ice of her intellectual resistance. The treatment could now be continued with satisfactory results. (Jung, 1952, para. 982)

Jung's narration of this synchronistic event focuses on the meaningful connection between inner (patient's dream) and outer (scarab beetle). However, the *context* of this connection was that of a specific event of transference/countertransference. This showed up as a sense of stuckness manifesting in the field between patient and doctor; the patient certainly feels stuck, but in terms of the analysis, so does Jung. In his account, Jung chooses to emphasise the subjectively experienced intrapsychic aspect of the patient's psychological breakthrough. He pays less attention to the simultaneous breakthrough that occurred in the *analytic process as a whole*. Yet, the latter breakthrough is arguably the important one, since, as we have seen, the stuckness was experienced not so much in either partner—Jung or the patient—as in the *field* connecting and containing the two of them. One is reminded of Jung's comment in *MDR*: "Unless both doctor and patient become a problem to each other, no solution is found." (Jung, 1989, p.143)

Evidently, in both the clinical arena and the synchronistic arena, and especially in the areas we have identified in which the two overlap, Jung is developing psychological ideas that move beyond the approach that we identified in the *Red Book* period, whereby inner was strictly segregated from outer.

If we now apply the dual lens perspective of the two personalities to these questions, we can see that Jung is bringing inner (personality No. 2) into relation to outer (personality No. 1), and thereby applying a binocular perspective to the issues, and it is this approach that constellates the transformative dimension of the process.

In the clinical encounter, as Jung's diagram makes clear, the analysand's personality No. 1 is in relation with the analyst's personality No. 1 (line a), the analyst's personality No. 1 is in relation with his/her own personality No. 2 (line c), and with the analysand's personality No. 2 (line e), and the analysand's personality No. 1 is in relation with his own No. 2 (line d) and with the analyst's No. 2 (line f). Finally, the personality No. 2 of both partners is in mutual relation (b). As Cambray pointed out, it is the relational field containing *all* of these connections that constitutes the transformative combination Jung describes as "the third": the arena in which both an inner (No. 2) process and an outer (No. 1) process come together.

In the classic synchronistic case of the scarab beetle, one way to understand the presenting problem of the client is that of a failure of connection between personality No. 1 and personality No. 2. Jung describes the client as "psychologically inaccessible." Her one-sidedness indicates that her personality No. 1 is out of touch with her No. 2. In the analytic context, this also means that there is some kind of blockage in the relationship between her No. 1 and Jung, who is acting as No. 2-by-proxy (via the transference). Although she (No. 1) is perfectly capable of communicating about the nature of her problem with Jung (No. 1), on a common-sense rational level (line a), that knowledge is not transformative because there is no active line of communication between her No. 1 and either her own No. 2 or Jung's No. 2. This means she has no access to the kind of intuitive insights that might enable her to break the psychological impasse that confronts her (and Jung). This also means that the field of "the third" (within which No. 1 and No. 2 would be able to communicate) remains unavailable, not only to her, but also to Jung. This is why the synchronistic event of the arrival of the scarab not only, as Jung puts it, "punctured the desired hole in her rationalism and broke the ice of her intellectual resistance" but simultaneously broke through whatever had simultaneously impeded the client's access to Jung's No. 2 and to her own No. 2, thus enabling access to "the third."

There remains another dimension of this synchronicity that we have yet to mention. As Roderick Main has pointed out, the image of the scarab had been particularly numinous for Jung long before this particular scarab flew into the consulting room. A scarab features in the vision that began Jung's 1913 confrontation with the unconscious (Jung, 1989, p.179), and its mythic/symbolic significance is explored in *The Red Book* (Jung, 2009, p.271). As Main has carefully traced, Jung was also well acquainted with the scarab's alchemical significance (Main, 2013, pp. 140ff.). In brief, the scarab powerfully evoked for Jung the personality No. 2 motifs of death and rebirth—because it had historically come to him at times of sterility. As Main puts it, this implies that the "incident involving the scarab beetle was a synchronicity not only for the patient but also for Jung." (Main, 2013, p.137) The rebirth constellated by the scarab that came to the window was not only relevant to the psyche of a one-sided patient, it was also significant for Jung. The subsequent psychic rebirth involved not only the patient's potential for wholeness, but Jung's own revivified link with his own unconscious. But the crucial point I want to make here is that it was an event of living relation between these two dimensions. In the overall context of the analysis, the breakthrough that enabled the treatment to "be continued with satisfactory results" therefore involved the simultaneous interaction of all of these multifaceted dimensions.

However, although these different aspects of the scarab synchronicity offer us a certain understanding of the nature of the problem and its solution, there remains a question as to why this problem occurred in this way within this particular therapy.

## Jung's Countertransferences

As it happens, Jung's account of the case contains a significant distortion. As we have already noted, when Jung recounted the scarab case, he directed the reader's attention toward the patient and her state of psychological stuckness. This focus has the effect of distracting the reader from the nature of Jung's involvement in that stuckness and how it might have contributed to the situation. We can gain a better understanding of the full context of this case if we look more closely into its biographical details.

Recent research by Vicente de Moura has revealed the identity of this particular client. According to de Moura, Madeleine Reichstein Quarles van Ufford (1894-1975) was not only the patient in the original case of synchronicity, but she also constellated a well-known dream of Jung's, which he recounts in *MDR* as an example of psychic compensation (Moura, 2014). In the dream, Jung craned his neck in order to see his patient far above him. Jung concluded that the dream image was compensating his own tendency to look down upon this particular patient. In *MDR*, Jung offered some personal background to the dream: "At first the analysis went very well, but after a while I began to feel that I was no longer getting at the correct interpretation of her dreams, and I thought I also noticed an increasing shallowness in our dialogue." (Jung, 1989, p.133) After the dream, Jung decided to inform his client of both dream and interpretation, and he tells us (in words that cannot help but remind us of those that concluded his account of the scarab synchronicity) that "[t]his produced an immediate change in the situation, and the treatment once more began to move forward." (Jung, 1989, p.133)

It would seem that this was a case that required, on at least two occasions, an unusually powerful intervention from the unconscious. We do not know which occurred first—dream or synchronicity—but what we can identify is a pattern whereby the analytic relationship between Jung and Reichstein became repeatedly stuck, and, with regard to the dream at least, the problem seems to have been related to Jung's attitude toward the client. This opens up the possibility that it was this same problem that lay behind the synchronistic event. What we do know is that more was going on in this case than Jung was acknowledging in his own published accounts. Peter Baynes records a conversation with Jung in about 1930 on the topic of the kinds of anima difficulties that can cause problems in analysis. Jung explained to Baynes:

[H]ow he had himself been caught by a counter-transference to a beautiful aristocratic girl [Reichstein] and how he had a dream in which she was enthroned very high on an Eastern temple, high above him. And this explained how all his knowledge and interest in Oriental ideas and feelings had developed out of his transference to the girl. He had, as he said, to cut off his head and learn to submit his ignorance to his patient. (Jansen, 2003, pp.244–45)

If Jung was indeed "caught by a counter-transference" to this particular patient (and as we know, it wouldn't have been the first or last time that such a thing occurred), then we can perhaps begin to understand the repeated impasses and subsequent unconscious interventions that seem to have characterised the case. By investigating these dynamics, we are neither resorting to gossip nor reducing the matter to a merely personal affair, but casting light upon the complicated interrelationships between the personal and the archetypal, and thereby achieving a better theoretical grasp of the role of synchronicities and compensatory dreams within analysis as a whole.

It would seem that in this case there was only one remaining psychological avenue through which transformation of both partners could occur, and that meant Jung needing to "cut off his head and learn to submit his ignorance to his patient," thus activating that field that Jung calls "the third." In *Psychology of the Transference,* Jung eloquently describes a situation of this kind: "The elusive, deceptive, ever-changing content that possesses the patient like a demon now flits about from patient to doctor and, as the third party in the alliance, continues its game, sometimes impish and teasing, sometimes really diabolical." (Jung, 1946, para. 384) In the Reichstein case, it was the scarab beetle that flitted about "from patient to doctor" (flitting also between literal and metaphorical!). The relational deadlock between the two partners thus became the very *prima materia* out of which insight could begin to emerge for both analyst and analysand.

However, this realisation brings with it a problem. It needs to be acknowledged that it has taken 90 years for us to get a glimpse of precisely how these insights came about, and we have achieved it *despite* Jung's attempts to disguise the truth of the matter. This situation is not unique, and it has had consequences for Jungian psychology. Jung's reluctance to acknowledge the role of countertransference problems in any of his accounts of the scarab beetle synchronicity has had the effect of significantly skewing the theoretical focus away from that of the therapeutic relationship between analyst and analysand and toward that of an intrapsychic difficulty *located within the patient alone*. In this case, we have been led to believe that it was *Reichstein's* problem alone and not a two-person problem within the therapy. Jung seeks to focus our attention on the stuckness of the client, thus distracting us from the trans-ference/countertransference difficulties that evidently characterised the case as a whole. The relational dimension of the problem has thereby become occluded. What is lost is the crucial information that, when it comes to clinical work, a synchronicity is an expression, as it were, of "the third"—which is why the synchronistic event occurs *outside* of either client or analyst, though *inside* the relationship between them.

When we looked at the relational complexities of the events described in Jung's doctoral dissertation and in his account of the birth of the anima, we noted a persistent tendency to suppress highly relevant details of the actual clinical settings out of which Jung's insights were constellated and that this tendency was intensified when those settings involved his own countertransference tangles. On the basis of the case we have been looking at here, it would seem that this pattern continued well into the period of Jung's mature psychology. As we will see later in the chapter, it is also to be found in one of Jung's most famous cases—that of Christiana Morgan.

## Universal and Particular

As Roderick Main has observed, Jung "only rarely—and never in detail—discussed the clinical dimension of synchronicities. The bulk of his writing on the topic is concerned with theoretical issues." (Main, 2007, pp.368–69) We have noted Jung's reluctance to divulge his own countertransferences, but the higher-order issue of which this is merely a particular instance is Jung's general tendency to maintain a segregation between that dimension of psychology that he categorises as archetypal from that described as personal. One way in which this shows up is as a preference, when it comes to discussing psychological theory, to approach it on the universal level, and to avoid specific clinical accounts—except when he judges that a clinical vignette can illustrate the general theoretical point. This emphasis upon the broadly archetypal dimension of his psychology has the inevitable effect of obscuring or even erasing the complexity and density of the relational dimension.

I would like now to focus on what occurred in Jung's therapeutic work with his patients. The possibilities for research on this topic are constricted by the fact that, as Sedgwick points out,

> Jung's opus is virtually devoid of clinical examples. It begs for the grounding in therapeutic reality that a practical example would give. The unconscious material in impersonal form … is given prominence over the "personal," just as it is in Jung's extended case studies." (Sedgwick, 1994, p.5)

James Hillman has also highlighted Jung's tendency, in those of his texts that deal extensively with a single case (series of visions or dreams), to choose patients who were not his own (Hillman, 2012, pp.31-32).[2] However, as we shall see, even the cases where Jung delivers a kind of proxy-analysis can tell us a great deal about Jung's approach to clinical work.

## Pauli

Let us take as our first example that of Wolfgang Pauli, the great physicist who provided the dreams that Jung analyses in his *Psychology and Alchemy* (Jung, 1966), and with whom Jung later actively collaborated while developing his work on synchronicity (Gieser, 2005). When Pauli, a prolific dreamer, first approached Jung for treatment in 1932, Jung took deliberate steps to avoid exerting any "influence" upon what he regarded as Pauli's unadulterated archetypal material. In the Tavistock Lectures, Jung describes the situation thus: "I saw he [Pauli] was chock-full of archaic material, and I said to myself: 'Now I am going to make an interesting experiment, to get that material absolutely pure, without any influence myself, I won't touch it.'" (Jung, 1935c, para. 402)

Jung therefore made the decision to entrust the case to Dr. Erna Rosenbaum, "a beginner ... who did not know much about archetypal material." (Jung, 1935c, para. 402) Jung's implication here is that his own understanding of archetypal symbolism—even when unarticulated - could be enough to risk influencing Pauli in ways that might taint the purity of his "archaic material." Jung appears to allude to this situation in a 1952 interview: "For fifteen years I studied alchemy, but I never spoke to anyone about it; I did not wish to influence my patients or my fellow workers by suggestion." (Jung, 1987, pp.227–28)

Jung tells us that for Dr. Rosenbaum this problem didn't occur on either conscious or unconscious levels since she offered no "interpretations worth mentioning ... because the dreamer, owing to his excellent scientific training and ability, did not require any assistance. Hence conditions were really ideal for unprejudiced observation and recording." (Jung, 1944, para. 45) One wonders exactly what kind of therapy Rosenbaum was able to supply, given that she had been assigned the status of a glorified laboratory assistant. Jung seems to have made the blithe assumption that during the period of Pauli's analysis with Rosenbaum, Pauli would continue to produce dreams that were "chock-full of archaic material" and (therefore?) empty of, for example, transferential material. This seems a particularly strange assumption given that Jung had specifically chosen a woman analyst for Pauli because of the physicist's anima problems. It would seem that the factor overriding all others here was Jung's need to gain proof of the archetypal nature of individuation. Interestingly, Jung seems to have assumed that Pauli's "natural process of individuation" would remain unaffected by the therapeutic relationship with Rosenbaum, since she "did not know much about archetypal material."

Although the analysis with Rosenbaum lasted only five months, it has been claimed that Paul did nonetheless develop "transferential feelings toward her." (Cohen, 2015, p.44) Certainly, when, years later, Pauli restarted analysis with Marie Louise von Franz, transference problems proliferated. Von Franz commented that Pauli "didn't submit to the transference" and that this "made our work together very difficult from the start." (Franz, 1991, p.56) Others have claimed that the relationship with von Franz was characterised by a mutual transference (Gieser, 2005, p.148), a claim possibly supported by the fact that, after Pauli's death, his widow burned all von Franz's letters.

Whatever the nature of the transference, it is clear that some kind of transferential relationship existed between Pauli and his analysts, and it is also clear that, when approaching the dreams that Pauli produced during these years, Jung deliberately chose to ignore this personal dimension. He tells us that in the "abbreviated" versions of the dreams presented in *Psychology and Alchemy*, he has "removed personal allusions and complications, as was necessary for reasons of discretion." (Jung, 1944/52, para 47) This presumably means that the material we get to see has been pruned so as to highlight the solely archetypal aspects of the dreams. We have to assume that the original uncensored versions would have constituted a fabric in which archetypal motifs were interwoven with personal motifs.

Jung is well aware that he is thereby distorting the dreams, and he draws our attention to it when he makes a point of contrasting his usual method of approaching dreams with the method he utilises here. Under normal circumstances (i.e., clinically), he tells us, he would seek to approach dreams with no preconceptions, aiming to discover the unique (personal) context in response to which this particular dream has appeared. In this case, however, as he puts it, his method runs "directly counter to this basic principle of dream interpretation." Because Jung was not Pauli's analyst when the dreams were dreamed, he is not acquainted with the personal context. He therefore proceeds, he tells us, by treating the dreams not as individual examples (which he acknowledges would require interpretation according to the particular context), but as an entire series. This justifies Jung in discerning their meaning within the series taken as a whole, which he performs by concentrating upon the resonances between images from different dreams, "throwing light from all sides on the unknown terms, so that a reading of all the texts is sufficient to elucidate the difficult passages in each individual one." (Jung, 1944/52, para. 50) This process, which as he himself acknowledges is "largely conjecture," is nonetheless aided (in a strikingly circular way) by Jung's amplificatory approach. For example, "in the third chapter we are concerned with a definite archetype—the mandala—that has long been known to us from other sources, and this considerably facilitates the interpretation." (Jung, 1944/52, para. 50) Jung reassures us as to the reliability of such an approach by telling us that "the series as a whole gives us all the clues we need to correct any possible errors in the preceding passages."

What Jung doesn't seem to be aware of is the strong possibility that such a hermeneutic will be extremely vulnerable to a viciously circular logic. The dreams and their interpretations by Jung are ungrounded in two related ways. First, outside their personal context, they can no longer be interpreted as compensatory to the conscious life of the dreamer. Second, because dreams are inevitably born out of and express something of the analytic relationship itself, their interpretation needs to take that relationship into account. Jung was well aware of this. In 1934, he wrote to James Kirsch, "With regard to your patient, it is quite correct that her dreams are occasioned by you. ... As soon as certain patients come to me for treatment, the type of dream changes. In the deepest sense, we all dream not out of ourselves but out of what lies between us and the other." (Jung, 1973b, p.172) Despite this important insight, Jung's primary intention here seems to be to give himself an entirely free hand to amplify the images as it pleased him, or as he described it, "as if I had had the dreams myself and were therefore in a position to supply the context," (Jung, 1944/52, para. 49) but he can achieve this only by keeping himself deliberately ignorant of this relational dimension, thus occluding a significant resource of meaning.

For all the virtuosic interpretations Jung provides us with in *Psychology and Alchemy*, what we are being offered is yet another example of Jung's persistent desire to keep the inner (No. 2) realm of the high archetypal compartmentalised away from the outer (No. 1) realm of the low personal (transference/countertransference). The net result of this segregation is that any scientific conclusions that Jung might have drawn from the "experiment" in question are not only distorted but fatally undermined.[3]

Betsy Cohen may well be right when she suggests that "Jung wanted to prove that Pauli's archetypal dreams and drawings, part of the objective psyche ('collective unconscious'), illustrated the blueprint for the natural process of individuation; and therefore, [he examined] the progression of the dreams in as pure and impersonal a way as possible" (Cohen, 2015, p.43). Nonetheless, as we have seen, such an approach was ultimately counterproductive.

## The Need to Compartmentalise

We have identified in Jung a consistent determination to keep the outer/personal/relational dimension separate from the inner/archetypal level: "It is therefore absolutely essential to make the sharpest possible demarcation between the personal and the impersonal attributes of psyche." (Jung, 1917b, para.150). By suppressing details about the counter-transferential involvement of the analyst in cases that he simultaneously held up as providing evidence of objective archetypal patterns, Jung's intention seems rather to distract his readers from the crucial connection between the personal and the collective unconscious.

As we have seen in those of Jung's texts that are devoted to the practice of psychotherapy, we find a contrasting emphasis upon the therapeutic necessity for the kind of complex, mutually transforming, encounter in which both archetypal and personal strands were inextricably intertwined (Jung, 1929, 1935b, 1946). However, of the 20 volumes of the *Collected Works*, there is only one volume devoted to psychotherapy as such; the remaining volumes focus upon theoretical matters and overwhelmingly upon symbolic and archetypal themes. These often occur in contexts which, on the face of it, have no obvious connection with practical psychology, such as Eastern religion, Gnosticism, flying saucers, parapsychology, Nietzsche's philosophy, astrology, mythology, anthropology, etc. To the bewilderment of many, the field that Jung most extensively worked, especially in his later works, was that of alchemy.

## Alchemy, etc.

It would be quite wrong, however, to represent Jung's interest in these obscure or marginal topics as merely a retreat into esotericism for its own sake. The red thread that runs through all Jung's interests is what he calls "the problem of the opposites"—a problem that had originally arisen in the context of his experience of the two personalities. For example, Jung's enthusiasm for alchemy in the last period of his creative life was directly relevant to precisely the issue we have been addressing in this book, the relation of outer to inner. We have seen how the topics of both counter-transference and synchronicity share an acknowledgment that the psychological dimensions of both *outer* world and *inner* world are intimately interwoven. It is this relationship (correspondence) between the two realms that drew Jung to alchemy, in which he saw a vital connection between the two.[4]

However, Jung's approach to alchemy seems on the face of it to maintain the same strict inner/outer compartmentalisation that we have observed elsewhere in his psychology. Here, as elsewhere, Jung relies heavily upon the concept of projection to articulate the relation of inner to outer. For example, he describes the alchemists as simply projecting inner psychic phenomena onto the outer material events they witnessed in their retorts:

> The real nature of matter was unknown to the alchemist: he knew it only in hints. In seeking to explore it he projected the unconscious into the darkness of matter in order to illuminate it. In order to explain the mystery of matter he projected yet another mystery—his own psychic background—into what was to be explained: *Obscurum per obscurius, ignotum per ignotius!* This procedure was not, of course, intentional; it was an involuntary occurrence. (Jung, 1944, para.345)

Jung seems to imply that the complex imagery of alchemy represents nothing but an outward representation of inner psychological dramas that unfolded unconsciously within the minds of the alchemists. There is also an implication that we moderns have now solved the mysteries that confused the alchemists—not only the psychological mysteries of individuation, but also the physical mysteries of matter. However, Jung's position is in fact not as reductive as this sounds; elsewhere, he implies that both modern physics and modern psychology (by which he means his own psychology) suffer from the limitations of a model that separates the inner world from the outer world. It is this realisation that lies behind Jung's project of reanimating the alchemical perspective, by giving it a new, psychological, form:

> [T]he moment when physics touches on the "untrodden, untreadable regions," and when psychology has at the same time to admit that there are other forms of psychic life besides the acquisitions of personal consciousness—in other words, when psychology too touches on an impenetrable darkness—then the intermediate realm of subtle bodies comes to life again, and the physical and the psychic are once more blended in an indissoluble unity. We have come very near to this turning-point today. (Jung, 1944, para. 394)

Here, just as in his contemporary writings on synchronicity, Jung seems to be keen to push psychology into a conceptual region within which the inner/outer division no longer holds. Von Franz describes such a perspective succinctly in an essay on the alchemical approach to the matter/psyche question:

> [I]t is to be suspected that our division into material versus mental, that which is observable from the outside versus that which is perceivable from the inside, is only a subjectively valid separation, only a limited polarization that our structure of consciousness imposes on us but that actually does not correspond to the wholeness of reality. In fact it is rather to be suspected that these two poles actually constitute a unitary reality. (von Franz, 1992, p.11)

It was in order to articulate this highly speculative holistic vision that Jung revived the concept of the *Unus Mundus* (Jung, 1955, paras. 659ff), first found in the alchemical writings of Gerhard Dorn (1530-84).

From this brief summary, it is possible to see that Jung, in his later psychology, made efforts to move beyond the limitations of a dichotomous perspective that insists upon imposing a categorical distinction between psyche and matter, or inside and outside. This was perhaps what Jung had in mind when he made his *MDR* comment that at the time of *The Red Book* he "could not yet see that interaction of both worlds which I now understand."

Unfortunately, it also brings us up against the fact that, for all Jung's attempts to twist free of such differentiations, he chooses to address these questions by utilising the kind of transcendental approach that is squarely aligned with his No. 2 personality. Such an approach necessarily excludes the personality No. 1 dimension.

For example, in his work on synchronicity, Jung attempts to transcend the opposition of matter vs. spirit by invoking the highly abstract principles of modern physics. As we have seen, he generally avoids making a direct connection between these speculations and clinical practice or even the psychological experience of the individual. Although Jung frequently claims that his aim is to avoid a reductive approach, his actual practice pulls him away from the relational and affective specificity of personal life—the dimension of existence in which the outer naturally dwells. References to the archetypal unity of spirit/matter have a nicely paradoxical sound, but to attain a truly binocular perspective, Jung would need to explore how and where the opposition is experienced in time by the concrete individual.[5] What this means is that Jung performs only half the psychological work. It is left to us, his readers, to take up the task of translating it back into the more grounded (No. 1) language of experience, thereby bringing the two personalities back into conversation.[6]

## The Yellowing

We can see the limitations of a one-sided Jungian approach if we look at Jung's writings on a crucially important moment in the alchemical process, the shift from the stage of albedo, or whitening, to the final stage of rubedo, or reddening.

Many alchemical texts describe three stages to the alchemical opus, first the nigredo, or blackening, second the albedo, or whitening, and third, the rubedo, or reddening. As we enter the albedo phase, Jung tells us, we emerge from the painful and dark stage of the nigredo. The albedo is the "first main goal of the process," a moment that is "highly prized by many alchemists as if it were the ultimate goal." (Jung, 1944, para. 334) However, it is in fact only the penultimate stage: "The albedo [whitening] is, so to speak, the daybreak, but not till the rubedo is it sunrise." (Jung, 1944, para. 334) In a 1952 interview conducted by Mircea Eliade, Jung explicates this in psychological terms:

> [In] this state of "whiteness" one does not live in the true sense of the word, it is a sort of abstract, ideal state. In order to make it come alive it must have "blood," it must have what the alchemists call the rubedo, the "redness" of life. Only the total experience of being can transform this ideal state of the albedo into a fully human mode of existence. (Jung, 1987, p.229)

For Jung, this transition represents the birth of a new personality through relationship with the self, an interior process that involves the bringing together of the opposites, and especially the opposites of conscious and unconscious. In the Eliade interview, Jung depicts the albedo/rubedo transition in quasi-theological terms as an intrapsychic shift whereby evil becomes fully integrated into consciousness so that "the devil no longer has an autonomous existence but rejoins the profound unity of the psyche." (Jung, 1987, p. 229) Jung may describe the rubedo as a "fully human mode of existence," but his emphasis is entirely on the achievement of wholeness on the *intrapsychic* level. For example, "inner conflict, … always the source of profound and dangerous psychological crises," (Jung, 1987, p. 230) may be transcended, Jung suggests, through an experience of God qua *coincidentia oppositorum*. Clearly, this is an approach that remains squarely within the inner dimension of personality No. 2.

We can detect a dissatisfaction with Jung's approach in James Hillman's post-Jungian treatment of the same topic (Hillman, 1991).[7] In his 1991 paper, *The Yellowing of the Work* Hillman noted that in early alchemy, the three stages—*nigredo, albedo* and *rubedo*—were sometimes augmented by a further transitional stage known as the yellowing (*citrinitas* or *xanthosis*). This stage denoted that moment in the process when the *albedo* (whereby "the anima or soul infuses the work with its whiteness" [Hillman, 1991, p.83]) lost its virginal purity and became yellow on its way toward the final reddening. In contrast with the abstract quality of Jung's approach, Hillman chooses to discuss the topic from a clinical perspective (thereby necessarily introducing a relational aspect to the discussion):

> In analysis, this whiteness refers to feelings of positive syntonic transference, of things going easily and smoothly, a gentle, sweet safety in the vessel, insights rising, synchronistic connections, resonances and echoes, the dead alive on the moon as ancestors who speak with internal voices of the activated imagination—all leading to the invulnerable conviction of the primacy of psychic reality as another world apart from this world, life lived in psychological faith. (Hillman, 1991, p.84)

It seems to me that with this depiction of the albedo-dimension Hillman is also describing the therapeutic setting under the enchanted sway of personality No. 2—when, that is, it is kept separate from personality No. 1. In alchemical terms, an albedo therapy of this sort, which Hillman depicts in its peculiarly Jungian form, is lacking something important; it awaits the final yellowing transition, which will move the therapy away from what Jungian analyst and writer Stanton Marlan describes as "the whiteness and abstractions of psychological insight," (Marlan, 2014, p.112) and into something more full-bloodedly worldly— something, we might suggest, that involves the personality No. 1 dimension of life.

This seems to be what Jason Butler is also pointing to when he suggests that "the yellowing of the work marks a needed shift from the *unio mentalis*, the union of soul and spirit, toward a meeting of soul in body and world." (Butler, 2014, p.120) We should not, however, understand this shift solely in linear developmental terms. In a binocular approach, the *inner* "abstractions of psychological insight," which we have observed dominating Jung's psychological works (and, by most accounts, his therapeutic work), are not merely left behind or replaced by the more worldly and relational *outer* engagement, in a swing from one pole to the other. This alchemical transition entails the colouring (yellowing) of psychological life through the meeting of opposites. However, these are not the purely *inner* opposites implied in Jung's account, but the opposites of 1) inner-facing personality No. 2 insight, and 2) outer-facing personality No. 1 engagement.

If the albedo is an inner-facing process, the yellowing, as Hillman puts it, is to be found "outside: wherever interest is kindled, wherever the active attention (or what Freud named "object libido") turns away from itself to things, things lighting up to be consumed," (Hillman, 1991, p.83) It points outward toward "anywhere that the different appears, anything outside subjective reflection, any moment that intrudes upon white conscious-ness's love of its own lunar illumination, which is precisely where its blindness lies." (Hillman, 1991, p.84) However, it is important to remember that this dimension of outer engagement is held in tension with an inner reflective quality, such that in the process ("the third") both inner and outer are mutually transformed. This transformed state is what the alchemists imagine as the *rubedo*.

It is interesting to note that by introducing a clinical vignette into his paper, Hillman goes against his usual practice. Like Jung, Hillman generally prefers to avoid case histories (Hillman, 2012). Here, however, he clearly feels the topic needs the injection of a more relational dimension.

As we have seen, Hillman's description of the albedo phase of the therapy chimes with Jung's descriptions of the personality No. 2 realm:

Hers had been a very white analysis: two or three times a week; many dreams each session which she worked on assiduously; hours of solitude; reading, reflection, reverie, imagination, memory, nature; few relationships; eating alone; isolation owing to language difficulties; feelings and fantasies focused on the analysis and on me, the analyst. (Hillman, 1991, p.89)

However, as the therapy enters its ending-phase, the relationship appeared to enter a more chaotic phase:

Our rapport had become complicated—she seemed suddenly so dense—by the increasing presence of indelible emotions that seemed bent on destroying the harmony and illuminating insights that nevertheless still kept coming. Then, I rationalized these perceptions by attending mainly to what we were achieving. Today, looking back through my yellow-tinted lens, I believe that what was also being achieved—besides the evident yellow illumination—was actually a thorough spoiling of the white harmony which her emotions and my perceptions were clearly indicating, a spoiling which my own analytic whiteness resisted and tried to smooth over. (Hillman, 1991, p.91)

The "the white harmony" of the previous highly syntonic analytic relationship was now being spoiled. Newly problematic differentiations of feeling emerged breaking up the albedo collusions—feelings of merger— that had hitherto been taken for granted. Importantly, Hillman notes his own resistance to the process and acknowledges the temptation to hang onto a "smooth" albedo (personality No. 2) dimension of the therapy for as long as possible. Looking back, however, he can see that this yellow "spoiling" was a necessary stage in the termination of the therapy.

I would also suggest that Hillman's introduction of the clinical illustration not only serves a rhetorical point, in that it supplies the reader with an amplification of motifs and insights which, according to his argument, characterise the yellowing, but it also performs a yellowing of its own, in that the entry of the outer other (the client) into the paper has the effect of spoiling the aesthetic euphony of Hillman's sometimes all-too-clever and all-too-learned fine writing. The patient's embodied presence cannot but make itself felt as "other" to Hillman's hitherto dominant voice. Hillman's crafted paradoxes now begin to seem precious and finicky. As readers, we are forced into an encounter with *her*, a living and breathing person. She may have been introduced as an example, but the fullness of her personhood transcends the limitations of exemplarity.

Hillman's paper derives from a period in his intellectual evolution in which he made an overt attempt to move psychology beyond what he saw as the navel-gazing of individual personal development and by shifting our attention "from mirror to window" to achieve a connection with "the world."[8] Hillman describes the project in this way:

> [A]s the alchemical opus rescues the soul of the individual, so this opus can rescue the psyche of psychology conceived only in terms of the individual human. From the alchemical perspective the human individual may be a necessary focus but cannot be a sufficient one; the rescue of the cosmos is equally important. Neither can take place without the other. Soul and world are inseparable: anima mundi. It is precisely this fact that the yellowing makes apparent and restores, a fact which the white state of mind cannot recognize because that mind has unified into itself the world, all things psychologized. (Hillman, 1991, p.91)

On the face of it, Hillman seems to be describing both problem and solution in a way that chimes with the argument of this book. Unfortunately, however, Hillman's attempts to free himself from the limitations he rightly observes in Jung's inward-facing psychology have the effect of embedding him more deeply within it. This is because, as the passage above makes clear, he diagnoses the problem as an overfocus on the individual person within psychology. Hillman's solution is to prioritise instead what he calls "soul"—autonomous imaginal activity untethered from the actual person.

By identifying world with *anima mundi*, Hillman makes a move in the direction of Neoplatonic idealism, and this inevitably takes him away from engagement with the "other" (i.e., whatever lies "outside"). Hillman thus exacerbates Jung's own problematic separation of archetypal and personal; in effect, he severs the transcendental (personality No. 2) Jung—

who prioritises image—from the immanent (personality No. 1) Jung—who is embedded in that relational network that constitutes world. This wrong turn involves Hillman in attempting to reconnect with "world" by waging a war on "ego-psychology" (Hillman, 1992a, p.48) and the "subjective." (Hillman 1992b, pp.93–94)

Hillman's "yellowing" turn toward the world reveals a genuine recognition of the need to reconnect with the "outside." However, by making Jung's identification of image and psyche into a core principle, Hillman also makes it impossible for this "outside" to function as genuinely exterior. As we have seen, such a psyche cannot genuinely meet the world; it can only introject it.

Wolfgang Giegerich's variant on Analytical Psychology, "Psychology as a discipline of interiority," marks an escalation in the decoupling of "soul" and person that Hillman's archetypal psychology pioneered.[9] We can gain a sense of how radically untethered Giegerich's psychology is from actual persons in the world when we look at the definition of "psyche" presented at the website of The International Society for Psychology as the Discipline of Interiority:

[T]he psyche is not only the object of psychological in-vestigation, but at the same time, and recursively so, its subject. Having no point of perspective outside the psyche to view it from objectively and no substrate or pre-suppositional base in anything more substantial, literal, or positively existing, a truly psychological psychology, it follows, must be internal to itself, a discipline of internal reflection. ('A Definitional Statement' n.d.)

In more ways than one, this approach takes to its logical conclusion a tendency that we have identified as active in Jung writings, whereby the personal is radically differentiated from the archetypal, thus achieving a compartmentalisation of personality No. 1 and personality No. 2.[10] Giegerich not only achieves a once-and-for-all radical scission between the world of Jung's personality No. 2 and the world of personality No. 1, *he deliberately banishes the latter from the realm of psychology.*

## Wotan

By maintaining a *cordon sanitaire* between the realms of the two personalities, Jung preemptively erases the possibility of inhabiting the creative tension between the two. I shall now focus upon the implications of this strategy by looking at two contrasting examples of Jung's approach.

The question of Jung's problematic response to the rise of Nazism in Germany in the 1930s has, for good reasons, tended to be subsumed into questions about his anti-Semitism or sympathy with fascism. Although I would like to approach it here from a rather different direction, I hope that this approach will shed some light on those issues, too.

Jung's essay "Wotan" (Jung, 1936c) (first published in the *Neue Schweizer Rundschau*) gives us the most elaborated version of Jung's approach to the German Revolution. In it, Jung imagines the German *volk* to be his patient and takes up the role of psychotherapist to the nation. Faced with an ordinary patient, Jung takes into account the conscious, objective situation of his client but also listens to the voice of the unconscious, in the form of dreams or active imaginations, and he encourages the patient to do the same. Such a patient may well find himself or herself in a place of great conflict, especially when undergoing major transitions such as the so-called midlife crisis. When dealing with such crises, Jung tends to invoke what he calls the problem of the opposites. This means that the patient is required to stay in touch with the conflict and endure the tension between the opposites until such time as a solution emerges that can enable the patient to find a new conscious perspective. This process is what Jung refers to as the transcendent function (Jung, 1916d). If, however, the patient rejects one of the opposites as unacceptable, irrational, or immoral, such a process cannot occur, and the result is that the patient's neurotic one-sidedness is perpetuated.

It is in the nature of the unconscious that it will produce images, ideas, and emotions that feel unacceptable to the conscious ego. Healing, however, involves conscious engagement with precisely these images, ideas, and emotions. It is this therapeutic approach that, in his Wotan essay, Jung takes toward his patient, the German people. Jung's diagnosis is that, for various reasons including a relatively superficial, conscious identification on the one hand with Christian values and on the other with Enlightenment values, Germans have in later modernity become neurotically one-sided. In such a situation, as Jung puts it in an earlier text, the unconscious "seeks to replace an attitude of a whole people that has become inadequate with a new one." (Jung, 1920, para. 597) Jung discerns in the collective psyche of the German people a revivification of unconscious forces that have simmered beneath the surface of its culture for centuries. In this essay, Jung takes the step of identifying the most powerful of these forces with Wotan, the ancient high god of the Teutonic tribes. Through this mythological parallel, Jung intends to amplify the explosion of primitive energy he now sees occurring within the race-psyche of the Germans. Like the god Wotan himself, this primitive energy is so far from civilised consciousness that it tends to be rejected (especially by non-Germans) as thoroughly unacceptable.

Jung's thesis is that in 1930s Germany, the historical/cultural form this primitive Wotanic resurgence has taken is that of the rise of Hitler and the Nazi party. However distasteful these events may be to the (one-sided hyperrational) consciousness of modern Europe, they are, in Jung's professional opinion, psychologically necessary in the same way that, in the case of an ordinary patient, primitive shadow components are required for a healthy rebalancing of the whole psyche. In short, they compensate one-sidedness. Any diagnosis of the German situation that does not take into account the psychological importance of these unconscious and irrational forces, and insists on utilising only economic, political, and psychological interpretations, will, as Jung sees it, necessarily fail to grasp the situation on a sufficiently profound level and therefore will miss the fundamental point of what is occurring. As Jung puts it, "The unfathomable depths of Wotan's character explain more of National Socialism than all ... reasonable factors put together" (Jung, 1936c, para. 385).

This analysis of the collective individuation process of the German people also involves Jung in interpreting what appear to be conscious choices (such as the election of Hitler as chancellor) as mere symptoms of unconscious possession by the Wotan archetype. It follows, according to Jung's argument, that the German people (qua patient) is not to be regarded as the perpetrator of dangerous and immoral actions but rather as the *victim* of autonomous phenomena taking place within a necessary depth-psychological process (Jung, 1936c, para. 398). As is often the case for a person undergoing individuation, the process sometimes takes on a highly regressive tone. However, Jung suggests, what the onlooker may mistake for a dangerous reversion to primitivity is for the Germans the kind of temporary backward move that always presages a forward leap. As Jung puts it, "Wotan's reawakening is a stepping back into the past; the stream was dammed up and has broken into its old channel. But the obstruction will not last for ever; it is rather a *reculer pour mieux sauter*, and the water will overleap the obstacle." (Jung, 1936c, para. 399)

There are numerous problems with Jung's argument here, most of which I have no space to go into.[11] I shall therefore narrow the discussion down to a particular problem that relates closely to the discussion that has taken up the first half of this chapter. In brief, my suggestion is that Jung's treatment of the Wotan question offers us a particularly clear example of the kind of difficulty we have seen surfacing in his treatment of individual patients. This difficulty is intimately bound up with Jung's insistence on segregating the personal from the archetypal, prioritising the latter and obviating communication between the two. Jung thereby fails to do justice to the psycho-logic of the two personalities, which, as we have seen, points toward the fact that it is precisely the conflict, tension, and communication between the two realms that creates conditions necessary for psychic transformation. There is more to be said about this. However, before doing so, it will be helpful to shift our focus from world affairs to Jung's actual clinical practice. I intend to examine Jung's treatment of one particular patient, whose case vividly illustrates where Jung's policy of segregating the archetypal from the personal can lead.

## Jung and His Patients

As we have seen, Jung's theoretical reflections on the subject of psychotherapy highlight the importance of mutual connection and influence between both partners, analyst and analysand. He thus clearly implies that the therapeutic event involves a complex interweaving of both conscious relations and unconscious transference and countertransference dynamics—i.e., of both inner and outer factors. However, Jung's actual therapeutic practice (as we can see both from his own accounts and from those of his patients) seems to have led him to maintain a radical separation between personal and archetypal aspects of the therapy.

In his 1935 Tavistock Lectures, Jung makes a clear distinction between the way he treats material that emerges from the *personal* unconscious and the way he approaches the products of the *collective* unconscious. In order to illustrate the first category, Jung gives an example of a patient presenting Jung with a dream containing an image of water. Since this is supposedly an image from the *personal* unconscious, Jung brings to bear an attitude of not knowing, reminiscent of Keats's negative capability, on the grounds that this is the approach that best elicits associations embedded in the context of the client's particular life. He asks the patient what his particular associations to water may be:

> Do I know what he means by 'water'? Not at all. When I put the test word or a similar word to somebody, he will say 'green'. Another one will say '$H_2O$', which is something quite different. Another one will say 'quicksilver' or 'suicide'. In each case I know what tissue that word or image is embedded in. (Jung, 1935c, para. 174)

However, confronted by dream material that he judges to be a product of the *collective* unconscious, Jung takes a completely different tack, enlisting a process he calls "amplification," which is intended to place the material in a wider archetypal context but which often entails, as Robin McCoy Brooks puts it, "a formulaic reduction of the expanded material to a presumed archetypal core." (Brooks, 2013, p.87) In this latter case, far from employing an approach of not knowing, Jung employs his understanding of the archetypal/symbolic world to make strong suggestions to the client as to the psychological meanings of the dream images in question. Jung feels authorised by his assumption that the transpersonal unconscious is shared by both client and analyst to impose his own interpretations (based upon his extensive knowledge of myth, fairy tale, etc.) on the material. In the example given in the Tavistock lecture, Jung mentions the image of a crab that has occurred in a patient's dream:

[T]he crab is not a personal experience, it is an archetype. When an analyst has to deal with an archetype he may begin to think … [I]nasmuch as [the client] is not a person, inasmuch as he is also myself, he has the same basic structure of mind, and there I can begin to think, I can even provide him with necessary context because he will have none, he does not know where that crab-lizard comes from and has no idea what it means, but I know and can provide the material for him. (Jung, 1935c, para. 190)

What is happening here is that Jung is imposing upon his clients a rigid hermeneutic template, albeit a template derived from Jung's own experiences.

## For Example, Christiana Morgan

I now want to take a closer look at the way Jung dealt with one of his own clinical cases, that of Christiana Morgan. Morgan, a talented and intelligent American woman of 28, arrived in Zurich in June 1926. Although she was accompanied by her husband, she was following in the steps of her lover, Henry Murray (also married).

As it happened, Murray had himself arrived in Zurich for analysis with Jung a year earlier. According to Morgan's biographer, Claire Douglas, Murray's analysis had begun with a "long" session, during which Jung explained his marital and romantic situation. In turn, Jung, utilising ideas to be found in his recently published "Marriage as a psychological relationship," (Jung, 1925b)

told Murray not only about his theory of the uncontained partner in a marriage needing to roam, and about the different types of women, the mother and hetaira, but … also about his personal life. Jung spoke of Emma Jung as filling the role of wife and mother for him, while Toni Wolff filled that of lover, mystical sister, and muse. Jung suggested that such an arrangement was difficult but possible and for some men psychologically advantageous. It had risks… but if handled honestly and clearly, and if Harry was up to it, it would only add to his creativity. (Douglas, 1997b, p.132)

When Christiana Morgan arrived in Zurich, she began an analysis with Jung that lasted from June to November 1926. There are several aspects to the analysis that I would like to draw attention to.

Douglas tells us that Morgan suffered with a father complex that left her with a tendency to look to older men to solve her problems. Her pattern was to idealise older men and seek their love by excelling in their world.[12] Not surprisingly, this pattern became powerfully reconstellated in the context of Morgan's analytic relationship with Jung. We can, of course, not know exactly what Jung felt toward his patient and least of all how he responded to her on an unconscious level. However, Morgan's account of her therapy with Jung indicates that her own idealising transference was met by a kind of anima-dominated countertransference.

Such an event would certainly not be surprising, given what we know of Jung's previous relationships with Preiswerk, Spielrein, Wolff, and, as we have seen, more recently with Reichenstein. Under these circumstances, we might have expected that the work of consciously unpicking these tangled mutual transference projections would have become Jung's focus in the therapy. Unfortunately, as Douglas puts it, "Jung never adequately dealt with [Morgan's] idealization of her father or himself." (Douglas, 1997b, p.149) Nor do we have any evidence that Jung was aware of his own countertransference reactions.

Instead, what seems to have developed is a powerful unconscious collusion between analyst and patient. On the one hand, this made "Morgan extremely receptive to all that Jung said," and on the other, Jung's "attraction for her made him willing to give her extra time and energy." (Douglas, 1997b, p.149) Jung instructed Morgan "to live her life very much in the same way Toni Wolff lived hers—as adjunct to and in the service of her lover," (Douglas, 1997b, p.150) telling her, "Your function is to create a man ... so you become a really wise woman a *femme inspiratrice*—and so you give to man what he has not." (Douglas, 1997b, p.151) Here we can clearly see Jung attempting to impose upon Morgan an "archetypal" template that, as he understood it, fitted both his own experience and his psychological theory. Unfortunately, as the analysis continued, Morgan began to increasingly experience this template as a straitjacket.

## The Visions

Jung considered Morgan's visions to be so interesting that he made them the subject of a four-year seminar, which took place four years after Morgan had left Zurich. A transcript of this seminar, which was attended by Jungian insiders, was privately published in 1957, republished in two volumes by Spring Publications in 1976 (Jung, 1976), and finally in 1997 given a scholarly edition (also in two volumes) in Princeton Press's Bollingen imprint (Jung, 1997).

In 1926, the practice of active imagination had only recently been introduced to Zurich. Morgan was "encouraged by Jung and by Toni Wolff" (Douglas 1997b, p.155) to take it up, and she began to produce visions that were immediately recognised as outstanding. As Douglas (the editor of the Bollingen edition of the Visions seminars) tells us (though without apparently realising the transferential implications of her statement), "Christiana came up with an unprecedented production of artistic and imaginative archetypal material *just when this was the very stuff that would most interest her doctor,*" (Douglas, 1997b, p.156. My italics) We are not entirely surprised when Douglas goes on to tell us, "Jung warmed to Morgan at this point, treating her with unusual delicacy and care. He welcomed her as a rare companion who explored the depths he, too, had sounded. ... [He] paid a great deal of attention to Christiana, changing his schedule so that he could see her almost daily." (Douglas, 1997b, p.158) This latter detail is very striking, given that, at this time, Jung's time and attention were in great demand. Clearly, whatever else they may have been, Morgan's visions were offerings to Jung that constituted highly successful attempts to maintain herself in his gaze and thereby to stand out in a very crowded field.

Of course, Jung's fascination with Morgan's visions was contingent upon the assumption that they were channelling archetypal/symbolic material. Neither Jung nor his followers seem to have evinced any doubt that active imagination is a reliable means to produce such material in a particularly pure form, uncontaminated by personal considerations. This was presumably because Jung's own experience during his confrontation with the unconscious left him with a high degree of confidence in the technique. Given that his whole psychology was based upon the need to maintain psychic health by accessing the unconscious, it was perhaps inevitable that active imagination, a process by which conscious and unconscious were enabled to make direct contact, should be held up as a primary technique. However, given that the technique involves a highly conscious engagement between the "personal" ego and "impersonal" unconscious material, it seems likely that a certain amount of cross-contamination between the "personal" realm and the "archetypal" realm would occur. If so, then the assumption that the material produced is purely "archetypal" begins to seem naïve. In Morgan's case, as we shall see, the assumption is shown to be particularly problematic.

As we have already seen, Jung was well aware that "in the deepest sense we all dream not out of ourselves but out of what lies between us and the other." (Jung, 1973b, p.172) The clear implication is that dreams do not represent a private unconscious realm belonging to the dreamer alone but are, on the contrary, constellated out of a complex interplay among the personal, relational, cultural and archetypal. If this is true for dreams, then it is also true for active imaginations produced in the clinical context.

What complicated matters in 1926 was that Morgan's positive transference to Jung provided her with a powerful incentive to provide the kind of material that Jung would find interesting. In order to retain Jung's ongoing attention and positive regard, such material would have to be produced not only once but repeatedly. What is more, the material in question would need to be expressed in precisely the "archetypal" form that Jung found most fascinating. By producing weekly or even daily episodes of such a narrative, Morgan, Scheherazadelike, could thus perpetually defer the moment when she would lose Jung's attention, and thus end the therapy that seemed to offer so much. On Jung's side, the anima problem that we have seen in his relationships with Preiswerk, Spielrein, Moltzer, Wolff and Reichstein evidently continued to be active in 1926.

Our faith in the purely archetypal nature of Morgan's active imaginations is further diminished when we read that she was "coached" in the technique by Robert Edmond Jones, who had arrived in Zurich shortly before Morgan.[13] Jones, together with Morgan and her husband, "discussed their creations intensely among themselves." Such discussions occurred in situations "where … other analysands … could not help but overhear. They would greet each other in the streets of Zurich with cries of 'How's your Indian?' 'Are you still in the cavern?' or 'What's your magician up to today?'" Jones would ask Morgan directive questions like, "Ah, but is it dark enough? Is it deep enough? Is it black? It must be dark, darker!" (Douglas, 1997b, p.155)

This is in marked contrast with Jung's description of active imagination as an interior journey to be undergone in deepest solitude (though as I have shown, even those experiences had a far more relational aspect than Jung admitted). At the very least, they highlight a conscious, and even collective, dimension in the visions. One could make the case that they are not so much documents of the collective unconscious as they are communications from the hothouse culture of 1920s Jungian Zurich.

The important point is that Jung resolutely ignored the relevance of these "external" factors, persisting in his assumption that because the archetypal transcends the personal, it could therefore be treated as a separate, more important realm. This assumption led him to overlook the fuller context - both personal and cultural—within which such products emerged.

### The Climax of a *folie à deux*

Apparently blind to the intensity and significance of Morgan's transference, Jung seems to have remained oblivious to the inflationary potential of his words to her. He encouraged her to follow directly in his own footsteps, telling her, "I would advise you to put it all down as beautifully and as carefully as you can—in some beautifully bound book." (Douglas, 1997b, p.159) As Morgan's visions reached their climax, Jung told her that they were a sacrament holding "material for the next two or three hundred years. It is a great *document humaine*. It is the rushing forth of all that has hitherto been unconscious." (Douglas, 1997b, p.161)

215

The excitement constellated by the resulting inflation merely disguised Jung's inability or unwillingness to see through and make conscious the powerfully mutual transference/countertransference developments that lay behind it. Had Jung been able to bring these interpersonal dynamics into creative tension with what he saw as an archetypal evolution within Morgan, he might yet have achieved the kind of mutual transformation that he was later to describe in *The Psychology of the Transference*.

Douglas tells us that as time passed the imagery in Morgan's visions began to render her "in assertive and aggressive activity that sometimes troubled her interpreter." (Douglas, 1997a, p.xvi) Douglas suggests that Jung had both personal and cultural difficulties with these images and, as a result, dismissed such unfeminine characteristics as merely a product of a negative animus. By persisting in bringing such material to Jung, Morgan might have been expressing her own aggression toward her analyst. By expressing the other "negative" pole to her unrealistically "positive" transference onto Jung, Morgan implicitly challenged the mutual collusion that had arisen between them.

From what we read in Morgan's accounts of her sessions with Jung, nothing of this kind was discussed. The only way that Jung could have explored these dynamics would have been to bring together the personal (transference) dimension and the impersonal (archetypal) dimension. Given Jung's fixed idea that the personal and the archetypal occupied radically different dimensions such an analysis inevitably remained unavailable.

The analysis laboured increasingly under the complexities of Morgan's unconscious transference reactions that inflamed and were in turn inflamed by Jung's own countertransference. The result was a full-blown *folie à deux*, which, as Douglas points out with devastating under-statement, "ultimately detracted from [Morgan's] therapeutic progress." (Douglas, 1997b, 149)

Eventually (and in retrospect unsurprisingly), the analysis simply unraveled. Unable or unwilling to consciously address the possible transference meanings bound up in Morgan's visions' imagery, Jung seems to have begun to act out some of the unconscious dynamics that had developed between them. Having first encouraged Morgan's relationship with her lover, Murray, Jung "now started to sound jealous, as if the force unleashed in the visions belonged to him." (Douglas, 1997b, p.163) He then attempted "to restrain the flow of Morgan's images ... suggesting that she buy an etymological dictionary and take up the study of the mythic parallels of her visions." (Douglas, 1997b, p.164) Next, he resorted to deflating the specialness of her visions by comparing them unfavourably to his own (Douglas, 1997b, p.165). Finally, he "suggested that she drop all the inner work she was doing and settle down and have another child." (Douglas, 1997b, p.166) As Douglas tells us, "[Morgan] was still immersed in her visions and still hadn't resolved many of her analytic issues but agreed with his suggestion; her analysis came to an end in early November." (Douglas, 1997b, p.168)[14]

## The Limits of Interpretation

In Doug las' account of this episode, Morgan's visions are represented as an unfolding depiction of "a fully engendered woman reclaiming all the possibilities inherent in her psyche." (Douglas, 1997a, p.xvi) Douglas's argument involves her in portraying the visions as a pure and authentic outpouring of Morgan's unconscious. She expertly reveals how Jung's imposition of the conventional aspects of his anima concept on Morgan worked like a kind of Procrustean bed, giving her no psychic space in which to open up "a new path in search of a more comprehensive feminine identity." (Douglas, 1997a, p.xxv) However, although Douglas criticises Jung for having failed to honour the full range of Morgan's creative imagination, she seems to share Jung's faith in the archetypal authenticity of the visions. Douglas acknowledges that the visions emerged in the context of a powerful field of transference/countertransference, and she recognises that for Jung "to deny the influence of all these personal currents was naïve." (Douglas, 1997a, p.xxiii) However, she holds back from acknowledging that the *context* of the visions might have made a real contribution to the shaping of their *content.*

As we have seen, Jung saw archetypal material as occupying a category radically segregated from the personal. During his therapy with Morgan, this approach authorised Jung to explain to her the symbolic meanings of her imagery without any reference to the personal context of their production (which, in this case, meant the transference-dominated situation out of which they had emerged). Jung's interpretations of the content of her visions, as Morgan reports them, take what we can immediately recognise as an orthodox "Jungian" form:

> The men against the wheel means the beginning of individuation. The 8 spokes here are the eight functions. The wheel is a very ancient symbol for the soul. … The moon & arrow is spirituality through sexuality. The wigwam is the abode of the primitive hence symbolizes the unconscious. (Douglas, 1997b, p.157)

When, four years later, Jung started to utilise Morgan's material in his Zurich seminars, many of his interpretations, severed as they were from the transferential and personal context, took on a similarly formulaic tone. Apparently, after several years of this, the seminar members began to become "restive." Douglas reports that they increasingly took every opportunity to distract themselves by pursuing alternative topics (Douglas, 1997a, p.xxiv). Even Jung began to lose interest. By 1934, we find him telling his audience: "Now we will go on with the visions, which are in part annoying, or worse, they are boring . . . exceedingly uninteresting." (Jung, 1997, p.1310) It is hard not to suspect that if the visions were boring, it was probably because of Jung's insistence on reading them solely on the archetypal level. As Douglas puts it:

> By repressing the personal and dealing with Morgan's visions as if they were universals, the seminar itself began to take on the disembodied quality that Jung projected onto the visions and explained as Morgan's animus problem. And the further Jung departed from his patient and her material, the more he imposed abstract theories onto them, until, finally, the abstractions themselves and their theoretical implications obscured the visions and blotted out the visioner. (Douglas, 1997a, p.xxiv)

## Anonymity

When Jung wrote in 1930 to ask Morgan's permission to use the visions in his English-speaking seminar, he admitted that he had already used them without her permission in a short German language seminar. He hastened to reassure her that her material had been used "from a purely impersonal point of view naturally, hiding any personal inferences." (Quoted in Shamdasani, 2005, p.114) There are two different difficulties with this statement. First, as we have suggested, to attempt to treat any psychic product as *purely* impersonal—i.e. to simply exclude the personal context—is arguably to subject the material to a fatal level of distortion. Second, given that this seminar was taking place a mere four years after Morgan's departure and given that Jungian Zurich was a hotbed of jealousies and rivalries, in which privacy was neither sought nor possible, Jung's suggestion that it would be possible for Morgan's material to remain safely anonymous seems absurdly optimistic. That Jung continued to have concerns about this issue is evident in a letter written to Morgan on August 15, 1932:

> Concerning the trances I am well aware of the personal side of it, but I carefully kept away from any hint to the personal implications. Otherwise people begin to find it too interesting and then they fall into the error to devour each others personal psychology instead of looking for themselves and learning the more difficult task of an impersonal attitude. There are some, quick enough to grasp something of the actual personal background and it is often difficult to keep them off the scent. Life on a personal level is the smaller affair, the higher level however is impersonal. And there is such a thing as responsibility to history. (Quoted in Shamdasani, 2005, p.114)

Here, Jung mixes up two quite different considerations: first, the quite proper requirement that Morgan's anonymity be prioritised; and second, his need to segregate the personal from the "impersonal," which he seeks to dignify with a grandiose invocation of his "responsibility to history." For all that, Jung put little actual effort into ensuring that Morgan remain anonymous. In fact, by the time of Jung's letter, Morgan's anonymity had already been compromised. In late 1931, Ralph Eaton, a young philosopher and rejected ex-lover of Morgan's, arrived in Zurich to consult with Jung about his affair with Morgan. Invited by Jung to attend the Visions seminar, Eaton immediately recognised the identity of their author.[15] We should also remember that Toni Wolff, who had been analyst to Morgan's husband, was present throughout the seminar.

Despite the incestuous nature of the proceedings, the seminar continued for another two years before Morgan, angry and upset at the fact that her identity had become common knowledge, insisted that Jung terminate it. Not surprisingly, Jung's attempt to utilise Morgan's material "from a purely impersonal point of view ... hiding any personal inferences" had failed. One can perhaps conclude that when the personal gets suppressed in favour of the archetypal in the way that Jung attempted, it tends to find a way to disrupt proceedings willy-nilly.

## Back to the Split

In the published version of the seminars, Jung opens proceedings with this interesting comment:

> I omit personal details intentionally, because they matter so little to me. We are all spellbound by external circumstances, and they make our minds deviate from the real thing, which is that we ourselves are split inside. Appearance blinds us and we cannot see the real problem. (Jung, 1997, p.7)

Jung here identifies the "real problem" with a state of splitness. As we have seen, this was the issue that he himself had wrestled with throughout his early years, and it was also the problem that, as I have argued, subsequently evolved into the foundational question behind his whole psychology. Unfortunately, I would argue, he here exacerbates that very splitness by insisting upon a strict differentiation between "external circumstances" (here identified with "personal details") which he claims have no importance, and what really matters: "the real thing ... the real problem." To be "spellbound" by the former, Jung suggests, is to be blind to the latter. What Jung doesn't seem to be willing to entertain is the possibility that one might also become "spellbound" by an archetypal realm, untethered to the personal. In both cases, to be spellbound means to be one-sided. What Jung dismisses here as unimportant are precisely the No. 1 concerns which, according to the logic of *MDR*'s storm lantern dream, need to be brought into relational tension with the "deep" reality of No. 2. In other words, even if Jung is right to claim that the "real problem" is one of inner splitness, the solution (i.e., Jung's own solution) is not to segregate No. 1 from No. 2 by making a radical differentiation of the archetypal from the personal, but to find ways to bring the two together. In practice, this might mean allowing the "personal" transferential dimension of the therapy to enter a field of play in which it could meet with the "archetypal" imagery produced by active imagination, or rather to acknowledge that the two dimensions are always already in play.

It might be argued that Jung's primary goal in conducting the seminar in question was not to provide insight about the complexities of this or any other therapeutic process, but rather to concentrate upon amplifying the symbolic content of Morgan's visions and to offer thereby educational insights into archetypal phenomena. The problem with this argument is that by imposing a *cordon sanitaire* between archetypal content and the personal context within which that content had been constellated, Jung distorts the material in such a way that its educational potential becomes extremely limited.

## What is Active Imagination?

I have questioned Jung's tendency to take Morgan's active imaginations as pure products of the collective unconscious, and I have suggested that a proper analysis of the "visions" would require not only an archetypal lens but both personal and cultural lenses, too. It follows that any really productive analysis of them would need to focus upon the interplay among personal, cultural, and archetypal elements. However, having acknowledged this much, the question that arises is this: If this is true of Morgan's active imaginations, then is the same not true of all active imaginations. If so, what of the creation myth of Jungian psychology, i.e., Jung's own confrontation with the unconscious? Surely, Jung's visions too need to be approached as a complex interweave of personal, cultural, and archetypal factors.

As we saw in the last chapter, the figures whom Jung meets in his confrontation with the unconscious are dressed up with archaic mythological or Gnostic names and thus appear to emanate from the far reaches of the collective unconscious. What this disguises, according to Wolfgang Giegerich, is the extent to which, in *The Red Book*, Jung is engaging with the intellectual, cultural, and political world of 1913, and specifically with the spiritual situation of contemporary Christianity in the wake of Nietzsche. What I would add to this is the suggestion that, as we saw in the earlier discussion of dream of the killing of the hero, Jung is also simultaneously working through some of the more personal issues that arose in his relationships with Freud and Spielrein. If any of this is true, then Jung's attempt to represent *The Red Book* as purely an engagement with the spirit of the depths and a rejection of the spirit of this time is not only naïve but profoundly misleading. What we witness in *The Red Book* is, in fact, a meeting between Jung's conscious thinking and Jung's unconscious thinking, and the latter contains a complex mixture of personal, cultural, and archetypal factors. As such, it can only be understood if we are willing to recognise that each of these factors is embedded inextricably in the others.

Jung's image of and response to his anima tells us a great deal about 1) his personal relationships with specific women (as we have already explored), 2) his culturally bound responses to women and the feminine, and 3) a personified contra-ego that opens Jung's eyes to those aspects of the psyche that transcend the limitations of the ego. None of these three has priority over the others, and each is bound up with both the others. If we understand the personal and cultural aspects as belonging to personality No. 1 and the archetypal as belonging to personality No. 2, then what becomes clear is that any real insight can only come from the interplay between both personalities.

## And Back to Wotan

I now want to return to a topic that would, at first glance seem, unrelated to the ins and outs of Jung's analysis of Christiana Morgan and her visions: Jung's attempts to provide a depth psychological analysis of contemporary events in 1930s Germany. However, if we place the two together, we can see that Jung's treatment of both brings about similar problems for very similar reasons. In the Wotan essay, Jung insists first that the mythological dimension of the issue should be seen as entirely separate from any historical/social/economic dimensions—in much the same way, and for the same reasons that in his therapeutic practice he seems to have compartmentalised archetypal and personal. Second, in both cases Jung prioritises the former and implicitly devalues the latter, an approach that seems to echo his treatment elsewhere of the realms of personality No. 2 and personality No. 1.

The extreme dichotomy that Jung establishes in the Wotan essay between the historical/social/economic dimension and the mythological dimension also recalls the way Jung in *The Red Book* dealt with the First World War and its causes. There, Jung suggested that current events should be approached not via the "spirit of this time," utilising the kind of rational approach to be found in historical discourse (characterised by Jung as "explaining and ordering things" [Jung, 2009, p.229]) but rather via the irrational "spirit of the depths," which, he claims, rules "the depths of everything contemporary" (Jung, 2009, p.229) and which is, according to Jung, "beyond justification, use, and meaning." (Jung, 2009, p.229) We can see another parallel to this approach in Jung's controversial comments during the 1930s on the differences between what he calls "Jewish psychology" (i.e., psychoanalysis) and German psychology (i.e., Analytical Psychology). Jung represents the former as possessing a "materialistic, rationalistic view of the world" (Jung, 1973b, pp.164–65) and as having therefore lost the connection to the creative depths of the soul, while he portrays the latter as uniquely able do justice to the "creative powers of the psyche labouring at the future; not just a dreary fragment but the meaningful whole." (Jung, 1934c, para. 354)[16]

At any rate, in all three of these examples, Jung sets up a clear dichotomy, in which one of the pair is highlighted as valuable and the other rejected as valueless. At no point does Jung appear to entertain the possibility that a more comprehensive understanding might be gained by bringing both of these apparently contradictory approaches together.

When it comes to Jung's attempt to account for the rise of Hitler, despite an insistence that he is providing a solely mythological approach, he does nonetheless assume a broadly historical context for the return of Wotan, although the history in question is in the service of a (Jungian) logic of compensation. The historical narrative that Jung likes to emphasise is one in which the dominant rationalism of the Enlightenment, with its emphasis upon consciousness, has, in the modern world, constellated an enantiodromic compensatory shift toward the dark unconscious psychic forces that Wotan expresses. As George Williamson among others has shown, post-Romantic, anti-Enlightenment, ideas, and specifically ideas highlighting Germanic mythology, were, throughout the 19th century, persistently intertwined with reactionary movements, nationalism, and even anti-Semitism (Williamson, 2004).

If Jung had taken a more nuanced approach toward the complex ebbs and flows that have characterised the history of modern German culture i.e., an approach that *engaged with* that history rather than rejecting it out of hand—he might perhaps have taken a more ambivalent attitude toward those energies he identifies with Wotan. He seems to have believed that his mythological/archetypal perspective on the phenomenon of the Nazi revolution offered him an objective view on what was occurring. Unfortunately, what it actually meant was that Jung, knowingly or not, was, in Walter Benjamin's words, supplying "auxiliary services to National Socialism." (Benjamin and Scholem, 1980, p.197) Moreover, defences of Jung's actions based upon the idea that he was merely a man of his time and that we are therefore critiquing his position from an anachronistic position, founder when we read Benjamin's words, which were written in 1937 (and those of, for example, Thomas Mann in 1935).[17]

Had Jung been able to bring the historical dimension into tension with the archetypal, he might also have achieved a far more fruitful analysis of to the question and one that furthered the psycho-logic of the two personalities.[18]

1 The best treatment of this subject is to be found in David Sedgwick's *The Wounded Healer: Countertransference from a Jungian Perspective* (Sedgwick, 1994)

2 In *Symbols of Transformation* (Jung 1912/1952), Jung uses the visions of "Miss Miller," (which he had found in a 1905 article in Flournoy's *Archives de Psychologie*); in "Psychology and Alchemy," he analyses the dreams of Wolfgang Pauli, whose case, as we shall see, he had deliberately handed over to another analyst. Even the famous "Solar Phallus Man" was not one of Jung's patients.

3 Perhaps, in truth, a more important consideration behind Jung's prophylactic attempts with Pauli was that of scientific plausibility: If Jung could show that Pauli's dreams (like, for example, the mythology of an obscure Amazonian tribe) were produced outside of Jung's influence, then they would function more effectively as evidence of the truth of Jung's claims. Hillman suggests that Jung's efforts were meant to ensure "that the demonstration of his theory by means of the case [should be] yet more objectively empirical." (Hillman, 2012, p.32) However, even this consideration doesn't seem to make much sense, since it would always be Jung's interpretations of the dreams that were under scientific scrutiny, rather than the dreams themselves

4 Jung was drawn to alchemy for several different reasons, including its imaginal richness, its linguistic complexity, its obscurity, and its paradoxicality. However, his central thesis is that alchemy performs a shadow role with regard to Christianity that is corrective of one-sidedness in the same way as that of Analytical Psychology (according to Jung) within modern Western culture. This involves it in "redeeming" topics that have been rejected by the dominant culture, such as the

feminine, evil, and matter. It utilises the premodern paradigm of *correspondence*, whereby macrocosm reflects and is reflected by microcosm. As the alchemical nostrum tells us, "As above so below." Such a paradigm predates the subject/object split of Descartes and the scientific perspective of modernity and overcomes (or ignores) the conceptual compartmentalisation of inner versus outer. As von Franz puts it, "[for the alchemists] the major part of what we call today the psyche was located outside the individual in the animated matter of the universe." (von Franz, 1992, p.177)

5 Roger Brooke approaches this issue from a different (phenomenological) direction but comes to a similar conclusion: for example, he describes Jung's theories of synchronicity and of the *unus mundus* as "a magical attempt on Jung's part to jump over the chasm that his separation of subject and object had already created." (Brooke, 2015, p.14, n. 3)

6 This work has been attempted in various ways by various different post-Jungian thinkers. Nathan Schwartz-Salant (Schwartz-Salant, 1998), Mario Jacoby (Jacoby, 1984) and Andrew Samuels (Samuels, 2006) have, in different ways attempted to spell out and develop Jung's alchemical intuitions in a specifically clinical setting. In an interesting paper bringing together Jung and Marx, David Holt has suggested that, for Jung, alchemy "belongs in the world of extraversion as well as of introversion, and ... its extraverted mode is expressed in the intercourse between man and nature ..." (Holt, 1992, p.141)

7 It is important to note that Hillman's essay "The Yellowing of the Work," was written at a point when he was turning away from a style of post-Jungian psychology that he felt had become too inward-looking, and attempting to extend his ideas outward, into the world. I introduce Hillman's personal equation and its vicissitudes here in an attempt to bring the personal into binocular play with the theoretical; it should not be seen as a reduction of one to the other.

8 For more developed presentations of this project, see Hillman's "Anima Mundi: The Return of the Soul to the World" (Hillman, 1982) and "From

Mirror to Window: Curing Psychoanalysis of Its Narcissism." (Hillman, 1989)

9 In fact, Giegerich himself identifies Hillman's paper on the "Yellowing of the Work" as offering support to his own emphasis upon *thinking* as the proper activity of soul: "My move from ontology and the pure imagination to logic corresponds to the emphasis on the intellectual (logical) form or status that Hillman, in his paper on the yellowing of the Work, relying on a statement by the alchemist Dorneus, correlates with the yellowing phase." (Giegerich, 1994, p.323)

10 In a previous article I suggested that by putting this differentiation at the center of his psychology, Giegerich was taking a step away from the Jungian tradition (Saban, 2015). It now seems to me that in fact Giegerich's psychology of interiority is all too true to Jung in ways that I had failed to see at that time and that it therefore functions as a kind of *reductio ad absurdum* of an important aspect of Jung's psychology.

11 These problems include, among others: 1) Jung's assumption that collective psychology behaves in exactly the same way as individual psychology; 2) the consequent lifting of collective responsibility from Hitler and the Germans who supported him; 3) the uninterrogated assumption that a mythic figure embedded in an ancient cultural context could "return" and become active in a modern context, and the ignoring of the historical fact that the Nazis' ideology involved them in a conscious and deliberate embracing of exactly such parallels (a process that relied upon a complex and ongoing historical relationship between nationalism and a revisioned mythology, in figures such as Grimm and Wagner (see for example, Williamson, 2004); 4) Jung's assumption that there exists such a thing as an identifiable German race-psyche that is somehow independent of German culture as socially/historically constructed.

12 Douglas tells us that Morgan "learned to attract [her father's] attention and please him. Even as a toddler she would run into him a breakfast and demand, 'Heed me, Papa,' as she climbed into his lap to talk." (Douglas, 1997b, p.33) She also informs us that "[Christiana] had a father complex, which kept her looking to strong and wise men to solve her

spiritual conflict in the same way she had looked to her father in childhood as the resolver of her problems." (Douglas, 1997b, p.146)

[13] Jones (1887-1954) was an American theatre designer, famous for his work with Eugene O'Neill

[14] Sonu Shamdasani, in the process of attempting to demolish Deirdre Bair's biography of Jung, also attacks Douglas's treatment of the Morgan case (Shamdasani, 2005, pp.112ff). In the face of Douglas's attempts to imply that there may have been sexual impropriety between Jung and Morgan (something I am not suggesting here), he attempts to show that Jung's behavior toward Morgan was proper and above board. In order to support his position, he quotes various letters from Morgan to Jung. In one, she apparently told Jung that "[s]he was not pleased that Peter Baynes had informed someone as to her identity, but ultimately had a sense that such experiences were not purely personal and belong to Jung and his work as much as to herself." (Shamdasani, 2005, p.114) In another, she informed "him of the gratitude in which she and Henry Murray held him. She informed him that it was through him, and in particular, his concept of the anima, that they found the "Way", and that they owed their creative life and joy to him." (Shamdasani, 2005, p.114) It seems naïve of Shamdasani to quote such letters as if they proved anything, other than Morgan's continuing desire to maintain Jung's approval. Morgan never seems to have entirely emerged from the idealising transference that accompanied her analysis with Jung. For example, having produced visions that echoed those in Jung's *Red Book*, Morgan went on to replicate Jung's Bollingen tower in New England (Douglas, 1997b, p.222). However, the fact that Morgan remained under Jung's influence cannot be used as evidence of either the effectiveness or the quality of Jung's therapeutic treatment. At any rate, the "creative life and joy" Morgan felt she owed to Jung was sadly not sufficient to avert her 1967 suicide (Douglas, 1997b, pp.313-5).

[15] Eaton, having himself become psychologically inflated by Jung's relentlessly archetypal interpretations of his material, returned to America in a full-blown psychosis and promptly killed himself (Douglas, 1997b, pp.209-10).

16 We might speculate that, just as Jung's own anima problem, unrecognised, powerfully affected the progress of the Morgan case, so, in this example, his Freud-complex affected his ability to engage in a balanced way with the question of national psychologies.

17 Mann wrote in his diary in 1935:

> If a highly intelligent man like Jung takes the wrong stand, there will naturally be traces of truth in his position that will strike a sympathetic note even in his opponents. ... His scorn for "soulless rationalism" has a negative effect only because it implies a total rejection of rationalism, when the moment has long since come for us to fight for rationality with every ounce of strength we have. Jung's thought and his utterances tend to glorify Nazism and its "neurosis." He is an example of the irresistible tendency of people's thinking to bend itself to the times—a high-class example . . . He swims with the current. He is intelligent, but not admirable. Anyone nowadays who wallows in the "soul" is backward, both intellectually and morally. The time is past when one might justifiably take issue with reason and the mind (Mann, 1982, pp. 201 and 235).

For this topic generally, see Jay Sherry's comprehensive *Carl Gustav Jung: Avant-Garde Conservative* (Sherry, 2012).

18 As it happens, post-Jungians pursuing the idea of the cultural complex have attempted to cultivate a perspective that is more historically (and politically) aware, although, in my opinion the results have been hampered by an insufficiently acute awareness of two kinds of related problems: first, those associated, as we have seen with the one-sidedness of Jung's approach to current events; and second, the category problems that show up when intrapsychic dynamics are applied to the world historical stage (See Singer and Kimbles, 2004; and for a critique Lu, 2013).

# A CONCLUSION

When I began to write this book, my aim was to investigate "the problem of the opposites" in Jung's psychology. But behind this question, as I look back now, I can see that I was engaged with another wider issue: Does Analytical Psychology constitute a coherent psychological approach, or is it merely a ragbag of different ideas that happened to have been thought up by C. G. Jung? If the former is the case, and my strong intuition told me that it is, then where do we locate the coherence of Jung's psychology?

I think this more fundamental question has been gradually gaining significance for me as a result of the years I have spent teaching under-graduates and master's degree students about Analytical Psychology. Of course, it is more than possible to teach Jung piecemeal; one can deliver a seminar on archetypes, a lecture on synchronicity, a talk on typology, and eventually one has covered the topics that seem to make up Analytical Psychology. However, does this mean that one has conveyed what Jung's psychology is really about? I think not.

If we read Jung's *Collected Works* and then push on through the canon of classical Jungian literature, I suspect we will be left wondering where, if anywhere, the center of gravity of this psychology lies. Most of Jung's texts concentrate upon the archetypes and the collective unconscious. He seems to be making enormous efforts to persuade his readers about those of his ideas that are unfamiliar to them, and these also seem to be the ideas that he himself identifies as central to his psychology. However, if we do take the archetypes to be the axial notion of Analytical Psychology, how then should we evaluate Jung's writings on typology or on synchronicity?

Are they therefore peripheral? If not, then what is the red thread that ties these apparently very different ideas together?

My conclusion is that it is Jung's notion of individuation that roots the whole psychology. Individuation goes deeper than the archetypes, the collective unconscious, the complexes, typology, and synchronicity, because it points us beyond concepts, things, or persons toward the notion of process. Individuation is process, is transformation. And transformation brings us back to another process—that of psychotherapy,

If we think about the archetypes or the complexes, we can see that in practice, in real life, they always show up in the context of the process of individuation because they always reveal themselves, whether in dream or active imagination, as the response to a problem. Complexes seek to draw our attention to what the conscious ego is missing, and synchronicities wake us up to the wider picture. Whatever our dominant type, it is the inferior function that will again and again draw our attention to the narrow one-sidedness of our perspective. When it really comes down to it, these phenomena are in the service of individuation. On the deepest level, there are no individuals, only individuations. This means that not only am I individuating, but my relationships are individuating, and my family is individuating, and my culture is individuating. Most importantly, for the purposes of this book, Analytical Psychology is individuating.

This book began with Jung's foundational statement about the two personalities: "Somewhere deep in the background I always knew that I was two persons." (Jung, 1989, p.44) What I have suggested here is nothing less than that his entire psychological project can be usefully seen as his attempt to work through this problem. In the first three chapters of *MDR*, we saw him trying to solve the problem in various ways. He tried to live within the limits of one personality, and then the other, but finally realised that neither of these attempted solutions allowed him to achieve the possibility of wholeness. Reluctantly he came to the conclusion that it was a psychological imperative for him find a way to allow both personalities, both dimensions of human existence, to coexist within his own life.

# A Conclusion

I have argued that it was this insight that, during Jung's "confrontation with the unconscious," led to the dialogical engagement between ego consciousness and various inner unconscious figures, and, on a more conceptual level, to the development of the transcendent function, whereby psychological transformation emerges from the meeting of what Jung calls "the opposites." As I hope I have made clear, the mature psychology that Jung subsequently developed has, at its center, the idea that the process of psychological development, or individuation, depends upon a repeated exposure to such experiences and that only in this way can the individual avoid falling into one-sidedness.

As I have researched these ideas, it has become increasingly apparent to me that while, on the one hand, Jung was extremely consistent in pursuing this basic notion within certain chosen arenas, there are, on the other hand, several important arenas within which different rules seem to apply, and within these arenas, Jung, instead of encouraging the bringing together of opposites, insists upon splitting the two apart and keeping them apart, by segregating them into radically different dimensions of psychological life. By drawing attention to these problems and showing the difficulties that have resulted from Jung's policy, I have tried to point to ways in which a post-Jungian psychology might itself, acting according to the logic of the two personalities, achieve a correction of the one-sidedness that has shadowed Analytical Psychology from the beginning.

This book can rightly be regarded as a fundamental critique of Jung's psychology. However, it can also be regarded as an attempt to apply to that psychology Jung's own dynamic of opposites. It therefore represents, in one sense, an *internal* critique, not because it is performed by an insider, someone who is by training and inclination a Jungian of many years standing, but, more importantly, because the critique in question brings to bear on Jung's psychology what is a fundamental principle of Jungian theory—the idea that psychological health is defined by the avoidance of one-sidedness. The implications of this internal critique point then toward the necessity for a meeting with and challenge by the outer other. The principle of individuation, as I understand it, requires a relentless process of exposure to what is "other," not only that domesticated "other" that we

233

like to set up as a straw man enemy, but, more importantly that frighteningly alien "other" that insists that we relinquish our comfort zone.

The comfort zones that are most dangerous to psychological development are those that have become ring-fenced as psychological. To the extent that Jung identifies individuation as a process that can only occur intrasychically, Jung builds a wall around psychological development and thereby rejects or demotes those psychological possibilities that come from, for example, relational engagement with outer others. This outer-relational realm of psychological life then becomes precisely the "other" with which his psychology needs to engage if it is serious about avoiding one-sidedness. This is no more and no less than the logic of individuation.

When Jung identifies the archetypal realm alone as the "real thing" and rejects or diminishes the personal realm, and then builds a conceptual wall between the two, he makes it impossible to follow his own logic of individuation, which would require that he bring the two together, and achieve thereby a binocularity of perspective that, by transcending each alone, creates a new three-dimensional viewpoint. When he insists that a mythological interpretation alone can bring insight to world events, and rejects historical, sociological, economic, and political interpretations as superficial, he loses the chance to follow the logic of individuation, whereby it is precisely by engaging with the tensions and contradictions between these two contrasting realms of interpretation that we can become midwives to the birth of a new kind of interpretation. In all these cases, Jung prefers to make a retreat into his fortified comfort zone (or as Giegerich puts it, makes a "flight into the unconscious"). He thereby not only ignores the psychological principle that he himself first articulated, but by shirking the challenge of the opposites, he allows his psychology to regress into one-sidedness.

In this book, I have spent a great deal of time and space focusing upon specific texts of Jung and specific details within those texts in order to understand how he came to develop his ideas the way he did. For some, this focus will seem to betray a regressive inability to outgrow Jung and move forward. My own opinion is that the individuation of Analytical

# A Conclusion

Psychology can only be furthered by paying proper attention to the problems and distortions that have been and remain deeply embedded within that psychology. They are inextricably bound up with that psychology because they were Jung's problems and distortions, and Analytical Psychology was Jung's psychology.

If we want that psychology to individuate, we need it to meet and engage with its own other; in this case, that requires it to face up to Jung's shadow. By this I mean not only the inevitable limitations of his personality (e.g., his racism, misogyny, and reactionary politics) but the shadow of Jung's personal equation, in the image of which Analytical Psychology was created. As I have tried to show, this linkage between the man and the psychology is one of the strengths of Jungian psychology, because it grounds it in a living experience of individuation. However, this strength is also its greatest weaknesses.

One aspect of this paradoxical problem has to do with what Jung identified as the *imitatio Christi*:

> Christ can indeed be imitated even to the point of stigmatization without the imitator coming anywhere near the ideal or its meaning. For it is not a question of an imitation that leaves a man unchanged and makes him into a mere artifact, but of realizing the ideal on one's own account—Deo concedente—in one's own individual life. (Jung, 1944/52, para. 7)

The problem is not that Jungians have, in a trivial or superficial way, aped Jung himself. Worse, by imitating the one-sidedness of Jung's ideas, they have chosen to lock themselves into a very narrow, inward-looking perspective. The dogmatisation of Jung's psychology, and the obsessive revisiting of those themes that Jung favoured, is precisely not "realizing the ideal on one's own account." What thus gets missed (and thus erased) is what is essential in Jung's psychology: individuation as an interminable engagement with the other.

In a previous article, I enlisted Harold Bloom's contrast between weak misreadings and strong misreadings (Bloom, 1975) as an aid in thinking about the ways that Analytical Psychology can individuate (Saban, 2014). According to (my misreading of) Bloom, when I read any canonical work, my reading must inevitably be a misreading, since the reading consists of me meeting that work with my own assumptions, challenges, under-standings—in other words, my own personal equation. However, the choice I can make is between performing a weak misreading, which will inevitably "have single, reductive, simplistic meanings," (Bloom, 1982, p.285) or a strong misreading whereby my reading owns its own partiality and goes on to create out of the encounter between it and me something new, strange, and complex.

According to Bloom's taxonomy, much of classical Jungian literature is offering a weak misreading of Jung. Because such a reading sets itself the unambitious task of clarifying or simplifying or merely re-presenting Jung's ideas, it fails to take on the challenge of engaging them creatively and thus fails to individuate them. The irony is that it thereby also fails to rise to the ideas themselves, which, according to Jung's own logic of individuation, need to meet and be brought into tension with whatever they lack. Unless Jung's ideas meet such a challenge, unless they are met by a strong misreading, they will calcify and die, or worse, become the dogma of a cult.

My goal here has been to present a strong misreading of Jung. However, ultimately it can only be *my* misreading. The best I can hope for from my readers is to be strongly misread in my turn. I therefore look forward to that challenge.

# REFERENCES

"A Definitional Statement". n.d. *International Society for Psychology as the Discipline of Interiority Homepage* (blog). Accessed January 30, 2019. https://www.ispdi.org/index.php.

Anthony, M. (1999) *Jung's Circle of Women: The Valkyries*. Lake Worth FL.: Nicolas-Hays.

Atwood, G. E., & Stolorow, R. D. (1977). Metapsychology, reification, and the representational world of C. G. Jung. *International Review of Psycho-Analysis*, 4, 197–214.

Bair, D. (2004). *Jung: A Biography*. London, England: Little, Brown.

Barreto, M. H. (2016). The riddle of Siegfried: Exploring methods and psychological perspectives in Analytical Psychology. *Journal of Analytical Psychology* 61 (1): 88–105.

Beebe, J., & Falzeder. E. (2013). Introduction. In Beebe, J., & Falzeder. E. (Eds.). *The Question of Psychological Types: The Correspondence of C. G. Jung and Hans Schmid-Guisan, 1915-1916*, (pp. 1-32). Princeton, NJ: Princeton University Press.

Benjamin, W. & Scholem G. (1980). *The Correspondence of Walter Benjamin and Gershom Scholem, 1932-1940*. Cambridge, MA: Harvard University Press.

Bennet, E. A. (1985). *Meetings with Jung: Conversations Recorded During the Years 1946-1961*. Zürich, Switzerland: Daimon Verlag.

Berry, P. (1978). Defense and telos in dreams. *Spring: An annual of archetypal thought*: 115-127.

Bleuler, E. (1918). Consciousness and Association. In Jung, C. G. (Ed.), *Studies in Word-Association*, (pp. 266-296). London, England: William Heinemann.

Bloom, H. (1975). The necessity of misreading. *The Georgia Review*, Vol. 29, No. 2 (Summer 1975), 267-288

Bloom, H. (1982). *Agon: Towards a Theory of Revisionism*. Oxford, England: Oxford University Press

Borch-Jacobsen M. & Shamdasani, S. (2011). *The Freud Files: An Inquiry into the History of Psychoanalysis*. Cambridge, England: Cambridge University Press.

Brenner, I. (2009). On splitting of the ego: A history of the concept. In Bokanowski, T. & Lewkowicz, S. (Eds.). *On Freud's "Splitting of the Ego in the Process of Defence,* (pp. 9-26). London, England: Karnac Books

Bromberg, P.M. (1996). The Multiplicity of Self and the Psychoanalytic Relationship. In: *Standing in the Spaces: Essays on Clinical Process Trauma and Dissociation*. (pp. 267-290) Hillsdale, NJ: Routledge

Brooke, R. (2013). Notes on the phenomenology of interiority and the foundations of psychology. *International Journal of Jungian Studies*, 5(1), 3-18.

Brooke, R. (2015). *Jung and Phenomenology*. Hove; New York, NY: Routledge.

Brooks, R. M. (2013). The ethical dimensions of life and analytic work through a Levinasian lens. *International Journal of Jungian Studies* 5 (1): 81-99.

Burleson, B. (2005). *Jung in Africa*. New York, NY: Bloomsbury Academic.

Butler, J. A. (2014). *Archetypal Psychotherapy: The Clinical Legacy of James Hillman*. New York, NY: Routledge.

Cambray, J. (2012). *Synchronicity Nature and Psyche in an Interconnected Universe*. College Station, TX: Texas A&M University Press.

Carotenuto, A. (1984). *A Secret Symmetry: Sabina Spielrein Between Jung and Freud*. New York, NY: Pantheon Books.

Carotenuto, A. (1985) *The Vertical Labyrinth: Individuation in Jungian Psychology*. Toronto, Ontario: Inner City Books.

Casement, A. (2010) Sonu Shamdasani Interviewed by Ann Casement. *Journal of Analytical Psychology* 55 (1): 35-49.

Champernowne, I. (1968). Interview by G. Nameche in C. G. Jung biographical archive, Countway Library.

# References

Clay, C. (2016). *Labyrinths: Emma Jung, Her Marriage to Carl and the Early Years of Psychoanalysis*. New York, NY: HarperCollins Publishers Limited.

Cohen, B. (2015). Dr. Jung and His Patients. *Jung Journal* 9 (2): 34-49.

Covington, C. & Wharton B. (2015). *Sabina Spielrein: Forgotten Pioneer of Psychoanalysis, Revised Edition*. Hove; New York, NY: Routledge.

Crabtree, A., (1993). *From Mesmer to Freud: Magnetic Sleep and the Roots of Psychological Healing*. New Haven, CT: Yale University Press.

Crabtree, A., (2009). Automatism and Secondary Centers of Consciousness. In *Irreducible Mind: Toward a Psychology for the 21st Century*, (pp. 301-365). Lanham, MD: Rowman & Littlefield Publishers.

Dalzell, T. G., (2007). Eugen Bleuler 150: Bleuler's reception of Freud. *History of Psychiatry* 18 (4): 471-482.

Dieckmann, H. (1976). Transference and countertransference. Results of a Berlin research group. *The Journal of Analytical Psychology* 21 (1): 25-36.

Douglas, C. (1997a). Introduction. In *Visions: Notes of the Seminar Given in 1930-1934*, (pp. ix-xxxiv). Princeton, NJ: Princeton University Press.

Douglas, C. (1997b). *Translate This Darkness: The Life of Christiana Morgan, the Veiled Woman in Jung's Circle*. Princeton, NJ: Princeton University Press.

Ellenberger, H. F. (1970). *The Discovery of the Unconscious: The History and Evolution of Dynamic Psychiatry*. New York, NY: Basic Books.

Ellenberger, H. F. (1993a). C. G. Jung and the Story of Helene Preiswerk: A Critical Study with New Documents. In M. S. Micale (Ed.) *Beyond the Unconscious: Essays of Henri F. Ellenberger*, (pp. 291-305). Princeton, NJ: Princeton University Press.

Ellenberger, H. F. (1993b). Psychiatry and Its Unknown History. In M. S. Micale (Ed.) *Beyond the Unconscious: Essays of Henri F. Ellenberger*, (pp. 239-253). Princeton, NJ: Princeton University Press.

Elms, A. C. (1997). *Uncovering Lives: The Uneasy Alliance of Biography and Psychology*. New York, NY: Oxford University Press.

Fordham, F. (1968). Interview by G. Nameche in C. G. Jung biographical archive, Countway Library.

Flournoy, T., (1899) Genese de Quelques Pretendus Messages Spirites. *Revue Philosophique de la France Létranger* XLVII, 144-158.

Flournoy, T., (1901) Observations psychologiques sur le spiritisme. In P. Janet (Ed.), *Quatrième Congrès international de psychologie, tenu à Paris du 20 au 26 août 1900*. Paris, France: Alcan.

Flournoy, T. (1903). Review: Zur Psychologie und Pathologie sogenannter occult Phanomen, de C. G. Jung. *Archives de Psychologie, 2*, 85-86.

Flournoy, T. (2015). *From India to the Planet Mars: A Case of Multiple Personality with Imaginary Languages*. Princeton, NJ: Princeton University Press.

Franz, M.-L. von. (1991). Love, war and transformation. *Psychological Perspectives* 24 (1): 54-63.

Franz, M.-L. von. (1992). *Psyche and Matter*. Boston, MA.: Shambhala.

Franz, M.-L. von. (1998). *C.G. Jung: His Myth in Our Time*. Toronto, Ontario: Inner City Books.

Freud, S., (1894). The Neuro-Psychoses of Defence. In J. Strachey (Ed.), *The Complete Psychological Works of Sigmund Freud, Vol. 3*, (pp. 45-61). London, England: Vintage.

Freud, S., (1893). On the Psychical Mechanism of Hysterical Phenomena (Preliminary Communication). In J. Strachey (Ed.), *The Complete Psychological Works of Sigmund Freud, Vol. 2*, pp. 3-17 London, England: Vintage.

Freud, S., (1910). The Future Prospects of Psychoanalytic Therapy. In J. Strachey (Ed.), *The Complete Psychological Works of Sigmund Freud, Vol. 11*, (pp. 139-151). London, England: Vintage.

Freud, S., (1912). A Note on the Unconscious. In J. Strachey (Ed.), *The Complete Psychological Works of Sigmund Freud, Vol. 12*, (pp. 260-266). London, England: Vintage.

Freud, S. (1923). The Ego and the Id. In J. Strachey (Ed.), *The Complete Psychological Works of Sigmund Freud, Vol 19*, (pp. 12-59). London, England: Vintage.

Freud, S., (1925) An Autobiographical Study. In J. Strachey (Ed.), *The Complete Psychological Works of Sigmund Freud, Vol. 20*, (pp. 7-70). London, England: Vintage.

# References

Freud, S., (1938) Splitting of the Ego in the Process of Defense. In J. Strachey (Ed.), *The Complete Psychological Works of Sigmund Freud, Vol. 13*, pp. 275-278. London, England: Vintage.

Freud, S., (1980). *The Interpretation of Dreams*. London, England: Penguin.

Freud, S. & Ferenczi, S. (1993) *The Correspondence of Sigmund Freud and Sándor Ferenczi: 1908-1914*. Cambridge, MA.: Harvard University Press.

Freud, S. & Jung C. G. (1977). *The Freud-Jung Letters: The Correspondence Between Sigmund Freud and C.G. Jung*. Princeton, NJ: Princeton University Press.

Frey-Rohn, L. (1986) Interview. In Transcript of Whitney, J. (Director), *Matter of Heart* [Film]. Retrieved from http://gnosis.org/gnostic-jung/Film-Transcript-Matter-of-Heart.html March 7, 2019

Ffytche, M. (2012). *The Foundation of the Unconscious: Schelling, Freud, and the Birth of the Modern Psyche*. Cambridge, MA; New York, NY: Cambridge University Press.

Gabbard, G. O., Lester E. P. (2016). *Boundaries and Boundary Violations in Psychoanalysis*. Arlington VA: American Psychiatric Association Publishing.

Gale, B.G., (2015). *Love in Vienna: The Sigmund Freud-Minna Bernays Affair*. Santa Barbara, CA: Praeger.

Giannoni, M. (2003). Jung's theory of dream and the relational debate. *Psychoanalytic Dialogues* 13 (4): 605-21.

Giegerich, W. (1994). Once More, the Reality/Irreality Issue: A Reply to Hillman's Reply. In *Collected English Paper Vol. III: Soul Violence*, (pp.317-336). New Orleans, LA: Spring Journal Books.

Giegerich, W. (2010). Liber Novus, that is, the New Bible: A first analysis of C. G.

Jung's Red Book, *Spring: A Journal of Archetype and Culture*, Vol. 83: pp. 361-411.

Gieser, S. (2005). *The Innermost Kernel: Depth Psychology and Quantum Physics. Wolfgang Pauli's Dialogue with C.G. Jung*. New York, NY: Springer.

Von Goethe, J. W. (1987) *Faust Part I*, trans. Luke, D. Oxford, England: Oxford University Press.

Goodheart, William B. (1984). C. G. Jung's First 'Patient': On the Seminal Emergence of Jung's Thought. *Journal of Analytical Psychology* 29(1), 1-34.

Graf-Nold, A. (2016). S. Shamdasani and the 'serial exemplarity of mediumship' in Jung's work: A critique. *History of Psychiatry* 27 (3): 381-83.

Gurney, E., (1887). Peculiarities of Certain Post-hypnotic States. *Proceedings of the Society for Psychical Research*. IV, 268-323.

Hannah, B. (1976). *Jung, His Life and Work: A Biographical Memoir*. Wilmette, IL: Chiron.

Hacking, I. (1997). Repression and dissociation—A comment on "memory repression and recovery." *Health Care Analysis*. 5, 117-120.

Hayman, R. (2002). *A Life of Jung*. New York, NY: W.W. Norton.

Haule, J.R. (1983). Archetype and integration: Exploring the Janetian roots of Analytical Psychology. *Journal of Analytical Psychology*. 28, 253-267.

Haule, J.R. (1984). From somnambulism to the archetypes: the French roots of Jung's split with Freud. *Psychoanalytic Review*. 71, 635-659.

Haule, J.R. (1986). Pierre Janet and dissociation: The first transference theory and its origins in hypnosis. *American Journal of Clinical Hypnosis*. 29, 86-94.

Haule, J. R. (1996). *The Love Cure: Therapy Erotic and Sexual*. Thompson, CT.: Spring Publications.

Healy, N. S. (2017). *Toni Wolff and C. G. Jung: A Collaboration*. Los Angeles, CA: Tiberius Press.

Hogenson, G.B. (2004) Archetypes: Emergence and the Psyche's Deep Structure. In J. Cambray & L. Carter (Eds.) (2004) *Analytical Psychology: Contemporary Perspectives in Jungian Analysis*, (pp. 32-55). Hove; New York, NY: Routledge.

Hillman, J. (1982). Anima mundi: The return of the soul to the world. *Spring, a Journal of Archetype and Culture*, 71-93.

Hillman, J. (1989). From Mirror to Window: Curing Psychoanalysis of Its Narcissism. In *Uniform Edition of the Writings of James Hillman Volume 2: City & Soul*, (pp. 66-79). Putnam, CT.: Spring Publications.

# References

Hillman, J. (1991). The Yellowing of the Work. In M. A. Mattoon (Ed.), *Personal and Archetypal Dynamics in the Analytical Relationship*, (pp. 77-102). Einsiedeln, Switzerland: Daimon.

Hillman, J. (1992a). *Re-Visioning Psychology*. New York, NY: HarperPerennial.

Hillman, J. (1992b). *The Thought of the Heart and the Soul of the World*. Putnam, CT.: Spring Publications.

Hillman, J. (2012). *Healing Fiction*. Putnam, CT.: Spring Publications.

Hillman, J. & Shamdasani S. (2013). *Lament of the Dead: Psychology After Jung's Red Book*. London; New York, NY: W.W. Norton.

Holt, D. (1992). Jung and Marx: Alchemy, Christianity, and the Work Against Nature. In *The Psychology of Carl Jung: Essays in Application and Deconstruction*, (pp. 139-157). Lewiston, NY: The Edwin Mellen Press.

Homans, P. (1995). *Jung in Context: Modernity and the Making of a Psychology*, Chicago, IL: University of Chicago Press.

Huskinson, L. (Ed.) (2008). *Dreaming the Myth Onwards: New Directions in Jungian Therapy and Thought*. London, England: New York, NY: Routledge.

Jacoby, M. (1984). *The Analytic Encounter: Transference and Human Relationship*. Toronto, Ontario: Inner City Books.

James, T. (1995). *Dream, Creativity, and Madness in Nineteenth-Century France*. Oxford, England: Clarendon Press.

James, W. (1891). *The Principles of Psychology Vol. 1*. London, England: Macmillan.

James, W. (1892). What Psychical Research Has Accomplished. In *William James: Writings 1878-1899*, (pp. 680-700). New York, NY: Library of America,

James, W. (1901). Frederic Myers' Service to Psychology. *Proceedings of the Society for Psychical Research*. 17, 13-23.

James, W. (1909). The Confidences of a "Psychical Researcher. In *Essays in Psychical Research, Works of William James,* (pp. 362-376). Cambridge, MA.: Harvard University Press.

Jansen, D. B. (2003). *Jung's Apprentice: A Biography of Helton Godwin Baynes*. Einsiedeln, Switzerland: Daimon Verlag.

Jung, C. G. (1895) Accounts of Séances Involving Hélène Preiswerk. Jung archive, Wissenschaftshistorische Sammlung, ETH, Zurich.

Jung, C. G. (1902) *On the psychology and pathology of so-called occult phenomena. CW1,* (paras. 1-151).

Jung C. G. (1903). Über die Psychologie des Unbewussten. *Correspondenz-Blatt für Schweizer Ärzte* XIII: 20-22.

Jung, C. G., (1906). Psychoanalysis and Association Experiments. In *CW 2,* (pars 660-727).

Jung, C. G. (1907). The Psychology of Dementia Praecox. In *CW3,* (paras. 1-316).

Jung, C. G. (1909). Psychic Conflicts in a Child. In *CW 17,* (paras. 1-79).

Jung, C. G. (1912a). The Theory of Psychoanalysis. In *CW 4,* (paras. 203-522).

Jung, C. G. (1912b). *Wandlungen und Symbole der Libido: Beiträge zur Entwicklungsgeschichte des Denkens.* Leipzig, Germany, & Vienna, Austria: F. Deuticke.

Jung, C. G. (1912/1952) *Symbols of transformation, CW 5.*

Jung, C. G. (1913). A Contribution to the Study of Psychological Types. In *CW 6* (paras. 858-882).

Jung, C. G. (1916a). Adaptation, Individuation, Collectivity. In *CW 18,* (paras. 1084-1106).

Jung, C. G. (1916b) General Aspects of Dream Psychology. In *CW 8,* (paras. 443-529).

Jung, C. G. (1916c). The Structure of the Unconscious. In *CW 7,* (paras. 442-521).

Jung, C. G. (1916d). The Transcendent Function. In J. C. Miller. *The Transcendent Function: Jung's Model of Psychological Growth through Dialogue with the Unconscious,* (pp. 145-178). New York, NY: SUNY Press.

Jung, C. G. (1917a). New Paths in Psychology. In *CW 7,* (paras. 407-441).

Jung, C. G. (1917b). On the Psychology of the Unconscious. In *CW 7* (paras. 1-201).

Jung, C. G. (1917c). The Psychology of the Unconscious Processes. In *Collected Papers,* 2nd ed., (pp. 354–444). London, England: Bailliere, Tindall & Cox.

# References

Jung, C. G. (1920). The Psychological Foundation of Belief in Spirits. In *CW8*, (paras. 570-600).

Jung, C. G. (1921). *Psychological Types*. In *CW 6*. London, England: Routledge & Kegan Paul.

Jung, C. G. (1925a). Analytical psychology and education. In *CW 17*, (paras 127-229).

Jung, C. G. (1925b). Marriage as a Psychological Relationship. In *CW 17*, (paras. 324-345).

Jung, C. G. (1928a). On Psychic Energy. In *CW 8* (paras 1-130).

Jung, C. G. (1928b). The Relations between the Ego and the Unconscious. In *CW7*, (paras. 202-406).

Jung, C. G. (1929). Problems of Modern Psychotherapy. In *CW 16*, (paras. 114-174).

Jung, C. G. (1931a). Introduction to Wickes's 'Analyse Der Kinderseele.' In *CW 17*, (paras. 80-97).

Jung, C. G. (1931b). The Stages of Life. In *CW8*, (paras.749-795).

Jung, C. G. (1935a). Preface to 'The relations between the ego and the unconscious.' In *CW 7*, (pp. 123–124).

Jung, C. G. (1935b). Principles of Practical Psychotherapy. In *CW 16*, (paras 1-27).

Jung, C. G. (1935c). The Tavistock Lectures. In *CW 18*, (Pars 1-415).

Jung, C.G. (1934a). Archetypes of the Collective Unconscious. In *CW 9i*, (paras 1-86).

Jung, C.G., (1934b). A review of the complex theory. In *CW 8*, (paras. 194-219).

Jung, C.G. (1934c). The State of Psychotherapy Today. In *CW 10*, (paras 333-370).

Jung, C.G. (1936a). Psychological Factors Determining Human Behaviour. In *CW 8*, (paras. 232-262).

Jung, C.G. (1936b). Wotan. In *CW 10*, (paras 371-399).

Jung, C.G. (1937). Psychology and Religion. In *CW 11*, (paras. 1-168).

Jung, C.G. (1939). "Conscious, Unconscious and Individuation" *CW 8*, (paras. 489-524).

Jung, C. G. (1941). Psychological Aspects of the Kore. In *CW 9i*, (paras 306-383).

Jung, C. G. (1943). On the Psychology of the Unconscious. In *CW 7 5th Edition*. (paras. 1-200).

Jung, C. G. (1944/52). Psychology and Alchemy. *CW12*

Jung, C. G., (1945). On the Nature of Dreams. In *CW 8*, (paras 530-569).

Jung, C. G. (1946). The Psychology of the Transference. In *CW16*, (paras 353-539).

Jung, C. G., (1947). On the nature of the psyche. In *CW 8*, (paras 343-442).

Jung, C. G., (1951). Aion: Researches into the phenomenology of the self. *CW9ii*

Jung, C. G. (1952). Synchronicity an Acausal Connecting Principle. In *CW 8*, (paras 816-967).

Jung, C. G. (1955). Mysterium Coniunctionis: An Inquiry into the Separation and Synthesis of Psychic Opposites in Alchemy. In *CW 14*. London: Routledge.

Jung, C. G. (1957). The Transcendent Function. In *CW 8*, (Paras 131-193).

Jung, C. G. (1958). Flying Saucers: A Modern Myth of Things Seen in the Skies. In *CW 10*, (Paras 589-824).

Jung, C. G. (1966). *Collected Works Vol 12: Psychology and Alchemy*. Princeton, NJ: Princeton University Press.

Jung, C. G. (1967). *Symbols of Transformation CW 5, 2nd Edition*. London, England: Routledge

Jung, C. G. (1973a). *Experimental Researches*. In *CW 2*. London, England: Routledge

Jung, C. G. (1973b). *Letters Vol. 1*. Princeton, NJ: Princeton University Press.

Jung, C. G. (1976). *Visions Seminars*. Zürich, Switzerland: Spring Publications.

Jung, C.G. (1987). *C. G. Jung Speaking: Interviews and Encounters*. Princeton, N.J: Princeton University Press.

Jung, C. G. (1990). *Analytical Psychology: Notes of the Seminar given in 1925 by C. G. Jung*. London, England: Routledge.

Jung, C. G. (1997). *Visions: Notes of the Seminar Given in 1930-1934*. Princeton, N.J: Princeton University Press.

# References

Jung, C. G. (2014). *General Bibliography - Revised Edition*. In *CW 19*. Princeton, N.J: Princeton University Press.

Jung, C. G. (2009). *Liber Novus*. London, England; New York, NY: W.W. Norton & Company.

Jung, C. G., and Jaffé A. (1962). *Erinnerungen, Träume, Gedanken Von C.G. Jung. Aufgezeichnet Und Herausgegeben Von Aniela Jaffé*. Zürich, Switzerland; Düsseldorf, Germany: Walter-Verlag.

Jung, C. G., and Jaffé A. (1989). *Memories, Dreams, Reflections*. New York, NY: Vintage Books.

Jung, C. G., and Schmid-Guisan H. (2013). *The Question of Psychological Types: The Correspondence of C. G. Jung and Hans Schmid-Guisan, 1915-1916*. Princeton, NJ: Princeton University Press.

Keeley, J.P. (2001). Subliminal promptings: Psychoanalytic theory and the Society for Psychical Research. *American Imago* 58, 767–791.

Kerr, J. (2011). *A Most Dangerous Method: The Story of Jung, Freud, and Sabina Spielrein*. New York, NY: Knopf Doubleday Publishing Group.

Kerslake, C. (2007). *Deleuze and the Unconscious*. London, England; New York, NY: Bloomsbury

Kris, E. (1956). The personal myth: A problem in psychoanalytic technique. *Journal of the American Psychoanalytic Association* 4 (4): 653-81.

Laplanche, J., & Pontalis, J.-B., (1988). *The Language of Psychoanalysis*. London, England: Karnac Books

Lehmann, H. (1986). Jung contra Freud/Nietzsche contra Wagner. *International Review of Psycho-Analysis, 13*, 201-209.

Loewald, H. W. (1977). Transference and countertransference: The roots of psychoanalysis: Book review essay on the Freud/Jung letters. *The Psychoanaltic Quarterly, 46*, 514–527.

Lothane, Z. (2015). Tender Love and Transference: Unpublished Letters of C. G. Jung and Sabina Spielrein. In C. Covington & B. Wharton (Eds.). *Sabina Spielrein: Forgotten Pioneer of Psychoanalysis,* (pp.126-57). Hove; New York, NY: Routledge.

Lu, K. (2013). Can individual psychology explain social phenomena? An appraisal of the theory of cultural complexes. *Psychoanalysis, Culture & Society*. v. 14, n. 4, p. 386-404

Main, R. (2007). Synchronicity and analysis: Jung and after. *European Journal of Psychotherapy & Counselling* 9 (4): 359-71.

Main, R. (2013) Myth, Synchronicity and Re-enchantment. In L. Burnett, S. Bahun & R. Main, (Eds.), *Myth, Literature and the Unconscious*, (pp. 129-146). London. England: Karnac Books

Mann, T. (1982). *Diaries, 1918-1939*. New York, NY: Harry N. Abrams.

Makari, G. J. (1992). A History of Freud's First Concept of Transference. *International Review of Psycho-Analysis* 19 (4): 415–32.

Makari, G. J. (2009). *Revolution in Mind: The Creation of Psychoanalysis*. New York, NY: Harper Perennial.

Marlan, S. (2014). The Philosophers' Stone: Alchemical Imagination and the Soul's Logical Life. Duquesne University. https://d sc.duq.edu/e td/874.

McLynn, F. (1998). *Carl Gustav Jung: A Biography*. London, England: St. Martin's Press.

Meier, C. A. (1989). *Consciousness: The Psychology of C.G. Jung, Vol. 3*. Boston, MA: Sigo Press.

Meredith-Owen, W. (2011). Jung's shadow: negation and narcissism of the Self. *Journal of Analytical Psychology*, 56(5), 674–691.

Mollon, P., (2011). The Foreclosure of Dissociation Within Psychoanalysis. In. V. Sinason (Ed.), *Trauma, Dissociation and Multiplicity: Working on Identity and Selves*, (pp. 8-20). Hove, East Sussex, England; New York, NY: Routledge.

Moltzer, M. (1912). Letter to Freud 12th April 1912. Sigmund Freud Archive, University of Essex.

Moura, V. de. (2014). Learning from the patient: The East, synchronicity and transference in the history of an unknown case of C.G. Jung. *Journal of Analytical Psychology* 59 (3): 391-409.

Mullen, S. (1982). *C.G. Jung, Emma Jung and Toni Wolff: a collection of remembrances*. Analytical Psychology Club of San Francisco.

Myers, F.W.H. (1882) Report of the literary committee. *Proceedings of the Society for Psychical Research*. 1, 116-155.

Myers, F.W.H. (1885) Automatic writing II. *Proceedings of the Society for Psychical Research*. III, 1-63.

# References

Myers, F.W.H. (1888) French experiments in strata of personality. *Proceedings of the Society for Psychical Research*. 5, 374-397.

Myers, F.W.H. (1891). The subliminal consciousness. *Proceedings of the Society for Psychical Research*. 7, 298-355.

Myers, F.W.H. (1894). The subliminal consciousness, chapter 6: The mechanism of hysteria. *Proceedings of the Society for Psychical Research*. 9, 3-25.

Myers, F.W.H. (1903a). *Human Personality and Its Survival of Bodily Death, Vol. 1.* London, England: Longmans, Green.

Myers, F.W.H. (1903b). *Human Personality and Its Survival of Bodily Death, Vol. 2.* London, England: Longmans, Green.

Owens, L. S. (2015). *Jung in Love: The Mysterium in Liber Novus.* Los Angeles, CA; Salt Lake City, UT: Gnosis Archive Books.

Papadopoulos, R.K. (1980). *The dialectic of the Other in the psychology of C. G. Jung: a metatheoretical investigation*, PhD thesis, University of Cape Town.

Papadopoulos, R. K. (1991). Jung and the Concept of the Other. In *Jung in Modern Perspective*, (pp. 54-88). Bridport, CT: Prism.

Papadopoulos R.K., (2002). The other other: when the exotic other subjugates the familiar other. *Journal of Analytical Psychology*, 47(2): 163-188).

Perry, C., & Laurence, J.-R. (1984). Mental processing outside of awareness: The contributions of Freud and Janet. In K. S. Bowers & D. Meichenbaum (Eds.), *The Unconscious Reconsidered* (pp. 9-48). New York, NY: John Wiley & Sons.

Pietikäinen, P. (1999). Jung's psychology in the light of his "personal myth." *Psychoanalysis and History* 1 (2): 237-51.

Post, L. van der. (2002). *Jung and the Story of Our Time.* London, England: Vintage Classics.

Prince, M. (1907). A symposium on the subconscious. *Journal of Abnormal Psychology*, 5, 67-80.

Prince, M. (1905). *The Dissociation of a Personality.* London, England: Longmans, Green, and Company.

Read, Sir H. E., Adler, G. & Fordham, M. (1953). Editorial Note to 1st Edition. In Jung, C. G. *CW 7, Two Essays on Analytical Psychology* (p. v).

Richardson, R. D. (2007). *William James: In the Maelstrom of American Modernism: A Biography*. Boston, MA: Houghton Mifflin Harcourt.

Roudinesco, É. (2016). *Freud: In His Time and Ours*. Cambridge, MA.: Harvard University Press.

Rowland, S. (2002). *Jung: A Feminist Revision*. Cambridge, England: Polity Press.

Rowland, S. (2003). Jung, myth, and biography. *Harvest, Journal for Jungian Studies* 49 (1): 22-39.

Rowland, S. (2005). *Jung as a Writer*. Hove, East Sussex, England; New York, NY: Routledge.

Rowland, S. (2011). *The Ecocritical Psyche: Literature, Evolutionary Complexity and Jung*. Hove, East Sussex, England; New York, NY: Routledge.

Saban, M. (2012). The dis/enchantment of C.G. Jung. *International Journal of Jungian Studies* 4 (1): pp.21-33.

Saban, M. (2013). Ambiguating Jung. In J. Kirsch & M. Stein (Eds.) *How and Why We Still Read Jung*, (pp. 6-25). Hove, East Sussex, England; New York, NY: Routledge.

Saban, M. (2014). A response to David Tacey's 'James Hillman: The unmaking of a psychologist.' *Journal of Analytical Psychology* 59: 524-528

Saban, M. (2015). Another serious misunderstanding: Jung, Giegerich and a premature requiem. *Journal of Analytical Psychology* 60 (1): 94-113.

Saban, M. (2016). Jung, Winnicott and the divided psyche. *Journal of Analytical Psychology* 61 (3): 329-49.

Saban, M. (2017a). Segrete e Bugie. Un'area Cieca Nella Psicologia Junghiana. *Rivista Di Psicologia Analitica* 95 (43): 39-76.

Saban, M. (2017b). The Dissociated Psyche and Its Politics. In S. Carta, A. Adorisio, and R. Mercurio (Eds.), *The Analyst in the Polis, Vol. 1*, (pp.184-97). Rome: Streetlib.

Samuels, A. (2006). Transference/Countertransference. In R. K. Papadopoulos (Ed.), *The Handbook of Jungian Psychology*, (pp.177-95). Hove, East Sussex, England; New York, NY: Routledge.

# References

Samuels, A., Shorter, B. & Plaut F. (1986). *A Critical Dictionary of Jungian Analysis*. Hove, East Sussex, England; New York, NY: Routledge.

Satinover, J. (1985). At the Mercy of Another: Abandonment and Restitution in Psychotic Character. *Chiron*, 47-86.

Schwartz-Salant, N. (1998). *The Mystery of Human Relationship: Alchemy and the Transformation of the Self*. London, England; New York, NY: Routledge.

Searle, J.R. (1992). *The Rediscovery of the Mind*. Cambridge, MA.: MIT Press.

Sedgwick, D. (1994). *The Wounded Healer: Counter-Transference from a Jungian Perspective*. London, England; New York, NY: Routledge.

Shamdasani, S. (1993). Automatic writing and the discovery of the unconscious. *Spring Journal of Archetype and Culture*. 54, 100–131.

Shamdasani, S. (1994). Introduction: Encountering Hélène. Théodore Flournoy and the Genesis of Subliminal Psychology. In T. Flournoy *From India to the Planet Mars: A Case of Multiple Personality with Imaginary Languages*. Princeton, NJ: Princeton University Press.

Shamdasani, S. (1998a). The lost contributions of Maria Moltzer to Analytical Psychology. Two unknown papers. *Spring: Journal of Archetype and Culture* 64: 103-20.

Shamdasani, S., (1998b) From Geneva to Zürich: Jung and French Switzerland. *Journal of Analytical Psychology*. 43, 115-126.

Shamdasani, S. (2000). Misunderstanding Jung: the afterlife of legends. *Journal of Analytical Psychology*. 45, 459-472.

Shamdasani, S. (2002). Psychoanalysis Inc. *Semiotic Review of Books* 13, 6-10.

Shamdasani, S., (2003a). *Jung and the Making of Modern Psychology: The Dream of a Science*. Cambridge, England: Cambridge University Press.

Shamdasani, S. (2003b). *Cult Fictions: C. G. Jung and the Founding of Analytical Psychology*. London, England; New York, NY: Routledge.

Shamdasani, S. (2005). *Jung Stripped Bare by His Biographers, Even*. London, England: Karnac Books.

Shamdasani, S. (2009). Introduction. In: Jung, C. G. *The Red Book: Liber novus*, (pp. 194-221). New York, NY: W.W. Norton & Company.

Shamdasani, S. & Beebe, J. (2010). Jung becomes Jung: A dialogue on Liber Novus (The Red Book). *Psychological Perspectives*. 53, 410–436.

Shamdasani, S. (2015) 'S.W.' and C.G. Jung: Mediumship, psychiatry and serial exemplarity. *History of Psychiatry* 26 (3): 288–302.

Shengold, L. (1976). The Freud/Jung Letters: Review. *Journal of the American Psychoanalytical Association* 24, 669–683.

Smith, R. C. (1997). *The Wounded Jung: Effects of Jung's Relationships on His Life and Work*. Evanston, IL.: Northwestern University Press.

Sherry, J. (2012). *Carl Gustav Jung: Avant-Garde Conservative*. London, England: Palgrave Macmillan.

Singer, T. & Kimbles, S. L. (2004). *The Cultural Complex: Contemporary Jungian Perspectives on Psyche and Society*. London, England; New York, NY: Routledge

Sommer, A. (2011). Trevor Hamilton, immortal longings: F.W.H. Myers and the Victorian search forlLife after death. *Medical History*. 55, 433-435.

Spielrein, S. (1994). Destruction as the cause of coming into being. *Journal of Analytical Psychology* 39 (2): 155-86.

Spielrein, S. (2001). Unedited extracts from a diary (1906/1907?). *Journal of Analytical Psychology* 46 (1): 155-71.

Starobinski, J. (1975). The inside and the uutside, *Hudson Review*, Vol. 28, No. 3 (Autumn, 1975)

Stephenson, C. (2009). Complex. In D. A. Leeming, K. Madden, S. Marlan (Eds.), *Encyclopedia of Psychology and Religion* (pp.165-68), New York, NY: Springer.

Stefana, A. (2017). *History of Countertransference: From Freud to the British Object Relations School*. Abingdon, Oxon, England; New York, NY: Routledge.

Stein, M. (2012) How to read The Red Book and why. *Journal of Analytical Psychology* 57 (3): 280-98.

Stevens, A. (1999). *On Jung*. Princeton, NJ: Princeton University Press.

Swan, W. (2009). *The Memoir of Tina Keller-Jenny: A Lifelong Confrontation with the Psychology of C. G. Jung*. New Orleans, LA: Spring Journal.

Taves, A. (2003). Religious experience and the divisible self: William James (and Frederic Myers) as theorist(s) ofrReligion. *Journal of the American Academy of Religion*. 71, 303-326.

# References

Taylor, E. (1980). William James and C. G. Jung. *Spring Journal of Archetype and Culture*. 157-67.

Taylor, E. (1986) C. G. Jung and the Boston Psychopathologists. In K. Gibson (Ed.) *Carl Jung and Soul Psychology*, (pp. 131-144) New York, NY: Haworth Press.

Taylor, E. (1996) The new Jung scholarship. *Psychoanalytic Review*. 83, 547-568.

Taylor, E. (1998) Jung before Freud, not Freud before Jung: The reception of Jung's work in American psychoanalytic circles between 1904 and 1909. *Journal of Analytic Psychology*. 43, 97-114.

Vandermeersch, P. (1991). *Unresolved Questions in the Freud/Jung Debate: On Psychosis, Sexual Identity and Religion*. Leuven, Belgium: Leuven University Press.

Wolff, Toni. (1956). *Structural Forms of the Feminine Psyche: (A Sketch)*. Students Association, C.G. Jung Institute.

Williamson, G. S. (2004). *The Longing for Myth in Germany: Religion and Aesthetic Culture from Romanticism to Nietzsche*. Chicago, IL: University of Chicago Press.

Winnicott, D.W. (1990). *The Maturational Processes and the Facilitating Environment*. Princeton, NJ.: Karnac Books.

Winnicott, D.W. (1992). Review of Jung's Memories, Dreams, Reflections. In R K. Papadopoulos (Ed.), *Carl Gustav Jung: Critical Assessments Vol. 1*. London, England; New York, NY: Routledge.

Williams, M. (1963). The indivisibility of the personal and collective unconscious. *Journal of Analytical Psychology* 8 (1): 45-50.

Witzig, J. S., (1982). Theodore Flournoy: A friend indeed. *Journal of Analytical Psychology*. 27, 131-148.

Wright, P., (1997). History of Dissociation in Western Psychology. In Krippner S., & Powers, S. M., (Eds.). *Broken Images Broken Selves: Dissociative Narratives in Clinical Practice*, (pp. 41-60). Washington, DC: Brunner/Mazel

Zumstein-Preiswerk, S. (1975). *C. G. Jungs Medium*. München, Germany: Kindler.

# ABOUT AUTHOR

Mark Saban is a Jungian analyst. He trained with the Independent Group of Analytical Psychologists, with whom he is a senior analyst. He sees clients in Oxford, and also enjoys teaching Jungian and post-Jungian studies.

For the last two years he has been employed as a lecturer in the Department of Psychosocial and Psychoanalytic Studies, University of Essex. Mark studied Classics at Oxford and then worked for twenty years as an actor, performing all over the world, doing everything from Shakespeare to street comedy.

He has published numerous papers and book chapters, and co-edited *Analysis and Activism - Social and Political Contributions of Jungian Psychology* with Emilija Kiehl and Andrew Samuels (Routledge 2016) (Finalist American Board and Academy of Psychoanalysis Book Prize, Nominated Gradiva Award for Best Edited Book). This is the first book he has written.